Camping Washington

A Comprehensive Guide to Public Tent and RV Campgrounds

Second Edition

Steve Giordano

FALCONGUIDES

GUILFORD, CONNECTICUT
HELENA, MONTANA
AN IMPRINT OF GLOBE PEQUOT PRESS

FALCONGUIDES®

Copyright © 2013 by Morris Book Publishing, LLC
Previously published in 2000 by Falcon Publishing, Inc.

FalconGuides is an imprint of Globe Pequot Press.
Falcon, FalconGuides, and Outfit Your Mind are registered trademarks of Morris Book Publishing, LLC.

All photos by Steve Giordano unless otherwise noted.
Maps © Morris Book Publishing LLC
Layout: Joanna Beyer
Project editor: Julie Marsh

Library of Congress Cataloging-in-Publication Data
Giordano, Steve, 1941-
  Camping Washington : a comprehensive guide to public tent and RV campgrounds / Steve Giordano. — Second edition.
     pages cm
  Includes bibliographical references and index.
  ISBN 978-0-7627-7800-3 (pbk.)
  1. Camping—Washington (State)—Guidebooks. 2. Washington (State)—Guidebooks. I. Title.
  GV191.42.W2G56 2013
  917.97'068—dc23
                          2012036901

Printed in the United States of America

10 9 8 7 6 5 4 3 2 1

Contents

Overview

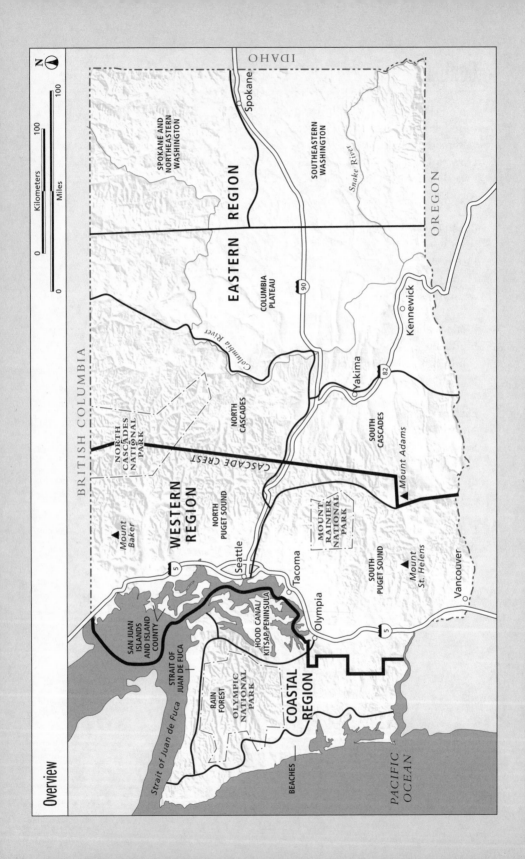

Acknowledgments

I could not have written this book without the extreme cooperation of the many public agencies that operate campground facilities in Washington State. These include the Washington State Parks and Recreation Commission, the USDA Forest Service, the US Army Corps of Engineers, the Washington Department of Natural Resources, the National Park Service, and many municipalities and public utility districts. The help of their staffs was invaluable.

I also owe great appreciation to my parents, Roy and Jeanne Giordano, for getting me started properly on a lifetime of camping. In the early days our equipment consisted of three war-surplus mummy bags, period. We slept on the beach or among the sand dunes, with me in the middle. Equipment added through the years, including a tent and stove, seemed like luxuries, and they still do today. I must confess, though, that the western Washington climate fairly calls out for an RV—they have theirs and I have mine.

I must also credit my FalconGuides editor, Julie Marsh, for seeing me through to the completion of *Camping Washington*. She never even got grumpy over the state of my submissions and did not cajole as the deadlines slipped by. Any mistakes in the book are mine, and she gets the credit for the way it works with you the reader in mind.

Happy camping!

Introduction

The popular image of Washington State, outside of the Pacific Northwest, is of a rain-soaked wilderness somewhere near Alaska. People know of Seattle and its high-tech coffee and its industries like Boeing and Microsoft, but they also tend to think the state is chock-full of mountains and forests with a few roads cut through the trees. In some parts of the state, that is true. For example, the famed North Cross State Highway, now known as the North Cascades Highway, opened as recently as 1972. However, it closes every winter, usually from November to March or April, because the mountain snows get too deep to plow and early-spring avalanches still cover the highway. Washington has about 81,300 miles of federal, state, and local roads, including 757 miles of interstate highway. Federal lands make up nearly 30 percent of the state's 71,300 square miles.

In 1942, when the immense Bonneville and Grand Coulee Dams on the Columbia River were completed, the Bonneville Power Administration produced a movie for Pacific Northwest residents in rural areas. The film encouraged them to electrify their homes and farms with the dams' newly generated power. Folk singer Woody Guthrie wrote twenty-six songs for the movie, for about $10 per song. The most famous of them is "Roll On, Columbia, Roll On."

Washington's mountains lack the height of the Rockies, but they excel by any standard of grandeur. Swift-moving streams fall away on all sides, rock walls jut straight up from the roadside, forest canopy hangs entirely over the road in some places, and in fall the changing of the leaves in the mountain passes creates a near-neon glow.

The scale of the mountains is enormous, their contrasting terrain is striking, their gorges and river valleys seem sculpted by giants, and their perpetually snow- and ice-covered peaks appear as beacons to everyone within 100 miles.

Western Washington's rain, in spite of its distressing reputation, is not really all that heavy. Seattle gets about 38 inches per year—less than New York City. In the "rain shadow" of the Olympic Peninsula, the town of Sequim (pronounced skwim) gets nearly 17 inches of rain per year, and some of the San Juan Islands get around 22 inches. Cactus grows on at least one of the islands. Of course the mountains that cause this dryness, the Olympics, absorb the southwesterly brunt of Pacific storms and receive up to 160 inches of rain per year. A two-story rain gauge behind the Quinault Lodge in Olympic National Forest measures the rainfall in FEET!

A popular activity for some hardy people is winter storm watching on the coast of the Olympic Peninsula. The experience is an actual tourism draw, as travelers pull their rigs into coastal campgrounds and Seattle weekenders rent cottages and lodge rooms—all for the sake of experiencing the brute beauty of a winter storm.

Two states border Washington: Idaho on the east and Oregon on the south. The Canadian province of British Columbia is to the north; the straits, Puget Sound, and the Pacific Ocean are to the west. A series of interlaced channels, the Straits of Juan de Fuca and Georgia, along with Haro Strait, separate the state from Canada's Vancouver Island.

The geographic center of Washington is the town of George. The Columbia River Gorge Amphitheater is nearby, a national-caliber concert venue during summer.

Forest covers about half of Washington's land area. The temperate rain forest extends down the western side of the Olympic Peninsula south to the Columbia River. It has a high biomass of spruce, cedar, and hemlock. The forest floor is dense with ferns and mosses.

The more heavily logged area from Puget Sound into the western Cascade Range contains cedar, hemlock, and Douglas fir. Higher in the Cascades the forest tends toward silver fir and Douglas fir. The eastern slope of the Cascades is ponderosa pine habitat. Douglas fir is the most common tree in northeastern Washington. The central Columbia Plateau is actually a steppe covered by short grasses. Much of southeastern Washington is a prairie of taller grasses.

Washington's major attractions are outdoors. They include three national parks (Mount Rainier, Olympic, and North Cascades), three national recreation areas (Lake Chelan, Lake Roosevelt, and Ross Lake), plus the Mount St. Helens National Scenic Monument and the Columbia River Gorge National Scenic Area. On the Olympic Peninsula alone, there are nearly a million acres of forest.

Not to make your eyes glaze over or anything, but here are the statistics on Washington's outdoor recreation possibilities (and these are just the parks):

186 state parks
3 state forests
6 state wildlife areas
1 state wildlife management area
26 state recreation areas
1 state natural area
6 state fish hatcheries
3 national parks
7 national forests
2 national historical parks
2 national historic sites
20 national wildlife refuges

Camping in Washington

Campgrounds in Washington are as diverse as the landscape. They include sites in the rain forest of the Olympic Peninsula; on the beaches of the Pacific Ocean, Hood Canal, and Puget Sound; in alpine forests and meadows; and, in some eastern sections of the state, in desertlike conditions. The vast majority of campgrounds are at the edge of a body of water; Washington is riddled with lakes and laced with rivers.

A high percentage of campgrounds are open year-round, offering access to both summer and winter recreation. Some parks close their campsites but remain open for day use through the winter.

Annual moorage permits, boat-launch permits, disability passes, and senior citizen passes are available by calling the Washington State Parks and Recreation Commission (360-902-8844). An application will be mailed to you.

The Washington State Parks system is one of the ten largest in the nation in terms of acreage managed (250,000 acres) and visitation (fifty-one million visits annually). Nearly all public parks in Washington have some degree of wheelchair accessibility, and almost all allow leashed pets. Pets must be on a leash no longer than 8 feet and under your control at all times.

During the busy summer months, you can reserve a campsite, yurt, cabin, rustic structure, vacation house, group camp, or group day-use facility in more than sixty Washington state parks. Drop-ins are welcome on a space-available basis. Reservations can also be made through e-mail. Instructions are posted on the parks commission website: www.parks.wa.gov/reservations.

The National Recreation Reservation Service takes reservations for most USDA Forest Service and US Army Corps of Engineers campgrounds. There is a fee to make reservations at forest service campgrounds but not at Corps of Engineers campgrounds.

The Discover Pass

It's no secret that financial hard times have hit Washington outdoor recreation budgets—more than a few state-owned parks have shortened their open seasons, been deeded to municipalities, or simply closed. In response the state legislature came up with the Discover Pass. Sort of a park user tax, as of publication, the price was set at $30 per year ($10 for a one-day pass). This pass is now required for motor-vehicle access to state parks and recreation lands managed by the Washington State Parks and Recreation Commission, the Washington Department of Fish and Wildlife (WDFW), and the Washington State Department of Natural Resources (DNR).

The happy exception for campers is that the pass is not required for camping in state parks: Your camping reservation stub or camping fee receipt will serve as your permit for the duration of your stay in the park where you have paid for a campsite, vacation house, environmental learning center, yurt, or cabin. If you visit other state

Kids make joyous jumps into the water from the Cascade Lake Lagoon Bridge (Campground 107) during warm summer months.

parks in the area, you will need to purchase an annual or one-day Discover Pass. You will need a pass if you are camping on lands managed by the DNR or WDFW.

The Discover Pass is available by phone at (866) 320-9933, or visit https://fish hunt.dfw.wa.gov/.

How to Use This Guide

Camping Washington is designed for quick and easy reference. You should be able to find what you are looking for at a glance, whether by location on one of the many campground locator maps or in the quick-reference tables for each region.

I have divided Washington into three broad regions, corresponding to the state's designated tourism regions, and each of these is further divided into several subregions:

The Coastal Region includes the entire Olympic Peninsula south to the border with Oregon. The Coastal Region contains the rain forest, coastal beaches, Hood Canal, the Kitsap Peninsula, and the Strait of Juan de Fuca.

The Western Region includes everything else in western Washington eastward to the crest of the Cascade Mountains. This region is divided into three subsections: the islands of the San Juans and Island County, from Everett north to the Canadian border, and from Seattle south to the Oregon border. The state's volcanoes, Mounts Baker, Rainier, St. Helens, and Adams, are all in the Western Region.

Kayaks and canoes wait to be rented near the Fairholm Campground on Olympic National Park's Lake Crescent.

The Eastern Region stretches from the crest of the Cascades eastward to the Idaho border. It includes the North and South Cascades, the Columbia Plateau, the northeastern highlands, the rolling Palouse, and the Blue Mountains in the state's southeastern corner.

Nearly 400 campgrounds are described in this guide. All of them are publicly owned, and all are accessible by car. A four-wheel-drive vehicle is not necessary to reach any of them. However, you may not be able to tow trailers to a few of the campgrounds, notably those in the Harts Pass area near Winthrop. When that is the case, the text will say so. Everything you need to know about any particular campground before setting out is discussed in the text. Complete driving directions are given from a nearby city, as are the number of campsites, RV length restrictions, a comprehensive list of amenities, nightly fee, elevation of the campground, the managing agency, things to do in the vicinity, and a narrative description of the campground.

Each campground description will tell you at a glance whether a campground offers tent sites, RV sites, or both. Most offer both, but many require RVs to be self-contained. The "Sites" listing will tell you when that's the case.

For easy comparison with other campgrounds in a subregion, the quick-reference guide gives the information in chart form. For example, if your camping style requires a restroom with showers, just scan the "Showers" column to find the campgrounds for you. From that point turn to the page of a campground you are interested in and read the complete description.

Since camping fees change frequently by a dollar or two, we have indicated overnight costs with dollar signs for comparative purposes. The key is:

$ = less than $10
$$ = $10 to $15
$$$ = $16 to $20
$$$$ = more than $20

Five Best Campgrounds in Six Categories

Families with Small Children

Fort Worden State Park, Port Townsend

This campground is easily accessed and offers beach walking, kayaking, biking and hiking trails, dining in Port Townsend on local cuisine, and a historic walk back in time.

Sol Duc, Olympic National Park

Sol Duc Campground's location close to the hot spring pools, Sol Duc Falls, and lack of cell phone service make it a great place for families to create memories.

Ocean City State Park, near Ocean Shores

The park is popular because of its sandy beach, easy accessibility, and proximity to shopping and restaurants in the town of Ocean Shores, 2 miles south.

South Whidbey State Park, near Greenbank on Whidbey Island

The 347-acre park offers plenty of room to play, plus 4,500 feet of saltwater shoreline on Admiralty Inlet on the western shore of Whidbey Island. It offers a sandy beach and views of Puget Sound and the Olympic Mountains.

Lewis and Clark Trail State Park, near Walla Walla

This 37-acre campground is on the Touchet River, which eventually joins the Walla Walla River on its way to the Columbia. Homesteaders used this site to hold post-harvest picnics and games. Park rangers host campfire interpretive programs in summer. There is a 1.0-mile interpretive trail and a 0.75-mile birding trail in the camp.

Families with Teenagers

Moran State Park, Orcas Island

Comprising 5,000 acres, with five lakes, 30 miles of foot trails, and 300 acres of old-growth forest, Moran State Park has more to offer than most parks, plus it's easy to set up multiple-family compounds in the camping areas. I know three extended families who have camped here together for more than fifty years running.

Pacific Beach State Park, near Hoquiam

The unusual in-town location of this park makes it very popular with campers who like the best of both worlds. There's plenty of clam digging, fresh- and saltwater fishing, kite flying, beachcombing, birding, kayaking, and surfing.

Grayland Beach State Park, near Aberdeen

On a hot summer day you would swear this was a Southern California beach—until you touch the water, which is a good 15 to 20 degrees colder here. Sand dunes stretch for a few miles to the south. This is a popular park, and families appreciate the large campsites.

Flowing Lake County Park, near Everett

This 38-acre county park is great for the whole family, including the dog (though it must be leashed). Entertainment is occasionally provided in the amphitheater. The nearby town of Snohomish is well known for its antiques shops.

Gifford on Franklin D. Roosevelt Lake, near Gifford

This large, nice campground sometimes seems like a waterskiing camp for children. It is an excellent facility for boaters. The Gifford-Inchelium ferry, just 1 mile south of camp, offers free passage across the Columbia to the Colville Indian Reservation every half hour.

Loners Who Really Want to Get Away from It All

Olympic National Park: Ozette

Open year-round, the campground is primitive, isolated, and very appealing because of the pristine lake. Cedar walkways lead 3 miles through dense forest to the beaches of the Pacific.

Cottonwood

Set on the banks of the Naches River, this wooded campground is just right for sitting around with or without a fishing rod and maybe taking a hike or two. The campground is open from April through November.

Boundary Dam

Four primitive year-round sites are located on 1,000 acres of wilderness terrain in northeastern Washington. The campground is in a beautiful forested setting on the west bank of the Pend Oreille River, which is hemmed in by precipitous rock walls that rise 100 to 200 feet. The Salmo Priest Wilderness is on the east side of the river.

Alder Thicket

Located, naturally, in an alder thicket in the middle of the proverbial nowhere, this campground is quite rustic, bordering on primitive. The choices are to kick back and commune with nature or go hiking and commune with nature.

Western Lakes, near Naselle

The Washington Department of Natural Resources knows how to build tiny, primitive campgrounds in the middle of nowhere, and this is one of the best and most private. The wooded site is located near tiny Western Lakes. The campground is open year-round.

Anglers

Bumping Lake, north of Yakima

The 1,300-acre lake holds kokanee salmon and rainbow trout. Some campsites are right at the water's edge. There are also some backpacking routes and day trails in the area that lead into the William O. Douglas Wilderness.

Bogachiel State Park, near Forks

With 2,800 feet of shoreline frontage along the Bogachiel River, this is a good location for steelhead fishing.

White Pass Lake (Leech Lake), near Yakima

The campground is at the summit across from the White Pass Ski Area. Fly fishing is good when the water warms a bit, but that is also when the mosquitoes swarm at this altitude (4,500 feet).

Cape Disappointment State Park, on the Long Beach Peninsula

With 8 miles of park shoreline on the Columbia River and Pacific Ocean, nearby Lake O'Neil, and fishing gear available right at the campground, what more could you ask for?

Howard Miller Steelhead, Rockport

This is steelhead country, and the fishing is reputed to be good here. The campground is open year-round.

Hikers

Heart o' the Hills, Olympic National Park

This is the closest campground to Hurricane Ridge and offers good access to the "rain shadow" side of Olympic National Park. The campground is in old-growth forest.

Falls Creek-Crest Horse Camp, 68 miles east of Vancouver

This camp for equestrians is close to the Pacific Crest National Scenic Trail and the Indian Heaven Wilderness in the Gifford Pinchot National Forest.

Clover Flats, near Yakima

Clover Flats is way out there, and therefore it is pretty quiet. It is a good base camp for hikers. Nearby trails head west into the Goat Rocks Wilderness. For winter users there are 60 miles of groomed snowmobiling trails in the area. The campground is open year-round, except during heavy snows.

Iron Creek, near Randle

This 32-acre campground is very popular because of its proximity to the east side of Mount St. Helens and its easy RV access.

Mount Spokane State Park, near Spokane

A ski area in winter, Mount Spokane offers 50 miles of hiking and equestrian trails and sweeping views of the Inland Empire.

Wildlife Viewers

Salt Creek Recreation Area, near Port Angeles

The wildlife here is on land, in the air, and both in and on the sea—the Strait of Juan de Fuca. The tidepools are considered some of the best in the Northwest. Depending on the time of year, campers can see gray whales, harbor seals, river otters, orcas, sea lions, bald eagles, and more.

Big Meadow Lake, 99 miles north of Spokane

Other than a wildlife-viewing platform, this campground doesn't have much in the way of amenities, and the road may give your passengers fits, but the location is idyllic. The campground sits at the edge of 70-acre Big Meadow Lake.

Deception Pass State Park, 18 miles west of Burlington

The state park features a few lakes, some old-growth Douglas fir forests, marshland, sand dunes, and a few smaller islands. Black-tailed deer are common, and bald eagles nest in the treetops.

Pearrygin Lake State Park, near Winthrop

Mountain lions and bears are spotted here from time to time, but deer, groundhogs, and ospreys are the usual wildlife enjoyed by campers.

Millersylvania State Park, near Olympia

Wildlife you may see here includes foxes, black-tailed deer, coyotes, red-tailed hawks, wood ducks, and porcupines.

Map Legend

Transportation

═〔25〕═   Interstate Highway

═〔40〕═   US Highway

═〔119〕═   State Highway

Land Management

▭   National Park/
National Forest

▭   National Monument/
National Recreation Area

Symbols

100   Campground

▲   Peak/Summit

○   Town

Water Features

⬭   Body of Water

∼   River/Creek

Help Us Keep This Guide Up to Date

Every effort has been made by the author and editors to make this guide as accurate and useful as possible. However, many things can change after a guide is published—campgrounds open and close, grow and contract; regulations change; facilities come under new management, and so forth.

We appreciate hearing from you concerning your experiences with this guide and how you feel it could be improved and kept up to date. While we may not be able to respond to all comments and suggestions, we'll take them to heart, and we'll also make certain to share them with the author. Please send your comments and suggestions to the following address:

Globe Pequot Press
Reader Response/Editorial Department
P.O. Box 480
Guilford, CT 06437

Or you may e-mail us at:

editorial@GlobePequot.com

Thanks for your input, and happy camping!

Coastal Region

There is a lot of watching to be done on the Olympic Peninsula: storm watching, whale watching, storm watching, bird watching, storm watching. From July through September the region is relatively dry, and temperatures get into the 70s. But the Olympic Peninsula is basically a temperate rain forest (nearly a million acres of it), and much of what there is to do there concerns water: fishing, boating, river rafting, beach walking, oyster harvesting. Even just going for a walk can mean wet feet. Good water-resistant boots and rain gear will keep you a happy camper.

An early-morning view looks east up the Quinault River on the Olympic Peninsula. Quinault means "wide spot in the river" (campground 10).

US 101 is the only way around the peninsula. The road makes a loop, starting just west of Olympia, but there are enough side trips to keep you busy for days.

Westport is well known for its charter fishing and whale watching, and Ocean Shores is a bit of a beach-resort paradise. On the north end of the peninsula, the community of Neah Bay attracts those interested in charter fishing, but the Makah Tribal Museum is another attraction worth visiting. It exhibits the best of the Ozette archaeological digs and has a good gift shop offering native artifacts.

On the peninsula it is sometimes hard to see the forest for the trees. Since there are only 38 miles of road in Olympic National Park, the best view of the park is from Hurricane Ridge, which is a 17-mile drive from Port Angeles on the north shore.

RV parks and campgrounds abound on the peninsula. There are as many campsites in Grays Harbor County (2,146) as motel rooms. So take a long weekend, or even a week or more, and explore the possibilities. The beaches and forests seem endless.

In the Olympic National Forest, many campsites go begging because campers assume they will all be full. Over one Labor Day Weekend, three-quarters of the campsites here were vacant, while all state park campgrounds were full. Even though no reservations are taken for Olympic National Forest campgrounds, be sure to call ahead and ask about campsite availability—do not assume they will be full.

Hood Canal is a long, narrow saltwater inlet that begins where the Juan de Fuca and Georgia Straits meet near Port Townsend. Hood Canal runs south along the eastern side of the Olympic Peninsula and bends northeast to the town of Belfair. US 101 runs most of the length of the western shore of the canal.

The Strait of Juan de Fuca separates the Olympic Peninsula from Vancouver Island. It is about 17 miles wide, and its shores collect an abundance of flotsam and jetsam during incoming tides from the Pacific Ocean.

Coastal Region: Rain Forest

	Group Sites	RV Sites	Total # of sites	Max RV Length	Hookups	Toilets	Showers	Drinking water	Dump station	Pets	Wheelchair	Recreation	Fee	Season	Can reserve	Stay limit
1 Big Creek	•		23	30		V		•		•		HFBS	$$	May–mid Nov		14
2 Bogachiel State Park	•		44	40	WES	F	•	•	•	•	•	HFB	$$$$	year-round		10
3 Brown Creek	•		20	21		V		•		•		HF	$$	year-round		14
4 Campbell Tree Grove	•		11	16		V		•		•		HF		year-round		14
5 Coho	•		58	36		F		•		•	•	HFBS	$$$	May–mid Nov		14
6 Collins	•		16	21		V		•		•		HFS	$$	mid May–Sept		14
7 Coppermine Bottom	•		9			V				•		FB		year-round		14
8 Cottonwood	•		9			V				•		HFB		year-round		14
9 Dungeness Forks			10			V		•		•		HF	$$	May–Sept		14
10 Falls Creek	•		31	16		F		•		•		FHBS	$$$	Mem Day–Lab Day		14
11 Falls View	•		30	21		F		•		•		HF	$$	mid May–mid Sept		14
12 Gatton Creek			5			V		•		•		HFBS	$$	mid May–Oct		14
13 Hamma Hamma	•		15	21		V		•		•	•	HFSC	$$	May–mid Nov		14
14 Hoh Oxbow	•		7			V					•	FB		year-round		14
15 Klahowya	•		55	20		F		•		•		HBFC	$$$	mid May–mid Oct		14
16 Lake Sylvia State Park	•		37	30		F	•	•	•	•	•	HFSB	$$–$$$$	Mar 15–Oct 31		10
17 Lena Creek	•		13	21		V		•		•	•	HF	$$	mid May–Sept		14
18 Minnie Peterson	•		8			V				•		HFB		year-round		14
19 Olympic Natl Park: Altair	•		30	21		F		•		•	•	HF	$$	Late May–Oct 25		14
20 Olympic Natl Park: Deer Park			14			V		•		•		H	$$	mid June–mid fall		14
21 Olympic Natl Park: Dosewallips			30			F		•		•		FH		mid May–late Sept		14
22 Olympic Natl Park: Elwha	•		40	21		F		•		•	•	HF	$$	year-round		14
23 Olympic Natl Park: Fairholm	•		88	21		F	•	•	•			HFB	$$	April–mid fall		14
24 Olympic Natl Park: Graves Creek	•		30	21		F		•		•	•	HF	$$	year-round		14
25 Olympic Natl Park: Heart o'the Hills	•		105	21		F		•		•	•	H	$$	year-round		14

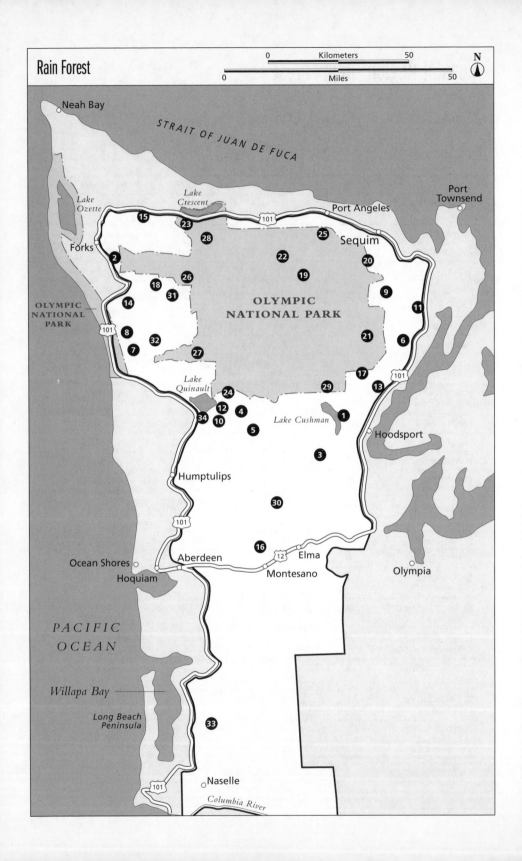

Rain Forest

Kilometers
0 50

Miles
0 50

N

Neah Bay

STRAIT OF JUAN DE FUCA

Lake
Ozette

Lake
Crescent

Port Angeles

Port
Townsend

15
23
101
25
Sequim

28

Forks

2

22

20

OLYMPIC
NATIONAL PARK

26
18
31
19

9

OLYMPIC
NATIONAL
PARK

14

11

101

8
32

21

6

7
27

17

Lake
Quinault

24

29

13

Hoodsport

34
12
4
Lake Cushman
1

10
5

3

Humptulips

30

101

16
12
Elma

Ocean Shores
Aberdeen
Montesano
Olympia

Hoquiam

PACIFIC
OCEAN

Willapa Bay

Long Beach
Peninsula

33

Naselle

101

Columbia River

	Group Sites	RV Sites	Total # of sites	Max RV Length	Hookups	Toilets	Showers	Drinking water	Dump station	Pets	Wheelchair	Recreation	Fee	Season	Can reserve	Stay limit
26 Olympic Natl Park: Hoh		•	88	21		F		•	•	•	•	HF	$$	year-round		14
27 Olympic Natl Park: Queets			20			V		•				HF	$$	year-round		14
28 Olympic Natl Park: Sol Duc		•	82	35		F	•	•	•	•	•	HF	$$	year-round		14
29 Olympic Natl Park: Staircase		•	47	21		F		•		•	•	HF	$$	year-round		14
30 Schafer State Park		•	59	40	WE	F	•	•	•	•	•	HFB	$–$$$$	May thru Sept		10
31 South Fork Hoh		•	3	21		V		•				HFB		year-round		14
32 Upper Clearwater		•	9			V		•				HFB		year-round		14
33 Western Lakes			3			V		•				H		year-round		14
34 Willaby		•	22	16		F		•		•		HFBCS	$$$$	mid April–mid Sept		14

Hookups: W=Water   E=Electric   S=Sewer
Toilets: F=Flush   V=Vault   P=Pit
Recreation: C = Bicycling/Mountain Biking   H=Hiking   S=Swimming   F=Fishing   B=Boating
O=Off-highway driving   R=Horseback Riding
Maximum Trailer/RV Length given in feet. Stay Limit given in days.
Fee $ = less than $10; $$ = $10–$15; $$$ = $16–20; $$$$ = more than $20.
If no entry under Fee, camping is free.

1 Big Creek

Location: 9 miles west of Hoodsport, near Lake Cushman
GPS: N47 29.692' / W123 12.682'
Elevation: 731 feet
Season: May through mid-Nov
Sites: 23 sites for tents or self-contained RVs no longer than 30 feet
Facilities: Drinking water, sheltered picnic tables, firewood, vault toilets, groceries, boat rentals, nature trails
Fee per night: $$
Management: Olympic National Forest, Hood Canal Ranger District, (360) 765-2200; no reservations
Activities: Hiking, fishing, boating, swimming, waterskiing
Finding the campground: From US 101 in the town of Hoodsport on Hood Canal, take WA 119 (Lake Cushman Road) west and then north for 9 miles to the campground.
The campground: The price is right at this 30-acre campground near Lake Cushman in Olympic National Park. The big sites offer more privacy than you find at most public campgrounds. The lake, which is about 8 miles long, is 1.5 miles south of camp.

2 Bogachiel State Park

Location: 6 miles south of Forks on the Bogachiel River
GPS: N47 48.826' / W124 18.811'
Elevation: 310 feet
Season: Year-round
Sites: 36 tent/RV sites, 6 sites with hookups for RVs no longer than 40 feet, 2 primitive sites
Facilities: Drinking water, picnic tables, fire grills, dump station, restrooms, coin-operated showers, boat ramp, kitchen shelter
Fee per night: $$$$
Management: Washington State Parks and Recreation Commission, (360) 902-8844 (information), (360) 374-6356 (park); no reservations
Activities: Hiking, fishing, boating, hunting, rafting
Finding the campground: Bogachiel State Park is 6 miles south of the town of Forks on US 101.
The campground: This sizable campground covers 123 acres and features 2,800 feet of shoreline frontage along the Bogachiel River. It is a good location for steelhead fishing along the river or hiking on 0.5 mile of marked trails nearby. The remote campground is located on both sides of US 101.

3 Brown Creek

Location: About 40 miles northwest of Olympia on the shore of the South Fork Skokomish River
GPS: N47 24.800' / W123 19.136'
Elevation: 650 feet
Season: Year-round
Sites: 8 tent sites, 12 sites for trailers and RVs no longer than 21 feet
Facilities: Drinking water, picnic tables, vault toilets
Fee per night: $$
Management: Olympic National Forest, Hood Canal Ranger District, (360) 765-2200; no reservations
Activities: Hiking, fishing
Finding the campground: Use a forest service map to find this remote campground. Drive west on US Highway 101 from I-5 exit 104 at Olympia. Continue for 29 miles, turn left onto Skokomish Valley Road, and drive 5 miles. Take FR 23 for 9 miles, then FR 2353 for 0.75 mile. Turn onto FR 2340 and drive into the campground.
The campground: Brown Creek Campground encompasses 6 acres within Olympic National Forest. It is rarely crowded because it is difficult to find and not many people know about it. Camping conditions are primitive. So is the access road, but four-wheel drive is not necessary, except perhaps in muddy weather.

4 Campbell Tree Grove

Location: 27 miles northeast of Humptulips, adjacent to the West Fork Humptulips River
GPS: N47 28.859' / W123 41.411'
Elevation: 200 feet
Season: Year-round
Sites: 8 tent sites, 3 sites for tents or self-contained RVs no longer than 16 feet
Facilities: Drinking water, picnic tables, vault toilets
Fee per night: None
Management: Olympic National Forest, Pacific Ranger District—Quinault, (360) 288 2525; no reservations
Activities: Hiking, fishing
Finding the campground: From Humptulips on US 101, drive 5 miles north and turn right (northeast) onto Donkey Creek Road (FR 22). Continue for 8 miles and turn left onto FR 2204. Stay on FR 2204 for 14 miles to the campground.
The campground: This 3-acre riverside campground is in Olympic National Forest next to the Colonel Bob Wilderness. This is way out in the boonies but small, nice, and peaceful. There are good hiking trails in the area.

5 Coho

Location: About 33 miles north of Montesano on the west shore of Wynoochee Lake
GPS: N47 23.412' / W123 36.303'
Elevation: 900 feet
Season: May to mid-Nov
Sites: 58 sites for tents or RVs no longer than 36 feet
Facilities: Drinking water, picnic tables, flush toilets, wheelchair-accessible restroom, boat docks, boat ramp
Fee per night: $$$
Management: Olympic National Forest, Hood Canal Ranger District, (360) 765-2200; no reservations
Activities: Hiking, fishing, canoeing, boating, swimming
Finding the campground: From Montesano, 37 miles west of I-5 on WA 8/US 12, turn north onto Wynoochee Valley Road/FR 22. After 32 miles bear west on FR 22 for 0.25 mile, then north on FR 2294 for just over 1 mile to the campground.
The campground: Wynoochee Lake is about 4 miles long and more than 0.5 mile wide. A hiking trail goes all the way around it. The campground is at the southern end of the lake on the west shore, near Wynoochee Dam. When the weather is nice, Coho is a wonderful campground for relaxing and exploring this part of Olympic National Forest.

6 Collins

Location: 26 miles north of Hoodsport on the Duckabush River
GPS: N47 40.950' / W123 01.182'
Elevation: 200 feet
Season: Mid-May through Sept
Sites: 6 sites for tents, 10 sites for RVs no longer than 21 feet
Facilities: Drinking water, picnic tables, vault toilets
Fee per night: $$
Management: Olympic National Forest, Hood Canal Ranger District, (360) 765-2200; no reservations
Activities: Fishing, hiking, swimming
Finding the campground: From Hoodsport on Hood Canal, drive 21 miles north on US 101. Half a mile south of Duckabush, turn left (west) onto Duckabush Road (FR 2510) and drive 5 miles to the campground.
The campground: Collins Campground is small, shady, and nicely situated on the shore of the Duckabush River in the Olympic National Forest.

7 Coppermine Bottom

Location: About 64 miles north of Hoquiam on the Clearwater River
GPS: N47 39.327' / W124 11.295'
Elevation: 620 feet
Season: Year-round
Sites: 9 sites for tents or self-contained RVs
Facilities: Picnic tables, fire grills, tent pads, vault toilets, group shelter, boat ramp; no drinking water
Fee per night: None
Management: Washington Department of Natural Resources, Olympic Region, (360) 374-6131
Activities: Fishing, boating
Finding the campground: From Hoquiam drive north on US 101 for about 50 miles. At milepost 147, midway between the towns of Amanda Park and Queets, turn north onto Hoh-Clearwater Mainline and drive for 12.6 miles. Turn right onto C-1010 Road and continue for 1.5 miles to the campground on the left. The last 1.5 miles are on a one-lane gravel road.
The campground: Well away from US 101, this secluded campground offers nice sites next to the Clearwater River. This is in the Olympic Experimental State Forest, also known as the Bert Cole State Forest.

8 Cottonwood

Location: About 18 miles south of Forks on the Hoh River
GPS: N47 46.735' / W124 17.537'
Elevation: 160 feet
Season: Year-round
Sites: 9 sites for tents or self-contained RVs
Facilities: Picnic tables, fire grills, tent pads, vault toilets, boat ramp; no drinking water
Fee per night: None
Management: Washington Department of Natural Resources, Olympic Region, (360) 374-6131
Activities: Hiking, fishing, boating, river rafting
Finding the campground: About 15 miles south of the town of Forks, between mileposts 177 and 178 on US 101, turn west onto Lower Hoh Road (also called Oil City Road). Drive for 2.3 miles and turn left onto H-4060, a gravel road. Continue 0.9 mile to the campground.
The campground: The Hoh is a swift, wide, and wondrous river, and this campground sits just above its bank. The camp is primitive but pleasantly isolated and peaceful. It is in the Olympic Experimental State Forest, also known as the Bert Cole State Forest.

9 Dungeness Forks

Location: About 12 miles south of Sequim at the confluence of the Dungeness and Gray Wolf Rivers
GPS: N47 46.735' / W124 17.537'
Elevation: 1,000 feet
Season: May through Sept
Sites: 10 tent sites
Facilities: Drinking water, picnic tables, vault toilets
Fee per night: $$
Management: Olympic National Forest, Hood Canal Ranger District, (360) 765-2200; no reservations
Activities: Hiking, fishing
Finding the campground: From Sequim, drive 3 miles southeast on US 101 and turn right (south) onto Palo Alto Road. Follow it for 7 miles, and then turn right (west) onto FR 2880. Continue 1.5 miles to the campground.
The campground: Situated in Olympic National Forest, Dungeness Forks Campground is comfortable, shady, and quiet. It is located at the confluence of the Dungeness and Gray Wolf Rivers, in the rain shadow of the Olympic Mountains. That means it is drier than campgrounds on the west side of the Olympic Peninsula.

Sailboats gather on the southern shore of Lake Quinault near Lake Quinalt Lodge, the Sitka Spruce Golf Course, and Falls Creek Campground.

10 Falls Creek

Location: About 45 miles north of Aberdeen on the south shore of Lake Quinault
GPS: N47 28.174' / W123 50.724'
Elevation: 200 feet
Season: Memorial Day through Labor Day
Sites: 15 tent sites, 16 sites for RVs no longer than 16 feet
Facilities: Drinking water, picnic tables, flush toilets; nearby boat rentals, docks, ramps
Fee per night: $$$
Management: Olympic National Forest, Pacific Ranger District—Quinault, (360) 288-2525
Activities: Fishing, hiking, boating, swimming
Finding the campground: From Aberdeen drive 42 miles north on US 101 to the Quinault turnoff (South Shore Road). Turn right (northeast) and drive 2.5 miles to the campground on the east shore of Lake Quinault.
The campground: Falls Creek Campground is located in Olympic National Forest, where Falls Creek flows into Lake Quinault. It is near the Quinault Ranger Station and Lake Quinault Lodge.

There is a boat ramp and a rocky beach. The lake is part of the Quinault Indian Nation, so a tribal fishing permit and boat decal are required. Both may be purchased at local merchants. The swimming is good in the warmer months of July and August. Signed nature trails go near and through the campground.

11 Falls View

Location: About 29 miles south of Port Townsend on the Big Quilcene River
GPS: N47 47.433' / W122 55.578'
Elevation: 400 feet
Season: Mid-May to mid-Sept
Sites: 30 sites for tents or RVs no longer than 21 feet
Facilities: Drinking water, picnic tables, flush toilets
Fee per night: $$
Management: Olympic National Forest, Hood Canal Ranger District, (360) 765-2200; no reservations
Activities: Hiking, fishing
Finding the campground: The entrance to Falls View Campground is on US 101, 3.5 miles south of Quilcene, which is 25 miles south of Port Townsend.
The campground: Within hiking distance of nearby Mount Walker, Falls View is a popular campground on the eastern side of the Big Quilcene River in Olympic National Forest.

12 Gatton Creek

Location: 45 miles north of Aberdeen on the south shore of Lake Quinault
GPS: N47 28.430' / W123 50.267'
Elevation: 200 feet
Season: Mid-May through Oct
Sites: 5 tent sites
Facilities: Drinking water, picnic tables, firewood, vault toilets, nature trail
Fee per night: $$
Management: Olympic National Forest, Pacific Ranger District—Quinault, (360) 288-2525; no reservations
Activities: Hiking, fishing, boating, swimming
Finding the campground: From Aberdeen, drive 42 miles north on US 101 to the Quinault turnoff (South Shore Road). Turn right (northeast) and drive 3 miles to the campground on the eastern shore of Lake Quinault.
The campground: Gatton Creek Campground was named for the creek that runs into Lake Quinault at this site. Situated in Olympic National Forest, the camp is small but lovely and peaceful. Signed nature trails pass through the rain forest nearby.

13 Hamma Hamma

Location: About 19 miles north of Hoodsport on the Hamma Hamma River
GPS: N47 35.712' / W123 07.367'
Elevation: 570 feet
Season: May to mid-Nov
Sites: 3 sites for tents, 12 sites for tents or self-contained RVs no longer than 21 feet
Facilities: Drinking water, picnic tables, vault toilets
Fee per night: $$
Management: Olympic National Forest, Hood Canal Ranger District, (360) 765-2200; no reservations
Activities: Hiking, fishing, swimming, mountain biking
Finding the campground: From Hoodsport on Hood Canal, drive 13 miles north on US 101. Two miles past Eldon, turn left (northwest) onto Hamma Hamma River Road (FR 25) and drive 6.5 miles to the campground.
The campground: This 5-acre, primitive camp is located in Olympic National Forest, just below the spot where Cabin Creek enters the Hamma Hamma River. The fishing is fine here on the "dry" side of the Olympic Mountains.

14 Hoh Oxbow

Location: About 16 miles south of Forks on the Hoh River
GPS: N47 48.679' / W124 15.049'
Elevation: 317 feet
Season: Year-round
Sites: 7 sites for tents or self-contained RVs, including 1 wheelchair-accessible site
Facilities: Picnic tables, fire grills, tent pads, vault toilets, boat ramp; no drinking water
Fee per night: None
Management: Washington Department of Natural Resources, Olympic Region, (360) 374-6131
Activities: Fishing, boating, river rafting
Finding the campground: The campground is about 16 miles south of the town of Forks between mileposts 176 and 177 on US 101. It is on the east side of the highway between the road and the Hoh River.
The campground: Hoh Oxbow, named for the oxbow made by the river here, is popular with anglers. The campground is very primitive and there is no water, but it is an easy trip north to Forks for supplies. This camp is in the Olympic Experimental State Forest, also known as the Bert Cole State Forest.

All the leaves seem to burst open at once in early spring on the Olympic Peninsula.

15 **Klahowya**

Location: About 20 miles northeast of Forks on the Soleduck River
GPS: N48 03.841' / W124 06.317'
Season: Mid-May to mid-Oct with full services; limited services rest of the year
Elevation: 800 feet
Sites: 35 sites for tents, 20 sites for RVs no longer than 20 feet
Facilities: Drinking water, picnic tables, vault and flush toilets, boat ramp
Fee per night: $$$
Management: Olympic National Forest, Pacific Ranger District—Forks, (360) 374-6522; no reservations
Activities: Hiking, boating, fishing, mountain biking
Finding the campground: From the town of Forks, drive 20 miles northeast on US 101.
The campground: This 32-acre campground in Olympic National Forest is quite popular because of its easy access from US 101 and its thickly forested surroundings. It is nicely situated on the comparative flats of the Soleduck River Valley next to the river.

16 Lake Sylvia State Park

Location: About 2 miles north of Montesano on Lake Sylvia
GPS: N47 00.000' / W123 35.400'
Elevation: 125 feet
Season: Mar 15 through Oct 31
Sites: 35 sites for tents or self-contained RVs no longer than 30 feet, 2 primitive tent sites
Facilities: Drinking water, picnic tables, fire grills, dump station, toilets, coin-operated showers, store, boat ramp, boat rentals, playground
Fee per night: $$-$$$$
Management: Washington State Parks and Recreation Commission, (360) 902-8844 (information), (360) 249-3621 (park)
Activities: Hiking, fishing, swimming, boating
Finding the campground: From US 12 in Montesano, head north at the sign for Lake Sylvia State Park. Drive 1.5 miles through town to reach the park.
The campground: Lake Sylvia State Park encompasses 234 acres and features 15,000 feet of shoreline, 270 feet of which are a developed swimming beach. Other attractions are a swimming float and 5 miles of hiking trails. The lake was formed when Sylvia Creek was dammed for log impoundment and power production. The power operated a downstream lumber mill for sixty years beginning in 1871. Individual campsites can be reserved from Apr 1 through Sept 30 by visiting https://secure.camis.com/WA/ or calling (888) 226-7688.

17 Lena Creek

Location: 21 miles northwest of Hoodsport on the Hamma Hamma River
GPS: N47 35.898' / W123 09.082'
Elevation: 700 feet
Season: Mid-May through Sept
Sites: 13 sites for tents or self-contained RVs no longer than 21 feet
Facilities: Drinking water, picnic tables, vault toilets
Fee per night: $$
Management: Olympic National Forest, Hood Canal Ranger District, (360) 765 2200; no reservations
Activities: Hiking, fishing
Finding the campground: From the town of Hoodsport on Hood Canal, drive 11 miles north on US 101 to Eldon. Continue 2 miles north on US 101 and then turn left (northwest) onto Hamma Hamma River Road (FR 25). Drive 8 miles to the campground.
The campground: This 7-acre campground is very basic, good for roughing it if you are so inclined. Save some energy for the 1.5-mile hike up Lena Creek past the Mason/Jefferson County line to Lena Lake. The lake is about 0.5 mile long, and 1 mile beyond the lake, the trail crosses from Olympic National Forest into Olympic National Park. From there it is another 3 miles to Upper Lena Lake.

A walk in the rain is part of the Hoh Rain Forest experience. Borrow an umbrella from the visitor center, and take the hour-long loop through a wonderland of flora.

18 Minnie Peterson

Location: About 18 miles southeast of Forks on the Hoh River
GPS: N47 48.679' / W124 15.049'
Elevation: 120 feet
Season: Year-round
Sites: 8 sites for tents or self-contained RVs
Facilities: Picnic tables, fire grills, tent pads, vault toilets; no drinking water
Fee per night: None
Management: Washington Department of Natural Resources, Olympic Region, (360) 374-2800
Activities: Hiking, fishing, boating, river rafting
Finding the campground: From Forks drive about 13 miles south on US 101. Turn left (east) between mileposts 178 and 179 onto Upper Hoh Road. Drive 4.5 miles to reach the campground on the left.
The campground: This campground sits at the edge of the Hoh Rain Forest in the Olympic Experimental State Forest (or Bert Cole State Forest). It is just outside the boundary of Olympic National Park. It is primitive and free, and the sites are nicely placed along the riverbank.

19 Olympic National Park: Altair

Location: About 13 miles southwest of Port Angeles on the Elwha River in Olympic National Park
GPS: N48 01.039' / W123 35.395'
Elevation: 450 feet
Season: Late May through Oct 25
Sites: 30 sites for tents or RVs no longer than 21 feet
Facilities: Drinking water, picnic tables, fire grills, restrooms, some wheelchair-accessible facilities
Fee per night: $$
Management: Olympic National Park, Elwha Ranger Station, (360) 565-3130
Activities: Hiking, fishing
Finding the campground: From Port Angeles on the Strait of Juan de Fuca, take US 101 west for 9 miles to the turnoff onto Olympic Hot Springs Road, just past Lake Aldwell. The campground is about 4 miles south on Olympic Hot Springs Road.
The campground: Altair feels more remote than it actually is. It is secluded and private, with good access to hiking trails in both Olympic National Forest and Olympic National Park.

20 Olympic National Park: Deer Park

Location: About 22 miles southeast of Port Angeles in Olympic National Park
GPS: N47 56.838' / W47 56.838'
Elevation: 5,400 feet
Season: Mid-June to mid-fall; limited winter facilities
Sites: 14 tent sites
Facilities: Drinking water, picnic tables, fire grills, vault toilets
Fee per night: $$
Management: Olympic National Park, (360) 565-3130
Activities: Hiking
Finding the campground: From US 101, 4 miles east of downtown Port Angeles, head south into the park on Deer Park Road. Continue for 18 miles to the campground.
The campground: Access to alpine hiking trails is the main appeal of Deer Park, a primitive campground for tents only. Its elevation of more than a mile allows you to get acclimated before tackling the trails. Unseasonable snows can close the winding dirt access road.

21 Olympic National Park: Dosewallips

Location: 39 miles northwest of Hoodsport on the Dosewallips River in Olympic National Park
GPS: N47 44.208' / W123 09.912'
Elevation: 1,540 feet
Season: Mid-May to late Sept

Sites: 30 tent sites for hikers only. The road to camp is washed out and closed 5.5 miles from the campground.
Facilities: Picnic tables, fire grills, restrooms; no water
Fee per night: None
Management: Olympic National Park, (360) 565-3130
Activities: Fishing, nature trails
Finding the campground: From Hoodsport on Hood Canal, drive north on US 101 for nearly 25 miles to just south of the town of Brinnon. Turn west onto Dosewallips Road (FR 2610) and drive along the Dosewallips River for 14 miles to the campground.
The campground: Dosewallips Campground is about the end of the road for cars, but you could hike along rivers to the Pacific Coast from here. The riverside campsites attract a lot of people who want to hike the trail network in Olympic National Park.

22 Olympic National Park: Elwha

Location: About 12 miles southwest of Port Angeles on the Elwha River in Olympic National Park
GPS: N48 01.674' / W123 35.262'
Elevation: 390 feet
Season: Year-round; primitive conditions in winter
Sites: 40 sites for tents or RVs no longer than 21 feet
Facilities: Drinking water, picnic tables, fire grills, restrooms, some wheelchair-accessible facilities
Fee per night: $$
Management: Olympic National Park, (360) 565-3130
Activities: Hiking, fishing
Finding the campground: From Port Angeles on the Strait of Juan de Fuca, take US 101 west for 9 miles to the turnoff onto Olympic Hot Springs Road, just past Lake Aldwell. The campground is about 2.5 miles south on Olympic Hot Springs Road.
The campground: The Elwha River is a lovely, north-draining river on the Olympic Peninsula, and this campground is right on the riverbank. It affords good access to hiking trails in both Olympic National Forest and Olympic National Park.

23 Olympic National Park: Fairholm

Location: About 22 miles west of Port Angeles on Lake Crescent in Olympic National Park
GPS: N48 04.074' / W123 54.978'
Elevation: 580 feet
Season: April through mid-fall
Sites: 88 sites for tents or RVs no longer than 21 feet
Facilities: Drinking water, picnic tables, fire grills, dump station, restrooms
Fee per night: $$
Management: Olympic National Park, (360) 565-3130
Activities: Hiking, fishing, boating

Finding the campground: From Port Angeles drive 22 miles west on US 101 to the western end of Lake Crescent. Turn right (north) onto North Shore Road. The campground is on the right within 0.5 mile.

The campground: Lake Crescent is a study in just how sublime a remote subalpine lake can be—except that it sits right next to the highway at a low elevation. Plenty of boaters use the lake; there is even a paddle wheeler for tourists. But if the lake were not in Olympic National Park, there would be subdivisions all around it. Fairholm's amenities make it one of the more comfortable campgrounds in the park.

24 Olympic National Park: Graves Creek

Location: 60 miles north of Aberdeen on the Quinault River in Olympic National Park
GPS: N47 34.272' / W123 34.908'
Elevation: 600 feet
Season: Year-round; limited amenities in winter
Sites: 30 sites for tents or RVs no longer than 21 feet
Facilities: Drinking water, picnic tables, fire grills, wheelchair-accessible restrooms
Fee per night: $$

It's not Disneyland; it's the remarkable Hall of Mosses Trail in the Olympic National Park Rain Forest. Take an umbrella and immerse yourselves in the mosses.

Management: Olympic National Park, (360) 565-3130

Activities: Hiking, fishing

Finding the campground: From Aberdeen drive 42 miles north on US 101 to the Quinault turnoff (South Shore Road). Turn right (northeast) and drive 18 miles to the campground. Graves Creek Ranger Station is here too.

The campground: Graves Creek Campground, located near the spot at which Graves Creek empties into the Quinault River, is a good base site for hikes into the Olympic backcountry.

25 Olympic National Park: Heart o' the Hills

Location: 6 miles south of Port Angeles in Olympic National Park

GPS: N48 02.040' / W123 25.560'

Elevation: 1,800 feet

Season: Year-round

Sites: 105 sites for tents or RVs no longer than 21 feet

Facilities: Drinking water, picnic tables, restrooms, wheelchair-accessible facilities

Fee per night: $$

Management: Olympic National Park, (360) 565-3130

Activities: Nature program, hiking

Finding the campground: From US 101 in Port Angeles, head south toward Hurricane Ridge on Mount Angeles Road. Continue 6 miles to the campground.

The campground: Heart o' the Hills covers just 35 acres, but it offers good access to the "rain shadow" side of Olympic National Park. The paved road continues to Hurricane Ridge, an alpine and cross-country ski area with excellent winter programs. Heavy snow can close Hurricane Ridge Road.

26 Olympic National Park: Hoh

Location: 33 miles southeast of Forks in Olympic National Park

GPS: N47 51.606' / W123 56.262'

Elevation: 500 feet

Season: Year-round

Sites: 88 sites for tents or RVs no longer than 21 feet

Facilities: Drinking water, picnic tables, fire grills, restrooms, wheelchair-accessible facilities, dump station

Fee per night: $$

Management: Olympic National Park, (360) 565-3130

Activities: Nature program, hiking, fishing

Finding the campground: From the town of Forks, drive 14 miles south on US 101. Turn left (east) onto Hoh River Road, and continue for 19 miles to the campground.

The campground: Hoh Campground, in the Hoh Rain Forest, can be one of the wettest places on Earth, but the surreal surroundings make this a very popular site, and no one seems to mind the rain. The visitor center even loans umbrellas. Visitors are surprised by how many shades of green can be found in this one place and by how big the plants grow here. There are two barrier-free loop trails nearby: One is 0.25 mile long, the other 1.25 miles. The Hall of Mosses Trail is a 0.75-mile loop that begins and ends at the visitor center. Don't miss it, even if it's pouring—it's well worth the experience.

27 Olympic National Park: Queets

Location: 75 miles north of Aberdeen on the Queets River in Olympic National Park
GPS: N47 37.554' / W124 00.864'
Elevation: 350 feet
Season: Year-round
Sites: 20 tent sites
Facilities: Picnic tables, fire grills, vault toilets; no drinking water
Fee per night: $$
Management: Olympic National Park, (360) 565-3130
Activities: Hiking, fishing
Finding the campground: From Aberdeen, drive 61 miles north on US 101, passing the turnoff to Lake Quinault. Just past the Jefferson County line, look for the campground sign on the right. Turn right here onto Queets River Road, a dirt road, and drive 14 miles along the Queets River to the campground at the end of the road.
The campground: The 2-acre Queets Campground is located as far into the Queets Rain Forest as you can drive. It is popular, nevertheless, for the rustic experience it offers.

28 Olympic National Park: Sol Duc

Location: 40 miles southwest of Port Angeles on the Soleduck River in Olympic National
GPS: N47 58.015' / W123 51.419'
Elevation: 1,700 feet
Season: Year-round; minimal services in winter
Sites: 82 sites for tents or RVs no longer than 35 feet
Facilities: Drinking water, picnic tables, fire grills, restrooms, dump station
Fee per night: $$
Management: Olympic National Park, (360) 565-3130
Activities: Hiking, fishing, nature programs
Finding the campground: From Port Angeles, drive west 28 miles on US 101. A few miles past Lake Crescent, turn left (southeast) onto Sol Duc River Road; continue for 12 miles to the campground.
The campground: Sol Duc Campground is very popular because of its proximity to Sol Duc Hot Springs, which are open to the public. The hot springs are fully developed and operated by a

Sol Duc Hot Springs, near the Sol Duc Campground in Olympic National Park, are open to the public.

resort, so there is an admission fee. The mineral pools are like giant hot tubs. The campground is nicely set on the west side of the Soleduck River, and the spaces offer some privacy.

29 Olympic National Park: Staircase

Location: 17 miles northwest of Hoodsport on the North Fork Skokomish River in Olympic National Park
GPS: N47 30.855' / W123 19.727'
Elevation: 820 feet
Season: Year-round; primitive Oct 26 through Apr 30
Sites: 47 sites for tents or self-contained RVs no longer than 21 feet
Facilities: Drinking water, picnic tables, fire grills, flush toilets, wheelchair-accessible facilities
Fee per night: $$
Management: Olympic National Park, (360) 565-3130
Activities: Hiking, fishing
Finding the campground: From US 101 in the town of Hoodsport on Hood Canal, drive 17 miles west and then north on WA 119 (Lake Cushman Road). The campground is 1 mile north of Lake Cushman, where Lake Cushman Road becomes FR 24.
The campground: The hiking is splendid around this 8-acre campground, which sits on the North Fork Skokomish River. The name Staircase comes from the Staircase Rapids at the site.

30 Schafer State Park

Location: 16 miles northwest of Elma on the East Fork Satsop River
GPS: N47 01.350' / W123 24.216'
Elevation: 235 feet
Season: May through Sept; park open year-round
Sites: 47 developed tent sites, 10 RV sites (40-foot maximum) with water and electrical hookups, 2 primitive tent sites
Facilities: Drinking water, picnic tables, fire grills, dump station, toilets, coin-operated showers, firewood (fee), playground
Fee per night: $–$$$$
Management: Washington State Parks and Recreation Commission, (360) 902-8844 (information); (360) 482-3852 (park)
Activities: Hiking, fishing, river floating, canoeing, kayaking, bird and wildlife watching
Finding the campground: From Elma drive 4 miles west on US 12 to the town of Satsop. Turn right (north) onto East Satsop Road and drive 12 miles to the campground.
The campground: This nice, 119-acre family campground features nearly a mile of shoreline on the East Fork Satsop River. The heavily wooded park was donated to the state by Schafer Brothers Logging Company.

31 South Fork Hoh

Location: About 27 miles southeast of Forks on the South Fork Hoh River
GPS: N47 48.238' / W123 59.428'
Elevation: 650 feet
Season: Year-round
Sites: 3 sites for tents or self-contained RVs up to 21 feet
Facilities: Picnic tables, fire grills, tent pads, vault toilets; no drinking water
Fee per night: None
Management: Washington Department of Natural Resources, Olympic Region, (360) 374-6131
Activities: Hiking, fishing, boating, river rafting
Finding the campground: From Forks drive about 13 miles south on US 101. Turn left (east) at milepost 176 onto Upper Hoh Road. Drive 6.6 miles on this paved road and turn left onto H-1000 Road, which becomes a one-lane gravel road for the last few miles. The campground is on the right, 7.4 miles from the turn onto H-1000 Road.
The campground: This campground is quite small and very remote, almost your own personal wilderness site. It is in the Olympic Experimental State Forest, also known as the Bert Cole State Forest. The Olympic National Park South Fork Trailhead is 2 miles beyond the campground.

32 Upper Clearwater

Location: About 66 miles north of Hoquiam on the Clearwater River
Sites: 9 sites for tents or self-contained RVs
GPS: N47 28.859' / W123 41.411'
Elevation: 1,574 feet
Season: Year-round
Facilities: Picnic tables, fire grills, tent pads, vault toilets, boat ramp; no drinking water
Fee per night: None
Management: Washington Department of Natural Resources, Olympic Region, (360) 374-6131
Activities: Fishing, hiking, boating
Finding the campground: From Hoquiam drive north on US 101 for about 50 miles. At milepost 147, midway between the towns of Amanda Park and Queets, turn north onto Hoh-Clearwater Mainline and drive for 12.9 miles. Turn right onto C-3000 Road, a one-lane gravel road, and continue for 3.2 miles to the campground on the right.
The campground: This well-appointed yet primitive campground on the Upper Clearwater is in a section of the rain forest not far from both Olympic National Forest and Olympic National Park. It is situated in the Olympic Experimental State Forest, also known as the Bert Cole State Forest.

33 Western Lakes

Location: About 6 miles north of Naselle
GPS: N46 22.230' / W123 46.894'
Elevation: 900 feet
Season: Year-round
Sites: 3 primitive tent sites
Facilities: Picnic tables, fire grills, tent pads, vault toilets; no drinking water
Fee per night: None
Management: Washington Department of Natural Resources, Pacific Cascade Region, (360) 577-2025
Activities: Hiking
Finding the campground: From the junction of US Highway 101 and WA 4, 5.5 miles northwest of Naselle, drive 3 miles south on WA 4 to milepost 3. Turn left (north) onto C-line Road. At the entrance to the Naselle Youth Camp, take the left fork and drive for 2.9 miles. Turn left onto C-2600 Road and drive for 0.9 mile. At C-2650 Road turn right; continue 0.3 mile to the campground. The road narrows to one lane and turns to gravel near the end.
The campground: The Washington Department of Natural Resources knows how to build tiny, primitive campgrounds in the middle of nowhere, and this is one of the best and most private. The wooded site is located near tiny Western Lakes.

34 Willaby

Location: About 44 miles north of Aberdeen on Lake Quinault
GPS: N 47 27.680' / W 123 51.633'
Elevation: 200 feet
Season: Mid-Apr to mid-Sept
Sites: 22 sites for tents or RVs no longer than 16 feet
Facilities: Drinking water, picnic tables, flush toilets, bathroom electricity, boat docks, boat ramp
Fee per night: $$$$
Management: Olympic National Forest, Pacific Ranger District—Quinault, (360) 288-2525; no reservations
Activities: Hiking, fishing, bicycling, boating, swimming. The lake is part of the Quinault Indian Nation, so a tribal fishing permit and boat decal are required. Both may be purchased at local merchants.
Finding the campground: From Aberdeen drive 42 miles north on US 101 to the Quinault turnoff (South Shore Road). Turn right (northeast) and drive 1.5 miles to the campground on the east shore of Lake Quinault.
The campground: This wooded campground covers 7 acres in Olympic National Forest. The swimming is good, and there is a boat ramp. The beach is rocky, but the water is "warm" according to the local forest ranger—45 to 50 degrees Fahrenheit. Ouch! That is comparable to the temperature of Puget Sound. Nevertheless, the water is clean and brisk.

Coastal Region: Beaches

	Group Sites	RV Sites	Total # of sites	Max RV Length	Hookups	Toilets	Showers	Drinking water	Dump station	Pets	Wheelchair	Recreation	Fee	Season	Can reserve	Stay limit
35 Cape Disappointment State Park	•	•	237	45	WES	F	•	•	•	•	•	HFB	$$–$$$	year-round	•	10
36 Grayland Beach State Park		•	120	40	WES	F	•	•		•	•	HFR	$$–$$$$	year-round	•	10
37 Ocean City State Park	•	•	178	50	WES	F	•	•	•	•	•	HFRS	$$–$$$	year-round	•	10
38 Olympic Natl Park: Kalaloch		•	177	21		F		•	•	•	•	HF	$$	year-round		14
39 Olympic Natl Park: Mora	•	•	95	21		F		•	•	•	•	HF	$$	year-round		14
40 Olympic Natl Park: Ozette		•	14	21		V		•		•		HFB		year-round		14
41 Pacific Beach State Park		•	66	60	E	F	•	•	•	•	•	FB	$$–$$$	year-round	•	10
42 Twin Harbors State Park	•	•	268	35	WES	F	•	•	•	•	•	FR	$$–$$$$	year-round	•	10

Hookups: W=Water E=Electric S=Sewer
Toilets: F=Flush V=Vault P=Pit
Recreation: C=Bicycling/Mountain Biking H=Hiking S=Swimming F=Fishing B=Boating
O=Off-highway driving R=Horseback Riding
Maximum Trailer/RV Length given in feet. Stay Limit given in days.
Fee $ = less than $10; $$ = $10–$15; $$$ = $16–20; $$$$ = more than $20.
If no entry under Fee, camping is free.

35 Cape Disappointment State Park

Location: About 3 miles southwest of Ilwaco on the Long Beach Peninsula
GPS: N46 17.467' / W124 04.333'
Elevation: Sea level
Season: Year-round
Sites: 137 standard campsites, 60 full hookup sites (45-foot limit), 18 sites with water and electricity only, 5 primitive campsites, 14 yurts, 3 cabins
Facilities: Drinking water, picnic tables, fire grills, flush toilets, coin-operated showers, dump station, boat ramps, groceries, fishing gear, interpretive center
Fee per night: $$–$$$
Management: Washington State Parks and Recreation Commission, (360) 902-8844 (information); (360) 642-3078 (park office)
Activities: Hiking, clam digging, surf fishing, beachcombing, seasonal whale watching, boating, interpretive center, nature program

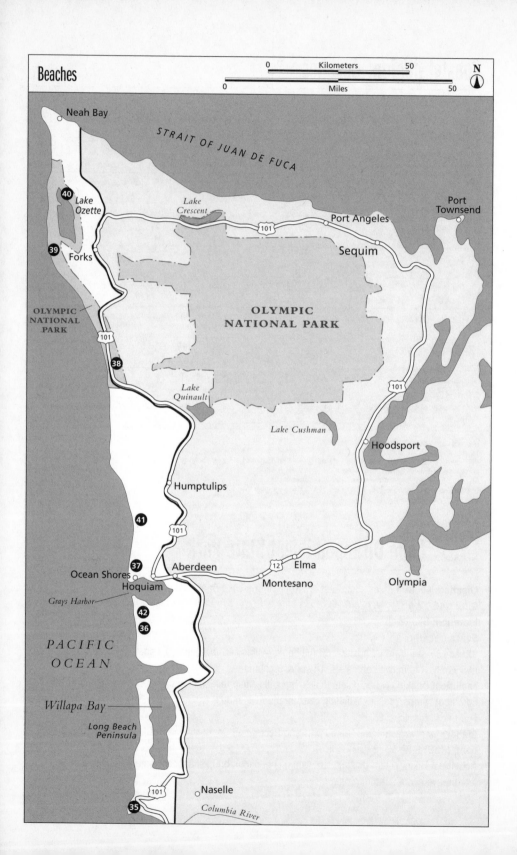

Beaches

Kilometers 0 — 50

Miles 0 — 50

N

Neah Bay

STRAIT OF JUAN DE FUCA

40 Lake Ozette

Lake Crescent

Port Angeles

Port Townsend

39 Forks

101

Sequim

OLYMPIC NATIONAL PARK

OLYMPIC NATIONAL PARK

101

38

Lake Quinault

Lake Cushman

Hoodsport

101

Humptulips

41

101

37 Ocean Shores

Aberdeen

12 Elma

Olympia

Hoquiam

Montesano

Grays Harbor

42

36

PACIFIC OCEAN

Willapa Bay

Long Beach Peninsula

101

Naselle

Columbia River

35

Finding the campground: From the town of Ilwaco on US 101, drive southwest on Fort Canby Road for 2.5 miles to the park.

The campground: This is a mighty nice campground considering the rugged terrain and brutish winter weather. It was here, at Cape Disappointment, that Lewis and Clark finally reached the Pacific Ocean in 1805. The campsites are on the sea side of this 1,882-acre park. Nearby Lake O'Neil has 1.3 miles of shoreline, and the park itself includes 8 miles of shoreline on the Columbia River and Pacific Ocean. Four miles of hiking trails lead through the park, to the beaches, to a pair of lighthouses (North Head and Cape Disappointment), and through old-growth forests. The Lewis and Clark Interpretive Center is open year-round, and tours are available of the North Head Lighthouse. Fort Canby was first armed during the Civil War and was dedicated as a state park nearly one hundred years later, in 1957. The Cape Disappointment area has been declared a National Historic District. Individual campsites can be reserved year-round by visiting https:// secure.camis.com/WA/ or calling (888) 226-7688.

36 Grayland Beach State Park

Location: About 20 miles southwest of Aberdeen
GPS: N46 47.322' / W124 05.574'
Elevation: Sea level
Season: Year-round
Sites: 58 sites with full hookups and 42 water sites with water and electric hookups for RVs no longer than 40 feet, 16 yurts, 4 primitive tent sites with a shared portable toilet
Facilities: Drinking water, picnic tables, flush toilets, fire grills, coin-operated showers
Fee per night: $$–$$$$
Management: Washington State Parks and Recreation Commission, (360) 902-8844 (information); (360) 267-4301 (park office)
Activities: Hiking, fishing, clam digging, kite flying, horseback riding, beachcombing
Finding the campground: From US 12 in Aberdeen, drive southwest for about 20 miles on WA 105. The campground is just south of Grayland.
The campground: This state park features nearly 1.5 miles of wide, sandy beach. On a hot summer day, you would swear this was Southern California—until you touched the water, that is. It is a good 15 to 20 degrees colder here. Sand dunes stretch for a few miles to the south, and to the north there is a cranberry bog on the other side of the highway. This is a popular park, and families appreciate the large campsites. Individual campsites can be reserved year-round by visiting https://secure.camis.com/WA/ or calling (888) 226-7688.

37 Ocean City State Park

Location: 17 miles west of Hoquiam, near Ocean Shores
GPS: N47 01.956' / W124 09.846'
Elevation: Sea level
Season: Year-round

Sites: 149 tent sites, 29 sites with full hookups for RVs no longer than 50 feet, 1 group site

Facilities: Drinking water, picnic tables, restrooms, dump station, coin-operated showers

Fee per night: $$–$$$

Management: Washington State Parks and Recreation Commission, (360) 902-8844 (information), (360) 289-3553 (park office)

Activities: Beachcombing, clam digging, fishing, horseback riding, kite flying, surfing, birding, mushroom picking, hiking, swimming

Finding the campground: From US 101 in Hoquiam, head west on WA 109 for 16 miles. At the intersection with WA 115, turn left (south) and drive for 1 mile to the park entrance on the right.

The campground: Ocean City State Park encompasses 170 acres, including 2,980 feet of coastline. The state's purchase of the land in 1960 ensured permanent public access to the beach. American Indians of the region traditionally made regular seasonal stops here to hunt for razor clams. Today the park is popular because of its sandy beach, easy accessibility, and proximity to shopping and restaurants in the town of Ocean Shores, 2 miles south. Individual campsites can be reserved year-round by visiting https://secure.camis.com/WA/ or calling (888) 226-7688.

38 Olympic National Park: Kalaloch

Location: 35 miles south of Forks in Olympic National Park

GPS: N47 36.784' / W124 22.483'

Elevation: Sea level

Season: Year-round

Sites: 177 sites for tents or self-contained RVs no longer than 21 feet

Facilities: Drinking water, picnic tables, fire grills, restrooms, wheelchair-accessible facilities, dump station

Fee per night: $$

Management: Olympic National Park, (360) 565-3130

Activities: Hiking, fishing, summer nature program

Finding the campground: From the town of Forks, drive 35 miles south on US 101 to the campground.

The campground: This is one of the few campgrounds on the Olympic Peninsula with access to Pacific beaches. Situated on a bluff above the beach, it is large enough that a walk around camp is an actual excursion. Some of the campsites feature an ocean view, and most are shielded from one another by scrub brush. Be prepared for wet weather, both fog and rain. During summer there is an overflow area 3 miles to the south on a gravel lot close to the beach. It has restrooms but no other facilities.

39 Olympic National Park: Mora

Location: 14 miles west of Forks on the Quillayute River in Olympic National Park

GPS: N47 55.104' / W124 36.430'

Elevation: 50 feet

Season: Year-round

Sites: 94 sites for tents or self-contained RVs no longer than 21 feet, 1 group site

Facilities: Drinking water, picnic tables, fire grills, restrooms, dump station

Fee per night: $$

Management: Olympic National Park, (360) 565-3130

Activities: Fishing, hiking, summer nature program

Finding the campground: From the town of Forks, drive north for 2 miles on US 101. Turn left (west) on La Push Road (WA 110) and continue for 8 miles. Bear right onto Mora Road at the Y junction and follow the signs for 4 miles to Mora Campground.

The campground: This is an isolated campground near the mouth of the Quillayute River. The nearby fishing community of La Push is home to the Quileute Indians. Mora Road continues past the campground to Rialto Beach, the only point between the Hoh River and Neah Bay with vehicle access to the coastline of Olympic National Park. The rocky headlands and offshore sea stacks are stark reminders of the wildness of this part of the coast. This stretch of the Pacific Ocean has been designated as the Quillayute Needles National Wildlife Refuge, a part of the Olympic Coast Marine Sanctuary. Nesting shorebirds and marine mammals find refuge here.

40 Olympic National Park: Ozette

Location: 75 miles west of Port Angeles on Ozette Lake in Olympic National Park

GPS: N48 08.821' / W124 38.997'

Elevation: 40 feet

Season: Year-round

Sites: 14 sites for tents or self-contained RVs no longer than 21 feet

Facilities: Drinking water, picnic tables, fire grills, vault toilets

Fee per night: None

Management: Olympic National Park, (360) 565-3130

Activities: Hiking, fishing, boating

Finding the campground: From downtown Port Angeles drive west on US 101 for 5 miles; bear right on WA 112 and drive another 49 miles. Two miles past the town of Sekiu, turn left (southwest) onto the Hoko-Ozette Road and drive 21 miles to Ozette, the campground, and a park ranger station.

The campground: The campground is primitive, isolated, and very appealing because of the pristine lake. Cedar walkways lead 3 miles through dense forest to the beaches of the Pacific.

41 Pacific Beach State Park

Location: 29 miles northwest of Hoquiam in Pacific Beach, on the Long Beach Peninsula

GPS: N47 12.429' / W124 12.134'

Elevation: Sea level

Season: Year-round

Sites: 64 sites for tents or RVs up to 60 feet long, 2 yurts

Facilities: Drinking water, restrooms, coin-operated showers, dump station

Fee per night: $$-$$$

Management: Washington State Parks and Recreation Commission, (360) 902-8844 (information); (360) 902-8844 (park office)

Activities: Clam digging, fresh- and saltwater fishing, kite flying, beachcombing, birding, kayaking, surfing

Finding the campground: From US 101 in Hoquiam, take WA 109 west for 16 miles. Turn north, still on WA 109, and drive for 13 miles to the park.

The campground: The unusual in-town location of this park makes it very popular with campers who like the best of both worlds. It tends to stay full in the warm months. Originally a private campground, it was purchased by the state to ensure public access to the beach and was completely renovated in 1995. The campground covers about 10 acres and features 2,300 feet of shoreline. Some of the sites have good ocean views. Individual campsites can be reserved year-round by visiting https://secure.camis.com/WA/ or calling (888) 226-7688.

42 Twin Harbors State Park

Location: 19 miles southwest of Aberdeen, near Westport

GPS: N46 51.408' / W124 06.408'

Elevation: Sea level

Season: Year-round

Sites: 261 tent/RV sites (3 are wheelchair-accessible and 42 have hookups for RVs up to 35 feet long), 4 hiker/biker sites, 2 yurts, 1 group site

Facilities: Drinking water, picnic tables, fire grills, restrooms, coin-operated showers, dump station, playground, clam-cleaning shed

Fee per night: $$-$$$$

Management: Washington State Parks and Recreation Commission, (360) 902-8844 (information); (360) 268-9717 (park office)

Activities: Surf fishing, clam digging, horseback riding, kite flying, beachcombing

Finding the campground: From Aberdeen take US 101 across the Chehalis River into South Aberdeen. Turn right (south) onto WA 105 and continue for 18 miles to the park, which is 3 miles south of Westport.

The campground: Named for its location between Willapa Bay and Grays Harbor, this park was a US Army training ground during the 1930s. The original park, created in 1937, had more than 0.5 mile of shoreline; the 12 miles of South Beach were added a piece at a time in 1973 and 1974. This is truly a beach lover's paradise, and the sand dunes are especially appealing. There is even a Shifting Sands Nature Trail. The park is very popular, and the campsites are relatively densely packed. Individual campsites can be reserved year-round by visiting https://secure.camis.com/WA/ or calling (888) 226-7688.

Coastal Region: Hood Canal / Kitsap Peninsula

	Group Sites	RV Sites	Total # of sites	Max RV Length	Hookups	Toilets	Showers	Drinking water	Dump station	Pets	Wheelchair	Recreation	Fee	Season	Can reserve	Stay limit
43 Belfair State Park		•	167	60	WES	F	•	•	•	•	•	HS	$$-$$$$	year-round	•	10
44 Camp Spillman		•	6	21		V		•		•		HFC		year-round		7
45 Dosewallips State Park	•	•	134	60	WES	F	•	•	•	•		HF	$-$$	year-round	•	10
46 Gold Creek Trailhead		•	6			V		•		•		HRC		May–Aug		7
47 Howell Lake		•	6	30		V		•		•		HBC		year-round		7
48 Illahee State Park		•	33	40		F	•	•	•	•	•	HB	$$-$$$$	May–Labor Day		10
49 Jarrell Cove State Park	•	•	23			F	•	•		•	•	HFBS	$$-$$$	April–Labor Day	•	10
50 Joemma Beach State Park		•	23	40		V	•	•		•	•	FB	$$-$$$$	Mem–Labor Day		10
51 Kitsap Memorial State Park	•	•	43	35	WE	F	•	•	•	•		HFB	$$-$$$$	year-round	•	10
52 Kopachuck State Park	•	•	42	35		F	•	•	•	•		HFSB	$$-$$$$	year-round		10
53 Manchester State Park		•	50	45		F	•	•	•	•		HFS	$$-$$$$	year-round		10
54 Penrose Point State Park	•	•	83	35		F	•	•	•	•	•	HFB	$$-$$$$	year-round	•	10
55 Potlatch State Park		•	75	60	WES	F	•	•	•	•	•	HFB	$$-$$$$	year-round	•	10
56 Scenic Beach State Park	•	•	55	60		F	•	•	•	•	•	HFB	$$-$$$	year-round	•	10
57 Seal Rock		•	41	21		F	•	•		•	•	HFBS	$$$	mid May–Sept		14
58 Tahuya River Horse Camp		•	9			V	•					HFR		year-round		7
59 Toonerville		•	4			V			•			HC		year-round		7
60 Twanoh State Park	•	•	48	35	WES	F	•	•		•	•	HFSB	$$-$$$$	year-round		10

Hookups: W = Water E = Electric S = Sewer
Toilets: F = Flush V = Vault P = Pit
Recreation: C = Bicycling/Mountain Biking H = Hiking S = Swimming F = Fishing B = Boating
O = Off-highway driving R = Horseback Riding
Maximum Trailer/RV Length given in feet. Stay Limit given in days.
Fee $ = less than $10; $$ = $10–$15; $$$ = $16–20; $$$$ = more than $20.
If no entry under Fee, camping is free.

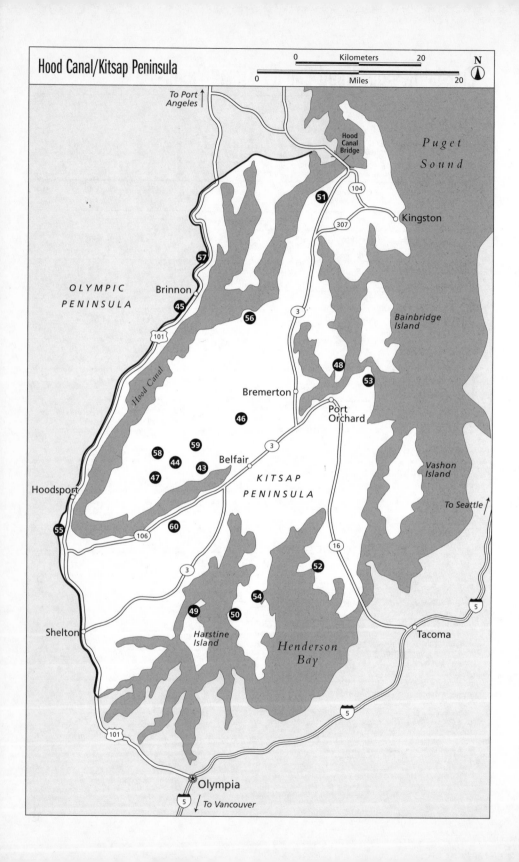

Hood Canal/Kitsap Peninsula

0   Kilometers   20
0   Miles   20

N

To Port
Angeles

Hood
Canal
Bridge

Puget
Sound

104

51

307

Kingston

57

101

Brinnon

45

OLYMPIC
PENINSULA

56

3

Bainbridge
Island

48

53

Bremerton

46

Hood Canal

Port
Orchard

59

3

58

44

43

Belfair

KITSAP
PENINSULA

47

Vashon
Island

Hoodsport

To Seattle

55

106

60

16

3

52

54

49

50

Shelton

Harstine
Island

Henderson
Bay

Tacoma

5

101

5

5

Olympia

To Vancouver

43 Belfair State Park

Location: 15 miles southwest of Bremerton on Hood Canal
GPS: N47 25.770' / W122 52.608'
Elevation: Sea level
Season: Year-round
Sites: 167 tent/RV sites (47 with full hookups for RVs no longer than 60 feet)
Facilities: Drinking water, picnic tables, fire grills, restrooms, coin-operated showers, playground
Fee per night: $$–$$$$
Management: Washington State Parks and Recreation Commission, (360) 902-8844 (information); (360) 275-0668 (park office)
Activities: Beachcombing, swimming, hiking, kite flying, horseshoes, crabbing
Finding the campground: From Bremerton on the Kitsap Peninsula, take WA 3 southwest for 12 miles to the town of Belfair. From there drive 3 miles southwest on WA 300 to the campground.
The campground: This 62-acre campground features 3,720 feet of shoreline on Hood Canal. A 300-foot swimming beach abuts an enclosed man-made saltwater basin, controlled by a tide gate. The beaches are closed to clam and oyster harvesting due to pollution at this end of the canal. Because of the many arrowheads found during the construction of park facilities, this beach was determined to have been a meeting place for many generations of Skokomish Indians. Two creeks run through the campground, Big Mission and Little Mission; salmon spawn in both during the fall. Individual campsites can be reserved year-round by visiting https://secure.camis.com/WA/ or calling (888) 226-7688.

44 Camp Spillman

Location: About 21 miles southwest of Bremerton on the Tahuya River
GPS: N47 48.679' / W124 15.049'
Elevation: 390 feet
Season: Year-round
Sites: 6 primitive sites for tents and small RVs no longer than 21 feet
Facilities: Drinking water, picnic tables, fire grills, tent pads, vault toilets
Fee per night: None
Management: Washington Department of Natural Resources, South Puget Sound Region, (360) 825-1631
Activities: Hiking, fishing, mountain biking, trail biking
Finding the campground: From Bremerton on the Kitsap Peninsula, take WA 3 southwest for 12 miles to the town of Belfair. From there take WA 300 southwest for 3.5 miles. Turn right onto Belfair-Tahuya Road and drive 2 miles. Turn right onto Elfendahl Pass Road and drive 2.5 miles to Twin Lakes Road. Turn left and drive nearly 1 mile to the campground.
The campground: This is a calm and remote wooded campground on the river. Trails in the area are inviting.

45 Dosewallips State Park

Location: 24 miles north of Hoodsport on Hood Canal, near Brinnon
GPS: N47 41.322' / W122 54.408'
Elevation: Sea level
Season: Year-round
Sites: 125 tent/RV sites (40 with full hookups for RVs no longer than 60 feet), 3 platform tents, 3 cabins, 1 bunkhouse, 2 group sites (one for 128 persons and one for 56)
Facilities: Drinking water, picnic tables, fire grills, restrooms, coin-operated showers, dump station, moorage
Fee per night: $-$$
Management: Washington State Parks and Recreation Commission, (360) 902-8844 (information); (360) 796-4415 (park office)
Activities: Hiking, fishing, oyster harvesting and clam digging (when water quality permits), shrimping, wildlife watching
Finding the campground: From Hoodsport drive 24 miles north on US 101 to reach the park.
The campground: This 425-acre park encompasses 5,500 feet of saltwater shoreline on Hood Canal and 5,400 feet of freshwater frontage on each bank of the Dosewallips River. The Dosewallips is the only glacier-fed river that flows into Hood Canal. It is clean and reputedly offers excellent fishing. The park beach is actually a large tidal flat with an abundance of clams and oysters. The beds open in January. Four miles of hiking trails wind up the steep hills that rise from the beach. Among the wildlife to be found here are deer, bald eagles, and a large seal population. An elk herd winters in the park. Fishing possibilities include steelhead trout in January and chum salmon in August. On the southeast side of the park, you can find old railroad beds—remnants of the logging heyday when logs were shipped by rail down the mountains to the water and then floated to mills and cargo ships. Individual campsites can be reserved year-round by visiting https://secure.camis.com/WA/ or calling (888) 226-7688.

46 Gold Creek Trailhead

Location: About 15 miles west of Bremerton on Gold Creek
GPS: N47 33.080' / W122 49.616'
Elevation: 340 feet
Season: May through Aug
Sites: 6 sites for tents or self-contained RVs
Facilities: Drinking water, picnic tables, fire grills, tent pads, vault toilets
Fee per night: None
Management: Washington Department of Natural Resources, South Puget Sound Region, (360) 825-1631
Activities: Hiking, horseback riding, mountain biking
Finding the campground: From the Seabeck Highway, which runs between Bremerton and Seabeck, turn south onto Holly Road and drive 2.2 miles. Turn left onto Tahuya Lake Road NW and

drive 1.3 miles. Turn left onto Gold Creek Road and drive 1.6 miles to the park entrance on the left.

The campground: Located in the Green Mountain State Forest on the Kitsap Peninsula, this basic DNR campground is wooded and not heavily used. Hiking and trail riding are the main activities, and there are plenty of hills to climb.

47 Howell Lake

Location: 21 miles southwest of Bremerton on Howell Lake
GPS: N47 25.822' / W122 59.476'
Elevation: 460 feet
Season: Year-round
Sites: 6 sites for tents or self-contained RVs no longer than 30 feet
Facilities: Drinking water, picnic tables, fire grills, tent pads, vault toilets, boat ramp
Fee per night: None
Management: Washington Department of Natural Resources, South Puget Sound Region, (360) 825-1631
Activities: Hiking, trail biking, mountain biking, boating
Finding the campground: From Bremerton on the Kitsap Peninsula, take WA 3 southwest for 12 miles to the town of Belfair. From there take WA 300 southwest for 3.5 miles. Turn right onto Belfair-Tahuya Road and continue 5.5 miles to the campground.
The campground: This campground has all the elements for a relaxed vacation experience. There are trails through the woods and a boat ramp to get out on the little lake.

48 Illahee State Park

Location: About 4 miles northeast of Bremerton on Port Orchard Bay
GPS: N47 35.820' / W122 35.922'
Elevation: Sea level
Season: May 1 through Labor Day
Sites: 25 sites for tents or self-contained RVs no longer than 40 feet, 8 primitive overflow tent sites
Facilities: Drinking water, picnic tables, fire grills, flush toilets, coin-operated showers, dump station, playground, ball field, fishing dock with 4 floats, concrete breakwater, 5 mooring buoys.
Fee per night: $$–$$$$
Management: Washington State Parks and Recreation Commission, (360) 902-8844 (information); (360) 902-8844 (park office); no reservations
Activities: Hiking, boating, waterskiing, oyster harvesting, clam digging, scuba diving
Finding the campground: From Bremerton on the Kitsap Peninsula, drive north on WA 303 for 2 miles through East Bremerton. Turn right onto Sylvan Way and drive nearly 2 miles to the park.
The campground: This park on the outskirts of Bremerton covers 75 acres and features 1,800 acres of saltwater frontage on Port Orchard Bay. The campsites are on a bluff above a relatively

rocky beach in a second-growth forest. Drink in the views across nearly a mile of water to Bainbridge Island.

49 Jarrell Cove State Park

Location: 17 miles northeast of Shelton on Harstine Island
GPS: N47 16.992' / W122 52.992'
Elevation: Sea level
Season: Apr through Labor Day
Sites: 22 sites for tents and one walk-in group site for up to 45 people
Facilities: Drinking water, picnic tables, fire grills, restrooms, coin-operated showers, marine pump-out, 2 docks and moorage piers, 14 mooring buoys
Fee per night: $$-$$$
Management: Washington State Parks and Recreation Commission, (360) 902-8844 (information); (360) 426-9226 (park office)
Activities: Hiking, fishing, boating, clam digging
Finding the campground: From US 101 in Shelton, head northeast on WA 3 and drive 10 miles. Turn right onto Pickering Road. In about 3 miles turn left and cross the bridge to Harstine Island. At the stop sign turn left onto North Island Drive; continue 4 miles to the park.
The campground: This wooded campground covers 43 acres and features 3,500 feet of saltwater shoreline on Pickering Passage. Swimming is possible, but the main attraction is boating in the protected cove. The site was named for the first woman settler on the island, Mrs. Philora Jarrell. One ADA-accessible campsite, 4 tent spaces (sites 9, 10, 11, and 12), and the walk-in group site can be reserved by visiting https://secure.camis.com/WA/ or calling (888) 226-7688.

50 Joemma Beach State Park

Location: About 28 miles west of Tacoma on Puget Sound
GPS: N47 13.557' / W122 48.459'
Elevation: Sea level
Season: Memorial Day through Labor Day
Sites: 19 tent sites for tents or self-contained RVs no longer than 40 feet, 2 water trail sites, 2 primitive walk-in sites
Facilities: Drinking water, picnic tables, fire grills, tent pads, vault toilets, coin-operated showers, large picnic shelter, boat ramp, 3 mooring buoys, 500-foot moorage dock (seasonal), camp host
Fee per night: $$-$$$$
Management: Washington State Parks and Recreation Commission, (360) 902-8844 (information); (253) 884-1944 (park office); no reservations
Activities: Boating, clam digging, crabbing, fishing, beachcombing
Finding the campground: You have to drive all the way around Henderson Bay and Carr Inlet to reach this park, but it is worth the drive. From I-5 in Tacoma drive 16 miles northwest on WA 16, crossing the Tacoma Narrows Bridge. Just before the town of Purdy, turn left onto WA 302 (Key

Peninsula Highway), also called the Gig Harbor–Longbranch Road. Be sure to stay on WA 302 when it bears left in about 5 miles. Continue south to the town of Home. From the bridge in Home, continue south on Longbranch Road for 1.3 miles; turn right onto Whiteman Road and drive 2.3 miles. Turn right onto Bay Road and drive 1 mile to the camp on the right.

The campground: This 122-acre park offers about 3,000 feet of saltwater frontage on Whiteman Cove. It was developed with help from the Olympia Outboard Motor Club and the Mission Creek Youth Camp. The oyster tracts off Whiteman Cove at Joemma Beach are operated by a local resident. The park is named for Joe and Emma Smith, who lived on the property from 1917 to 1932. This is a fine park for relaxation and exploration of Case Inlet.

51   Kitsap Memorial State Park

Location: 19 miles north of Bremerton on Hood Canal
GPS: N47 49.065' / W122 39.092'
Elevation: Sea level
Season: Year-round
Sites: 21 tent sites, 18 sites with water and electric hookups for RVs no longer than 35 feet, 4 cabins
Facilities: Drinking water, picnic tables, fire grills, dump station, flush toilets, playground, boat buoys, coin-operated showers, firewood (fee)
Fee per night: $$–$$$$
Management: Washington State Parks and Recreation Commission, (360) 902-8844 (information); (888) 226-7688 (park office)
Activities: Hiking, baseball, volleyball, fishing, marine recreation
Finding the campground: From Bremerton on the Kitsap Peninsula, drive north on WA 3 for 19 miles. The entrance to the park is on the left, 3 miles before you reach the Hood Canal Floating Bridge.
The campground: Trails to the beach offer sweeping views of Hood Canal and the Olympic Peninsula. There is also a 1-mile wooded trail. Bottom fishing is reportedly good. Individual campsites and cabins can be reserved year-round by visiting https://secure.camis.com/WA/ or calling (888) 226-7688.

52   Kopachuck State Park

Location: 12 miles northwest of Tacoma on Puget Sound
GPS: N47 18.990' / W122 40.710'
Elevation: Sea level
Season: Year-round
Sites: 41 sites for tents or self-contained RVs no longer than 35 feet, 1 tent-only group site for up to 60 people
Facilities: Drinking water, picnic tables, fire grills, restrooms, coin-operated showers, dump station, boat buoys, underwater marine park

Fee per night: $$–$$$$
Management: Washington State Parks and Recreation Commission, (360) 902-8844 (information); (253) 265-3606 (park office); no reservations except for group site. Call the office to reserve it.
Activities: Hiking, fishing, clam digging, birding, swimming, boating, waterskiing, scuba diving
Finding the campground: From I-5 in Tacoma, take exit 132 and drive north on WA 16 for 7 miles to the sign for Kopachuck State Park. Turn left (west) and drive 5 miles to the camp situated on Henderson Bay.

The campground: This 109-acre park has 5,600 feet of saltwater shoreline made mostly of fine gravel, as well as 1,500 feet of unguarded beach. There are numerous trails, some with views of Henderson Bay and the Olympic Mountains. The underwater marine reef is actually a barge that sank years ago. It is host to all kinds of marine life and is a very popular Puget Sound dive site. The campground is on the forested bluffs above Carr Inlet. This site was used for seasonal fishing and clam digging by the Puyallup and Nisqually Indians.

53 Manchester State Park

Location: 35 miles northwest of Tacoma on Puget Sound, near Port Orchard
GPS: N47 34.542' / W122 33.090'
Elevation: Sea level
Season: Year-round; limited winter facilities
Sites: 50 sites for tents or self-contained RVs up to 45 feet long, including 15 utility sites
Facilities: Drinking water, picnic tables, fire grills, restrooms, coin-operated showers, dump station
Fee per night: $$–$$$$
Management: Washington State Parks and Recreation Commission, (360) 902-8844 (information); (360) 871-4065 (park office)
Activities: Hiking, fishing, clam digging, scuba diving
Finding the campground: From I-5 in Tacoma take exit 132 and head north on WA 16 toward Bremerton. Drive 24 miles; just before reaching Port Orchard, take the WA 160/Southeast Sedgwick Road exit. Follow the signs for 11 miles to the park. Alternatively, from downtown Port Orchard proceed east on Bay Street (WA 166) until it becomes Mile Hill Drive. Continue for 3.2 miles on Mile Hill Drive until it ends at Colchester. Turn left (north) onto Colchester Drive Southeast and drive 3 miles north to the park, on the right.

The campground: Manchester is a stop on the Cascadia Marine Trail, a sea kayaking route that stretches from Olympia north to Vancouver Island, British Columbia. The park covers 111 acres and offers 3,400 feet of saltwater shoreline on Rich Passage. Well off the beaten track for campers, the campground is usually not crowded. Yet it is just 6 miles northeast of Port Orchard, a popular antiques-shopping town. At the dawn of the twentieth century, this site was a US Coast Artillery Harbor Defense installation for the protection of Bremerton. During World War II it was converted to a Navy fuel supply depot and Navy fire fighting station. In 1970 the state bought the land and converted it to a park. The Torpedo Warehouse remains to this day as a park attraction. Individual campsites can be reserved in summer only by visiting https://secure.camis.com/WA/ or calling (888) 226-7688.

There's always time for a peaceful walk in the woods when you're camping.

54 Penrose Point State Park

Location: About 26 miles northwest of Tacoma on Carr Inlet
GPS: N47 15.522' / W122 44.640'
Elevation: Sea level
Season: Year-round
Sites: 82 sites for tents or self-contained RVs no longer than 35 feet, 1 group site for up to 50 people in tents or RVs
Facilities: Drinking water, picnic tables, dump station, flush toilets, coin-operated showers, 8 mooring buoys
Fee per night: $$–$$$$
Management: Washington State Parks and Recreation Commission, (360) 902-8844 (information); (253) 884-2514 (park office)
Activities: Fishing, clam digging, boating, hiking, beachcombing
Finding the campground: You have to drive all the way around Henderson Bay and Carr Inlet to reach this park, but it is worth the drive. From I-5 in Tacoma take exit 132 and drive 16 miles northwest on WA 16. Just before the town of Purdy, turn left (west) onto WA 302 (Key Peninsula Highway), also called the Gig Harbor–Longbranch Road. Be sure to stay on WA 302 when it bears

left in about 5 miles. Continue through the towns of Key Center and Home to Lakebay. Turn left (east) onto Cornwall Road KPS. Drive 1.25 miles and turn left (north) onto 158th Avenue KPS and into the park.

The campground: This park was built out of a former swamp. A petroglyph etched into the rock in inner Mayo Cove indicates that American Indians once occupied the area. The majority of the park is covered in natural forest and is crisscrossed by 2.5 miles of hiking trails. The beach is 1,700 feet long. Individual campsites can be reserved year-round by visiting https://secure.camis.com/WA/ or calling (888) 226-7688.

55 Potlatch State Park

Location: 12 miles north of Shelton on Hood Canal, near Hoodsport
GPS: N47 21.708' / W123 09.576'
Elevation: Sea level
Season: Year-round
Sites: 38 tent sites, 2 primitive sites for hikers and bikers, 35 utility sites for trailers no longer than 60 feet
Facilities: Drinking water, picnic tables, fire grills, restrooms, coin-operated showers, dump station, boat ramp, dock, 5 moorage buoys
Fee per night: $$–$$$$
Management: Washington State Parks and Recreation Commission, (360) 902-8844 (information); (360) 877-5361 (park office)
Activities: Hiking, fishing, clam digging, crabbing, scuba diving, boating
Finding the campground: From Shelton drive north on US 101 for 12 miles to the park.
The campground: Potlatch covers 57 acres and features 9,570 feet of saltwater shoreline on Hood Canal. Skokomish and Twanoh Indians once gathered here to hold potlatches, or gift-giving ceremonies. Later the cabins and hotel of Minerva Resort were built on the site. This is a terrific boaters' campground. The camping area is located across US 101 from the day-use area. Individual campsites can be reserved in summer only by visiting https://secure.camis.com/WA/ or calling (888) 226-7688.

56 Scenic Beach State Park

Location: About 9 miles northwest of Bremerton on Hood Canal
GPS: N47 38.988' / W122 50.742'
Elevation: Sea level
Season: Year-round
Sites: 52 sites for tents or self-contained RVs no longer than 60 feet, 2 primitive tent sites, 1 primitive group site for up to 50 people
Facilities: Drinking water, picnic tables, fire grills, restrooms, showers, dump station, dock, boat ramp, horseshoe vault, volleyball courts
Fee per night: $$–$$$

Management: Washington State Parks and Recreation Commission, (360) 902-8844 (information); (360) 830-5079 (park office)

Activities: Hiking, fishing, boating, oyster harvesting

Finding the campground: From Bremerton drive north on WA 3 for about 5 miles. Before the town of Silverdale, take the Newberry Hill Road exit and drive west for 3 miles to the intersection with Seabeck Highway. Turn right (north) and proceed to the town of Seabeck, turning south when you reach Warrenville. Just past the Seabeck Elementary School, turn right onto Stavis Bay Road; drive 1 mile to the campground at the end of the road.

The campground: This 88-acre campground, one of the loveliest in the Washington system, features 1,500 feet of gravelly saltwater frontage, a nature trail, and great views of the Olympic Mountains. It sits on the bluff in a forest of western red cedars, madrones, and western hemlocks. The park also is home to a 460-plus-year-old Douglas fir. This spot was originally developed as a homesite and later converted to Scenic Beach Resort, offering cabins, campground, boat rentals, and picnic facilities. Birders should watch for varied thrushes and waterfowl, willow goldfinches, and pileated woodpeckers. Orcas and pilot whales roam the waters. Individual campsites can be reserved year-round by visiting https://secure.camis.com/WA/ or calling (888) 226-7688.

57 Seal Rock

Location: 27 miles north of Hoodsport on Hood Canal

GPS: N47 42.557' / W122 53.405'

Elevation: 100 feet

Season: Mid-May through Sept

Sites: 41 sites for tents or self-contained RVs no longer than 21 feet

Facilities: Drinking water, picnic tables, tent pads, flush toilets, nearby boat docks and ramp

Fee per night: $$$

Management: Olympic National Forest, Hood Canal Ranger District, (360) 765-2200; no reservations

Activities: Hiking, fishing, nature trails, clam digging, swimming, boating

Finding the campground: From Hoodsport drive 25 miles north on US 101 to the town of Brinnon. Continue 2 miles farther north to the campground.

The campground: This 6-acre campground sits nicely on a rocky beach on Dabob Bay and is a natural for boaters. It is very popular, and all facilities are barrier-free. On the forested bluff is a nature trail through the woods.

58 Tahuya River Horse Camp

Location: About 22 miles southwest of Bremerton on the Tahuya River, near Belfair

GPS: N47 28.065' / W122 56.596'

Elevation: 320 feet

Season: Year-round; call the DNR at (360) 825-1631 for seasonal closures.

Sites: 9 primitive sites for tents or self-contained RVs

Facilities: Drinking water, picnic tables, fire grills, tent pads, vault toilets, horse trails
Fee per night: None
Management: Washington Department of Natural Resources, South Puget Sound Region, (360) 825-1631; no reservations
Activities: Hiking, fishing, horseback riding, motorbiking
Finding the campground: From Bremerton on the Kitsap Peninsula, take WA 3 southwest for 12 miles to the town of Belfair. From there take WA 300 southwest for 3.5 miles. Turn right onto Belfair-Tahuya Road and continue 3.2 miles. Then turn right onto Spillman Road and drive 2.1 miles. Turn left and drive 0.8 mile to the campground.
The campground: This way-out-of-the-way campground will appeal especially to hikers and trail riders, including both equestrians and dirt bikers. The rustic campsites are set along the river in the Tahuya State Forest.

59 Toonerville

Location: 21 miles southwest of Bremerton, near Belfair
GPS: N47 32.226' / W122 51.936'
Elevation: 340 feet
Season: Year-round
Sites: 4 sites for tents or self-contained RVs
Facilities: Picnic tables, fire grills, tent pads, vault toilets; no drinking water
Fee per night: None
Management: Washington Department of Natural Resources, South Puget Sound Region, (360) 825-1631
Activities: Hiking, mountain biking, trail biking
Finding the campground: From Bremerton on the Kitsap Peninsula, take WA 3 southwest for 12 miles to Belfair. From there take WA 300 southwest for 3.5 miles. Turn right onto Belfair-Tahuya Road; drive 2 miles and turn right onto Elfendahl Pass Road. Drive another 3.3 miles, past the Tahuya Trailhead and through the intersection with Goat Ranch Road, to reach the campground.
The campground: It is back to the basics at this campground, which does not even have a creek for distraction. Mostly used by hikers and trail riders, Toonerville may best serve as a base camp, unless you brought some good books to read.

60 Twanoh State Park

Location: 21 miles northeast of Shelton on Hood Canal, near Belfair
GPS: N47 22.374' / W122 58.440'
Elevation: Sea level
Season: Year-round; limited facilities in winter
Sites: 47 sites, including 22 sites with full hookups for RVs no longer than 35 feet and 1 non-RV group site (steep, winding access road) for up to 50 people

Facilities: Drinking water, picnic tables, fire grills, restrooms, coin-operated showers, store, playground, tennis court, horseshoe vaults, boat dock, 7 mooring buoys, marine pump-out, 2 boat ramps, 580 feet of swimming beach, kiddie wading pool

Fee per night: $$-$$$$

Management: Washington State Parks and Recreation Commission, (360) 902-8844 (information); (360) 275-2222 (park office); no reservations except for group site

Activities: Hiking, fishing, swimming, oyster harvesting, boating, waterskiing

Finding the campground: From Shelton drive north on US 101 for 10 miles. Turn right (east) onto WA 106 and continue for 11 miles to the park.

The campground: Twanoh State Park covers 182 acres and features 3,167 feet of beautiful saltwater shoreline. It has good hiking trails, and fishermen appreciate the proximity to oysters, crabs, and perch. The park buildings were constructed by the Civilian Conservation Corps in the early 1930s and are still preserved in their original beauty. Because of the abundance of wildlife, early American Indians here were among the few hunting and gathering societies in the world that produced wealth beyond their needs. The basis for their economy was fishing, and salmon was the main commodity.

Coastal Region: Strait of Juan de Fuca

	Group Sites	RV Sites	Total # of sites	Max RV Length	Hookups	Toilets	Showers	Drinking water	Dump station	Pets	Wheelchair	Recreation	Fee	Season	Can reserve	Stay limit
61 Fort Flagler State Park	•	•	120	50	WE	F	•	•	•	•	•	HFBS	$$-$$$$	year-round	•	10
62 Fort Worden State Park		•	83	50	WES	F		•		•	•	HFBSC	$$-$$$$	year-round	•	10
63 Lyre River		•	11			V		•				HF		year-round		14
64 Old Fort Townsend State Park		•	43	40		F	•	•	•	•		HF	$$-$$$$	May 1–Oct 2	•	10
65 Salt Creek Recreation Area		•	92			F	•	•	•	•		HFSR	$$-$$$$	year-round	•	14
66 Sequim Bay State Park	•	•	65	30	WES	F	•	•	•	•	•	HFB	$$-$$$$	year-round	•	10

Hookups: W = Water E = Electric S = Sewer
Toilets: F = Flush V = Vault P = Pit
Recreation: C = Bicycling/Mountain Biking H = Hiking S = Swimming F = Fishing B = Boating
O = Off-highway driving R = Horseback Riding
Maximum Trailer/RV Length given in feet. Stay Limit given in days.
Fee $ = less than $10; $$ = $10–$15; $$$ = $16–20; $$$$ = more than $20.
If no entry under Fee, camping is free.

61 Fort Flagler State Park

Location: About 19 miles southeast of Port Townsend on Marrowstone Island
GPS: N48 05.838' / W122 41.694'
Elevation: Sea level
Season: Year-round
Sites: 59 tent sites, 58 sites with water and electric hookups for RVs no longer than 50 feet, 2 primitive sites, 1 Cascadia Marine Trail site
Facilities: Drinking water, picnic tables, fire grills, restrooms, coin-operated showers, dump station, store, cafe, 2 boat ramps, buoys, floats, underwater scuba diving park, fishing pier, American Youth Hostel, Cascadia Marine Trail campsite, 2 wheelchair-accessible vacation houses
Fee per night: $$-$$$$
Management: Washington State Parks and Recreation Commission, (360) 902-8844 (information); (360) 385-1259 (park office)
Activities: Hiking, bottom and salmon fishing, boating, beachcombing, scuba diving, clam digging, crabbing, sailboarding
Finding the campground: Although the park is only 2 miles across Port Townsend Bay from Port Townsend, it is a 19-mile drive around the bay and across two islands. The road is paved the whole way. From Port Townsend drive south on WA 20 for 5 miles and turn left (southeast) onto WA 19 (Rhody Road). In 3.5 miles turn left (west) onto WA 116 to the town of Hadlock. From Hadlock

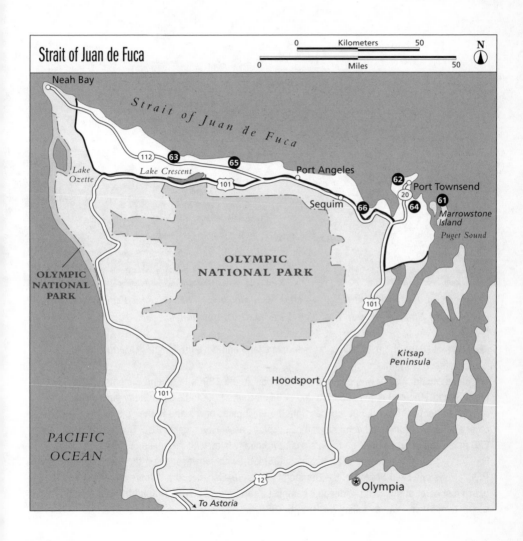

Strait of Juan de Fuca

Kilometers 0 — 50

Miles 0 — 50

N

Neah Bay

Strait of Juan de Fuca

112 63 65

Lake Ozette

Lake Crescent

101

Port Angeles

62

20

Port Townsend

66

61

Sequim

64

Marrowstone Island

Puget Sound

OLYMPIC NATIONAL PARK

OLYMPIC NATIONAL PARK

101

Kitsap Peninsula

Hoodsport

101

PACIFIC OCEAN

101

12

To Astoria

Olympia

Passengers on the Black Ball Ferry can view the north shore of the Olympic Peninsula as they cross the Strait of Juan de Fuca from Victoria, British Columbia.

stay on WA 116 for about 10 miles; cross Indian Island and drive the length of Marrowstone Island to reach the park.

The campground: Flagler was one of three forts built in the 1890s to defend the entrance to Puget Sound. (The others were Fort Worden and Fort Casey.) The fort's big artillery guns were scrapped after World War II, but replicas from the Philippines now stand in their place. There are other abandoned gun emplacements you can explore, as well as a lighthouse. The park covers 780 acres and is surrounded on three sides by Admiralty Inlet, with 3.6 miles of saltwater shoreline. This is definitely a complete park, almost luxurious, with activities to suit the whole family. The Marrowstone Field Station of the Bureau of US Sports Fisheries and Wildlife is located on the beach just north of the camp. Individual campsites can be reserved year-round by visiting https://secure.camis.com/WA/ or calling (888) 226-7688.

62 Fort Worden State Park

Location: In Port Townsend
GPS: N48 08.141' / W122 45.736'

Elevation: Sea level

Season: Year-round

Sites: 80 sites for tents or self-contained RVs no longer than 50 feet, 3 primitive tent sites for campers who hike or bike in

Facilities: Drinking water, picnic tables, firewood (fee), restroom, dock, 2 mooring floats, 9 mooring buoys, 2 boat ramps, underwater scuba park, 2 tennis courts, ball field, snack bar/grocery, restaurant (dinners, Sunday brunch), coin-operated laundry, 3 dormitories, youth hostel, 25 units of vacation housing, Cascadia Marine Trail campsite, Marine Science Center

Fee per night: $$–$$$$

Management: Washington State Parks and Recreation Commission, (360) 902-8844 (information); (360) 344-4431 (park office)

Activities: Hiking, fishing, boating, sea kayaking, scuba diving, swimming, bicycling, kite flying

Finding the campground: The park is within the city limits of Port Townsend at the north end of town. The directional signage from downtown is good.

The campground: This big, magnificent park encompasses 434 acres and offers 2 miles of saltwater shoreline on Admiralty Inlet and the Strait of Juan de Fuca. The fort is listed on both the State and National Register of Historic Places and has been designated a National Historic Landmark. The abandoned concrete bunkers and artillery vaults are a real curiosity. The old military buildings house conferences such as the Sea Kayak Symposium, held annually in September. The campground itself is very popular with sea kayakers and scuba divers, and there are 6 miles of hiking trails. The sites are on a sandy peninsula that can get quite windy. Wildlife includes black-tailed deer, great blue herons, bald eagles, gray whales, and orcas. Call (360) 344-4431 for individual campsite reservations.

63 Lyre River

Location: About 20 miles west of Port Angeles, on the Lyre River

GPS: N47 39.327' / W124 11.295'

Elevation: Near sea level

Season: Year-round

Sites: 11 sites for tents or self-contained RVs

Facilities: Picnic tables, fire grills, tent pads, vault toilets, group shelter; no drinking water

Fee per night: None

Management: Washington Department of Natural Resources, Olympic Region, (360) 374-6131

Activities: Hiking, fishing, rockhounding

Finding the campground: From Port Angeles take US 101 west for 5 miles. Turn right (west) onto WA 112 and continue driving about 15 miles. The paved entrance road is on the right, between mileposts 46 and 47.

The campground: This primitive campground is right on the Lyre River, not far from where it pours into the Strait of Juan de Fuca. A promontory forms a good catch-point for flotsam treasures from the strait, and the rockhounding is good here.

64 Old Fort Townsend State Park

Location: About 6 miles south of Port Townsend on Port Townsend Bay
GPS: N48 04.404' / W122 47.358'
Elevation: 150 feet
Season: May 1 through Oct 2
Sites: 40 sites for tents or self-contained RVs no longer than 40 feet, 3 primitive tent sites
Facilities: Drinking water, picnic tables, fire grills, restrooms, coin-operated showers, playground, boat buoys, firewood (fee), dump station
Fee per night: $$–$$$$
Management: Washington State Parks and Recreation Commission, (360) 902-8844 (information); (360) 385-3595 (park office)
Activities: Hiking, fishing, clam digging, historical walk
Finding the campground: From downtown Port Townsend, drive south on WA 20 for 4.5 miles. Turn left (east) at the sign for the park and drive 1.5 miles. To get there from the junction of US 101 and WA 20 at the southern end of Discovery Bay, take WA 20 north for 9 miles toward Port Townsend. Turn right at the sign for the park and drive 1.5 miles to the park entrance.
The campground: This 377-acre park sits above a 150-foot cliff, overlooking Port Townsend Bay, the islands of central Puget Sound, and the Cascade Mountains. The US Army fort, built in 1856 from hand-hewn logs and clamshell plaster, was established to protect settlers in the area from the American Indians. This is a nice campground, not well known outside the area. There is a good beach below the bluffs. Reservations can be made up to 12 months in advance by sending an e-mail to Fort Worden State Park at fwcamping@parks.wa.gov; mailing a letter to 200 Battery Way, Port Townsend, WA 98368; or faxing a letter to (360) 385-7248. Reservations can be made up to 11 months in advance in person at Fort Worden or by calling (360) 344-4431 from 8:30 a.m. to 4 p.m. daily. Reservations must be made at least 24 hours in advance.

65 Salt Creek Recreation Area

Location: 15 miles west of Port Angeles on Crescent Bay
GPS: N48 09.539' / W123 41.295'
Elevation: Sea level
Season: Year-round
Sites: 92 sites for tents or self-contained RVs
Facilities: Drinking water, picnic tables, toilets, showers, playground, firewood, dump station, swimming beach
Fee per night: $$–$$$$
Management: Clallam County Parks, Salt Creek Recreation Area, (360) 928-3441
Activities: Hiking, fishing, swimming, horseshoes, beachcombing, horseback riding
Finding the campground: From Port Angeles take US 101 west for 5 miles. Turn right (west) onto WA 112 and continue about 7 miles to Camp Hayden Road. Turn right (north) onto Camp Hayden Road and drive 3 more miles to the campground.

The campground: Tongue Point, just west of the campground, juts into the Strait of Juan de Fuca toward Vancouver Island, about 12 miles away. Nearby Agate Bay is named for the treasures that can be found on local beaches. This is one of only a few campgrounds on the strait, and it is a good stopover for people driving around the Olympic Peninsula. For reservations visit www.clallam .net/Parks/SaltCreek.html.

66 Sequim Bay State Park

Location: 4 miles southeast of Sequim on Sequim Bay
GPS: N48 02.436' / W123 01.830'
Elevation: Sea level
Season: Year-round
Sites: 49 tent sites, 15 sites with full hookups for RVs no longer than 45 feet in the upper area and 30 feet in the lower area, 1 summer-only group site for up to 40 people
Facilities: Drinking water, picnic tables, fire grills, restrooms, showers, playground, dump stations, boat ramp, docks, moorage camping
Fee per night: $$–$$$$
Management: Washington State Parks and Recreation Commission, (360) 902-8844 (information); (360) 683-4235 (park office)
Activities: Hiking, fishing, boating, clam digging, scuba diving, beach walking, marine life study, field and group sports, tennis, flora study, birding
Finding the campground: The park is along US 101, 4 miles southeast of the town of Sequim.
The campground: Sequim (pronounced skwim) is a Coast Salish word meaning "quiet waters," and Sequim Bay truly is calm. That is due to a pair of naturally occurring and overlapping sand spits at the bay's entrance that force sailors to take a zigzag course into the bay from the Strait of Juan de Fuca. The park covers 92 acres and features nearly a mile of tidelands. It is in the rain shadow of the Olympic Mountains, which means that clouds release their precipitation mostly on the western slopes, forcing farmers on this side to irrigate. The bay is 5 miles long, so this park offers a lot of opportunity for safe recreation on the water. For landlubbers there are 2.5 miles of hiking trails. Individual campsites can be reserved year-round by visiting https://secure.camis .com/WA/ or calling (888) 226-7688.

Western Region

One of the nation's largest inland waterways, Puget Sound was sculpted by glaciers at the end of the last ice age. To the east lie the volcanic Cascade Range and its preeminent peaks: Mounts Baker, Rainier, Adams, and St. Helens. North Cascades National Park, in the northern part of the range, has one of the most extensive glacier systems in the contiguous states. Glaciers flow in all directions, supplying unbelievably beautiful mountain lakes and streams. The National Park Service wants to maintain the park in as natural a state as possible. As a consequence, the only traveler services

A pedestrian bridge crosses to an island in Cascade Lake in Moran State Park on Orcas Island. A trail continues around the lake (campground 107).

along one 80-mile stretch of the North Cascades Highway are some occasional campgrounds.

Mount Rainier National Park and Mount St. Helens National Volcanic Monument each features terrain and activities appropriate to any level of interest. It would be tough to exhaust the rangers' and volunteers' knowledge of the areas; they are a great resource for travelers and campers alike. Be sure to take extra film or memory cards and keep the camera ready, because the photo ops are unlimited. Seeing is believing, and by camping in or near the parks you will gain a real sense of the spectacular scope and grandeur of this nearly untouched part of the world.

Only serious hikers, packers, and skiers venture far beyond the few available roads through the wilderness. They soon learn just how primitive the Washington backcountry can be. For the rest of us Washington offers a multitude of state parks with campgrounds and many more that are designated for day use only. There are hundreds of other publicly owned campgrounds in Washington. Their administration ranges from local municipalities to the forest service. These public agencies are guardians of these snowcapped peaks, glaciers, alpine lakes, cascading rivers, and conifer-blanketed hills and valleys that seem to go on forever.

Western Region: North Puget Sound

	Group Sites	RV Sites	Total # of sites	Max RV Length	Hookups	Toilets	Showers	Drinking water	Dump station	Pets	Wheelchair	Recreation	Fee	Season	Can reserve	Stay limit
67 Bay View State Park	•	•	76	50	WE	F	•	•	•	•	•	HS	$$-$$$$	year-round	•	10
68 Beckler River		•	27	21		V		•		•		HF	$$$	Mem Day–Lab Day	•	14
69 Bedal		•	21			F				•	•	HFB	$$	Jun–early Sept	•	14
70 Birch Bay State Park	•	•	170	60	WE	F	•	•	•	•	•	HFB	$$-$$$$	year-round	•	10
71 Boardman Creek Group Campground	•	•	8			V				•		HF	$$$$	May 1–Sept 30	•	14
72 Boulder Creek	•		11			V				•		HF	$$	mid May–mid Sept	•	14
73 Buck Creek		•	25	30		V				•		HF	$$	late May–Oct	•	14
74 Clear Creek		•	13			V				•		HF	$$	late May–Oct	•	14
75 Douglas Fir		•	29	26		V				•		HF	$$	May–Sept	•	14
76 Fay Bainbridge Park		•	36	30		F	•	•	•	•		HFB	$$-$$$$	Apr–Aug		10
77 Flowing Lake County Park		•	39	25	WE	F	•	•		•		FSB	$$$-$$$$	RVs all year/ Tents mid May–Sept	•	14
78 Gold Basin		•	88	31		F	•	•		•	•	HF	$$$$	May–Sept	•	14
79 Hannegan		•	0			V		•		•		H		May–Sept		14
80 Horseshoe Cove		•	35	34		F	•	•		•		HFBC	$$$	May–Sept	•	14
81 Howard Miller Steelhead Park		•	56		WES	F	•	•	•	•		FCH	$$$$	year-round	•	14
82 Hutchinson Creek		•	11			V				•		HF		year-round		7
83 Kayak Point County Park		•	39		WE	F		•		•		HFBS	$$$$	May–late Sept	•	14
84 Larrabee State Park	•	•	86	60	WES	F	•	•	•	•	•	HFBC	$$-$$$$	year-round	•	10
85 Marble Creek		•	23	22		V				•		HF	$$	mid May–mid Sept	•	14
86 Mineral Park			7			V				•		HF	$$	mid May–Sept	•	14
87 Money Creek		•	17	21		V		•		•	•	HFS	$$$	May 1–Sept 30	•	14
88 Northern Cascades Natl Park: Colonial Creek		•	142	32		F		•	•	•	•	HF	$$	late May– late Sept		14
89 Northern Cascades Natl Park: Goodell Creek	•	•	21	22		V		•			•	F	$	year-round		14
90 Northern Cascades Natl Park: Hozomeen		•	75+	22		V		•		•		HFB		late May– late Oct		14

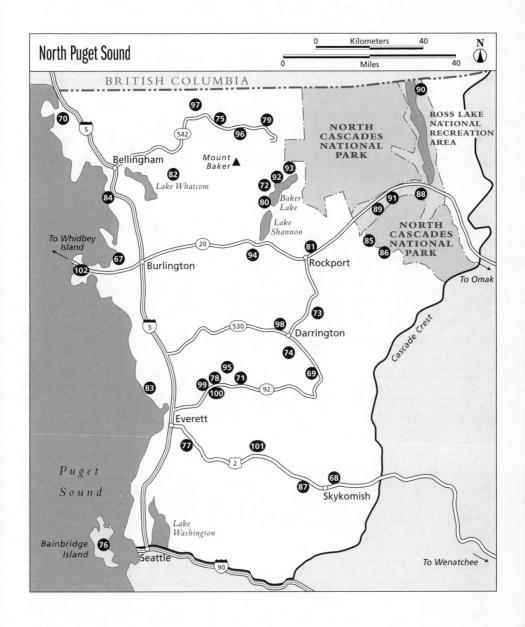

North Puget Sound

0   Kilometers   40

0   Miles   40

N

BRITISH COLUMBIA

70

5

97

75

79

96

542

82

Lake Whatcom

Mount
Baker

92

93

72

80

Baker
Lake

Lake
Shannon

NORTH
CASCADES
NATIONAL
PARK

90

ROSS LAKE
NATIONAL
RECREATION
AREA

91

88

89

85

86

NORTH
CASCADES
NATIONAL
PARK

84

To Whidbey
Island

67

102

20

94

Burlington

81

Rockport

To Omak

5

73

530

98

Darrington

74

69

95

99 78   71

100

92

83

Everett

77

101

2

87   68

Skykomish

Cascade Crest

Puget

Sound

Lake
Washington

To Wenatchee

Bainbridge
Island

76

Seattle

90

	Group Sites	RV Sites	Total # of sites	Max RV Length	Hookups	Toilets	Showers	Drinking water	Dump station	Pets	Wheelchair	Recreation	Fee	Season	Can reserve	Stay limit
91 Northern Cascades Natl Park: Newhalem Creek		•	128	32		F	•	•	•		•	HF	$$$$	mid May–mid Sept		14
92 Panorama Point		•	15	21		V	•		•			HFBC	$$$	May–mid Sept	•	14
93 Park Creek		•	12	22		V			•			HFB	$$	mid May–early Sept	•	14
94 Rasar State Park		•	49	40		F	•	•	•		•	HF	$$–$$$$	year-round	•	10
95 Red Bridge		•	16	31		F			•			HFS	$$	late May–early Sept		14
96 Silver Fir		•	20	31		V	•		•			H	$$$	May–Sept	•	14
97 Silver Lake Park	•	•	148		WE	F	•		•			BFSR	$$–$$$	year-round	•	14
98 Squire Creek County Park		•	33	25		F	•	•	•			HF	$$$–$$$$	year-round	•	14
99 Turlo		•	18	31		F	•		•			HFS	$$$	mid May–late Sept	•	
100 Verlot		•	26	31		F	•		•			HFS	$$$	mid May–late Sept	•	
101 Wallace Falls State Park			7			F	•		•			HFC	$$–$$$$	year-round	•	10
102 Washington Park		•	70	70	WES	F	•	•	•	•		HFBC	$$$$	year-round		

Hookups: W=Water E=Electric S=Sewer
Toilets: F=Flush V=Vault P=Pit
Recreation: C=Bicycling/Mountain Biking H=Hiking S=Swimming F=Fishing B=Boating
O=Off-highway driving R=Horseback Riding
Maximum Trailer/RV Length given in feet. Stay Limit given in days.
Fee $ = less than $10; $$ = $10–$15; $$$ = $16–20; $$$$ = more than $20.
If no entry under Fee, camping is free.

67 Bay View State Park

Location: 7 miles west of Burlington on Padilla Bay
GPS: N48 29.278' / W122 28.825'
Elevation: Sea level
Season: Year-round
Sites: 46 tent sites, 29 sites with water and electrical hookups for RVs no longer than 50 feet, 1 tent-only group site for up to 64 people
Facilities: Drinking water, picnic tables, flush toilets, coin-operated showers, dump station
Fee per night: $$–$$$$
Management: Washington State Parks and Recreation Commission, (360) 902-8844 (information); (360) 757-0227 (park office)

Activities: Beach walking, swimming, sailboarding

Finding the campground: From I-5 in Burlington take exit 231 and drive 7 miles west on Josh Wilson Road. In the town of Bay View, the road comes to a T junction with Bayview-Edison Road. Turn north onto Bayview-Edison Road and the state park is right there. The entrance is on your right.

The campground: This 25-acre park was formerly a baseball field, racetrack, and local picnic area. It features a grassy expanse plus 1,300 feet of saltwater shoreline on Padilla Bay. The camping area is nestled on a hill above the road. To get to the gravel beach, you must walk through a highway underpass. This stretch of beach, part of the Padilla Bay National Estuarine Research Reserve, connects with the Padilla Bay Trail to form an 8-mile shoreline walk. Individual campsites can be reserved year-round by visiting https://secure.camis.com/WA/ or calling (888) 226-7688.

68 Beckler River

Location: 2 miles northeast of Skykomish on the Beckler River
GPS: N47 44.035' / W121 19.926'
Elevation: 900 feet
Season: Memorial Day through Labor Day
Sites: 7 tent sites, 20 sites for tents or RVs up to 21 feet long
Facilities: Drinking water, picnic tables, fire grills, vault toilets
Fee per night: $$$
Management: Mount Baker-Snoqualmie National Forest, Skykomish Ranger District, (360) 677-2414
Activities: Hiking, fishing
Finding the campground: From Skykomish drive 1 mile east on US 2 and turn right (north) onto FR 65. Drive 1 mile to the campground.
The campground: Beckler River Campground is about 50 miles east of Everett. It occupies a very pleasant site that includes 12 forested acres on the river, where the fishing is reputed to be good. For a minimal fee you can make reservations by contacting the National Recreation Reservation Service at www.recreation.gov or (877) 444-6777.

69 Bedal

Location: About 50 miles east of Everett on the Sauk River, near Darrington
GPS: N48 06.049' / W121 23.366'
Elevation: 1,300 feet
Season: June to early Sept
Sites: 21 sites for tents or self-contained RVs
Facilities: Picnic tables, flush toilets, firewood; no drinking water
Fee per night: $$
Management: Mount Baker–Snoqualmie National Forest, Darrington Ranger District; (360) 691-7791
Activities: Hiking, fishing, canoeing, kayaking

The beach is not far from the Larrabee State Park camp sites. The rocky beach has warmer, swimmable water during summer and lots of tide pool critters year-round.

Finding the campground: From I-5 in Everett, take exit 194 and go east for 2 miles on US 2. Stay in the left lane over the causeway that crosses Ebey Island and go left onto WA 204 toward Lake Stevens. In another 2 miles, at WA 9, turn north and go 2 more miles to WA 92 (Mountain Loop Highway). Turn right onto WA 92 and continue for 8 miles into the town of Granite Falls. Head north out of town and then east on what is now the Mountain Loop Highway (CR 92/FR 7). Continue 36.5 miles to the campground. FR 7 becomes FR 20 at the 30-mile point, but it is still the Mountain Loop Highway. The last 6.5 miles are on a narrow gravel road, but it is well graded.

The campground: The Verlot Public Service Center, 11 miles east of Granite Falls, is a good place to check for local maps and get information on road conditions and campsite availability. The North and South Forks of the Sauk River meet at this 6-acre campground. Rustic and remote, it offers access to the Glacier Peak and Henry M. Jackson Wildernesses.

The drive to Bedal is part of a Forest Service Scenic Byway that runs for 50 miles between Granite Falls and Darrington. The roadside woods are thick with second- and third-growth western hemlock, Douglas fir, western red cedar, black cottonwood, red alder, vine and bigleaf maple, and some Sitka spruce. These form a green canopy for nearly the entire route. With an average annual rainfall of 140 inches, this forest has no problem staying green. You may spot mountain goats on the upper slopes, as well as dogwood, trillium, and queen's cup on the forest floor. For a minimal fee you can make reservations by contacting the National Recreation Reservation Service at www .recreation.gov or (877) 444-6777.

70 Birch Bay State Park

Location: About 10 miles south of Blaine on Birch Bay
GPS: N48 54.192' / W122 45.894'
Elevation: Sea level
Season: Year-round
Sites: 147 sites for tents or self-contained RVs up to 60 feet, 20 sites with water and electrical hookups, 3 group sites
Facilities: Drinking water, picnic tables, fire grills, flush toilets, coin-operated showers, firewood, 2 dump stations
Fee per night: $$–$$$$
Management: Washington State Parks and Recreation Commission, (360) 902-8844 (information); (360) 371-2800 (park office)
Activities: Fishing, picnicking, hiking, clam digging, crabbing, birding, waterskiing, beachcombing, scuba diving, sailboarding, kite flying, photography
Finding the campground: From I-5, 10 miles southeast of Blaine, take the Grandview exit (exit 270). Go west on WA 548 (Grandview Road) for about 7 miles. Turn right (north) onto Jackson Road. At 0.7 mile turn left onto Helwig Road and into the park.
The campground: A mile-long, sandy beach along Birch Bay is the major draw of this 200-acre park. Kayaking is popular, and there is a primitive boat ramp. The campground is nestled among tall cedars and hemlocks, and large fir stumps remain from logging done at the turn of the twentieth century. Birch Bay was once inhabited by Semiahmoo, Lummi, and Nooksack Indians. In prehistoric days as well as today, an abundance of shellfish, migratory waterfowl, and salmon drew people to harvest these resources.

Terrell Creek Marsh is one of the few remaining saltwater/freshwater estuaries in northern Puget Sound. On the beach at the north end of the park is a natural sanctuary acquired through The Nature Conservancy under the condition that no development be permitted there. Residents include migratory waterfowl, bald eagles, and great blue herons. A 0.5-mile nature trail skirts the marsh. Also inside the park are nearly 3 miles of freshwater shoreline on Terrell Creek. Individual campsites can be reserved year-round by visiting https://secure.camis.com/WA/ or calling (888) 226-7688.

71 Boardman Creek Group Campground

Location: About 30 miles east of Everett on the South Fork Stillaguamish River, near Granite Falls
GPS: N48 04.189' / W121 40.691'
Elevation: 1,470 feet
Season: May 1 to Sept 30
Sites: 8 sites for tents or self-contained RVs
Facilities: Picnic tables, vault toilets, firewood; no drinking water
Fee per night: $$$$ for the entire campground
Management: Mount Baker–Snoqualmie National Forest, Darrington Ranger District, (360) 691-7791

Activities: Hiking, fishing

Finding the campground: From I-5 in Everett take exit 194 and go east for 2 miles on US 2. Stay in the left lane over the causeway that crosses Ebey Island, and go left onto WA 204 toward Lake Stevens. In another 2 miles, at WA 9, turn north and go 2 more miles to WA 92 (Mountain Loop Highway). Turn right onto WA 92 and continue for 8 miles into the town of Granite Falls. Head north out of town and then east on what is now the Mountain Loop Highway (CR 92/FR 7). Continue for 16.5 miles to the campground.

The campground: This campground on the South Fork Stillaguamish River is shady and roomy but always full in the summer. It is very popular because it offers easy access to the river. For a minimal fee you can make reservations by contacting the National Recreation Reservation Service at www.recreation.gov or (877) 444-6777.

72 Boulder Creek

Location: 15 miles north of Concrete near Baker Lake
GPS: N48 42.000' / W121 41.983'
Elevation: 730 feet
Season: Mid-May to mid-Sept
Sites: 9 tent sites, 1 double site, 1 group site
Facilities: Picnic tables, fire grills, vault toilets; no drinking water
Fee per night: $$
Management: Mount Baker–Snoqualmie National Forest, Mount Baker Ranger District, (360) 599-2714
Activities: Fishing, hiking
Finding the campground: From the town of Concrete on WA 20, drive 9.5 miles north on CR 25 and then 5.5 miles north on FR 11.
The campground: This 5-acre, wooded campground sits next to Boulder Creek, 1 mile west of Baker Lake. There are some good mountain views, especially of 10,778-foot Mount Baker. The camp is relaxing and makes a good base from which to explore the 9-mile-long lake or the nearby trails. For a minimal fee you can make reservations by contacting the National Recreation Reservation Service at www.recreation.gov or (877) 444-6777.

73 Buck Creek

Location: About 70 miles east of Everett on Buck Creek, near Darrington
GPS: N48 16.050' / W121 19.961'
Elevation: 1,150 feet
Season: Late May to Oct
Sites: 25 sites for tents and self-contained RVs no longer than 30 feet
Facilities: Picnic tables, vault toilets, firewood; no drinking water
Fee per night: $$

*Campsite #27 in Larrabee State Park near Bellingham is a favorite even with the locals! Campers with tents and RVs check in all year-round.*PHOTO BY LYNN ROSEN

Management: Mount Baker–Snoqualmie National Forest, Darrington Ranger District, (360) 691-7791

Activities: Hiking, fishing

Finding the campground: From Everett drive north on I-5 for 15 miles. Take exit 208 and drive east on WA 530 for 32 miles to the town of Darrington. Continue on WA 530, now heading north, for 7.5 miles. When the road forks bear right onto FR 26. It follows the Suiattle River for 15 miles to the campground.

The campground: Situated on the western boundary of the Glacier Peak Wilderness, this campground is on Buck Creek not far from where it flows into the Suiattle River, which drains Huckleberry and Green Mountains. The real attraction, though, is the nearby wild and woolly Suiattle River and the steelhead that it hosts. Campground conditions are primitive, but then so is the wilderness. Call the Darrington Ranger District (360-691-7791) for current conditions; there are occasional road washouts in winter. For a minimal fee you can make reservations by contacting the National Recreation Reservation Service at www.recreation.gov or (877) 444-6777.

74 Clear Creek

Location: 50 miles east of Everett on the Sauk River, near Darrington
GPS: N48 13.215' / W121 34.130'
Elevation: 650 feet
Season: Late May to Oct
Sites: 13 sites for tents or self-contained RVs
Facilities: Picnic tables, fire grills, vault toilets, firewood; no drinking water
Fee per night: $$
Management: Mount Baker–Snoqualmie National Forest, Darrington Ranger District, (360) 691-7791
Activities: Hiking, fishing
Finding the campground: From Everett drive north on I-5 for 15 miles. Take exit 208 and drive east on WA 530 for 32 miles to the town of Darrington. From there turn south onto FR 20 (Mountain Loop Highway) and drive 3 miles to the campground.
The campground: This section of the Mountain Loop Highway is neither as thickly forested nor as populated as the section along the Stillaguamish River on the south side of the Boulder River Wilderness. But the highway is every bit as nice, the fishing is good, and trails lead into the wilderness. The campground is situated at the confluence of the Sauk River and Clear Creek in Mount Baker-Snoqualmie National Forest. For a minimal fee you can make reservations by contacting the National Recreation Reservation Service at www.recreation.gov or (877) 444-6777.

75 Douglas Fir

Location: 33 miles east of Bellingham on the North Fork Nooksack River, near Glacier
GPS: N48 54.122' / W121 54.798'
Elevation: 1,000 feet
Season: May through Sept
Sites: 29 sites for tents or self-contained RVs no longer than 26 feet
Facilities: Drinking water, picnic tables, fire grills, vault toilets
Fee per night: $$
Management: Mount Baker–Snoqualmie National Forest, Mount Baker Ranger District, (360) 599-2714
Activities: Hiking, fishing
Finding the campground: From I-5 in Bellingham drive 31 miles east on WA 542 (Mount Baker Highway) to the town of Glacier. The campground is 2 miles beyond Glacier on the left (north) side of WA 542.
The campground: This little forested campground sits right on the North Fork Nooksack River a few miles from a spot where bald eagles congregate to feed on the salmon that migrate upriver to spawn. The rushing waters are a bit noisy, but a lot of campers like it that way. The Mount Baker Ski Area is about 15 miles up the highway, and the town of Glacier has a couple of very good

restaurants. Nineteen of the 29 sites can be reserved. For a minimal fee you can make reservations by contacting the National Recreation Reservation Service at www.recreation.gov or (877) 444-6777.

76 Fay Bainbridge Park

Location: On Bainbridge Island in Puget Sound, near Seattle
GPS: N47 42.108' / W122 30.456'
Elevation: Sea level
Season: Campground open Apr through Aug; park open for day use only rest of the year
Sites: 10 tent sites, 26 sites for tents or self-contained RVs no longer than 30 feet
Facilities: Drinking water, picnic tables, fire grills, coin-operated showers, flush toilets, dump station, playground, firewood (fee), boat ramp, 2 mooring buoys
Fee per night: $$–$$$$
Management: Bainbridge Island Metro Park & Recreation District, (206) 842-2306; no reservations
Activities: Hiking, fishing, scuba diving, boating, clam digging, crabbing, beachcombing
Finding the campground: From the Seattle waterfront take the Winslow ferry to Bainbridge Island. Disembark at the town of Winslow and take WA 305 north for 4 miles. Turn right (northeast) onto Phelps Road Northeast and drive about 2 miles through Port Madison and around Point Monroe to the park.
The campground: This 17-acre waterfront park on the northeastern shore of Bainbridge Island is the only park on the island with camping facilities. It features a sandy beach, kitchen shelters, and a boat ramp. A hiking trail winds past old bunkers and sword ferns under a canopy of coniferous trees. From the camping and day-use areas, there are scenic views of Puget Sound, the Cascade Range, and the Seattle metropolitan area.

77 Flowing Lake County Park

Location: About 12 miles southeast of Everett on Flowing Lake, near Snohomish
GPS: N47 57.200' / W121 59.300'
Elevation: 300 feet
Season: Year-round for self-contained RVs; mid-May to late Sept for other campers
Sites: 5 tent sites, 30 hookup sites for RVs no longer than 25 feet, 4 cabins
Facilities: Drinking water, picnic tables, flush toilets, dump station, firewood, playground; boat docks and launch nearby
Fee per night: $$$–$$$$
Management: Snohomish County Parks, (360) 568-2274
Activities: Swimming, sunbathing, boating, waterskiing, fishing
Finding the campground: From I-5 in Everett take exit 194 and head east on US 2 for 10 miles. Turn left onto 100th Street Southeast (Westwick Road). Just after the French Creek Grange, bear

left (north) as 100th Street becomes 171st Avenue Southeast. Continue to 48th Street Southeast and turn right (east). The park entrance is at the end of the road.

The campground: This 38-acre county park will appeal to the whole family, including the dog (though it must be leashed). The park also gets a lot of day use from people who come to fish, picnic, or hike the trails. Entertainment is occasionally provided in the amphitheater. The nearby town of Snohomish is well known in the state for its antiques shops. For reservations visit www.reserveamerica.com.

78 Gold Basin

Location: About 28 miles east of Everett on the South Fork Stillaguamish River, near the town of Granite Falls
GPS: N48 04.692' / W121 44.052'
Elevation: 1,100 feet
Season: May to Sept
Sites: 10 tent sites, 78 sites for tents or self-contained RVs no longer than 31 feet
Facilities: Drinking water, picnic tables, flush toilets, firewood
Fee per night: $$$$
Management: Mount Baker–Snoqualmie National Forest, Darrington Ranger District, (360) 691-7791
Activities: Hiking, fishing
Finding the campground: From I-5 in Everett take exit 194 and go east for 2 miles on US 2. Stay in the left lane over the causeway that crosses Ebey Island and go left (north) onto WA 204 toward Lake Stevens. In another 2 miles turn north onto WA 9 and go 2 more miles to WA 92 (Mountain Loop Highway). Turn right onto WA 92 and continue for 8 miles into the town of Granite Falls. Drive north out of town and then east on what is now the Mountain Loop Highway (CR 92/FR 7). Continue 13.5 miles to the campground.
The campground: The Boulder River Wilderness lies north of this 30-acre riverside campground. Forest roads and nearby trails offer good access for hardy explorers, but be sure to get a map before taking off. The Verlot Public Service Center, 11 miles east of Granite Falls, is a good place to get local maps as well as information on road conditions and campsite availability. Gold Basin is a large campground, and it is very popular, but only some of the campsites are on the river. There is a wheelchair-accessible interpretive trail. For a minimal fee you can make reservations by contacting the National Recreation Reservation Service at www.recreation.gov or (877) 444-6777.

79 Hannegan

Location: About 50 miles east of Bellingham on Ruth Creek
GPS: N48 54.608' / W121 35.525'
Elevation: 906 feet
Season: May through Sept

Sites: No designated campsites

Facilities: Vault toilet; no drinking water

Fee per night: None

Management: Mount Baker–Snoqualmie National Forest, Mount Baker Ranger District, (360) 599-2714

Activities: Hiking

Finding the campground: From I-5 in Bellingham, take exit 255 and head northeast on WA 542 (Mount Baker Highway). Continue for about 46 miles and then turn left (east) onto FR 32 just before the bridge over the North Fork Nooksack River. Drive 5 miles to the campground at the end of FR 32.

The campground: You can really rough it at the Hannegan Campground, which is really nothing more than a clearing in the woods. In winter the access road is a cross-country ski trail. This beautiful woodsy spot is used mainly as a base camp for backpackers headed into the Mount Baker Wilderness and North Cascades National Park. Check for conditions and maps at the Glacier Public Service Center, which is 0.5 mile east of Glacier on Mount Baker Highway. The center is a joint operation of the Mount Baker–Snoqualmie National Forest and North Cascades National Park.

80 Horseshoe Cove

Location: About 14 miles north of Concrete, on Baker Lake

GPS: N48 40.228' / W121 40.622'

Elevation: 730 feet

Season: May through Sept

Sites: 35 sites for tents or self-contained RVs no longer than 34 feet

Facilities: Drinking water, picnic tables, flush toilets, boat ramp

Fee per night: $$$

Management: Mount Baker-Snoqualmie National Forest, Mount Baker Ranger District, (360) 599-2714

Activities: Fishing, boating, waterskiing, hiking, mountain biking

Finding the campground: From WA 20 in Concrete, drive 9.5 miles north on CR 25 (Baker River Road), cross the Upper Baker Dam, and then drive a bit over 1 mile on FR 1106 to its intersection with FR 11 (Baker Lake Road). Turn right and drive 1.5 miles on Baker Lake Road. Turn right onto FR 1118 and drive 1.5 miles to the campground.

The campground: This busy lakeside campground appeals primarily to boaters, including those with personal watercraft. Baker Lake is 9 miles long and covers about 5,000 acres. The fishing is good, and the catch might include Dolly Varden trout, cutthroat trout, and kokanee salmon. The site is shady, and the views of 10,778-foot Mount Baker are inspiring. For a minimal fee you can make reservations by contacting the National Recreation Reservation Service at www.recreation.gov or (877) 444-6777.

81 Howard Miller Steelhead Park

Location: 38 miles east of Burlington on the Skagit River, in the town of Rockport
GPS: N48 29.064' / W121 35.886'
Elevation: 500 feet
Season: Year-round
Sites: 54 sites with full hookups, 2 cabins
Facilities: Drinking water, picnic tables, restrooms, showers, dump station, clubhouse, Adirondack shelters, playground, boat ramp
Fee per night: $$$$
Management: Skagit County Parks and Recreation, (360) 853-8808 (park office)
Activities: Fishing, river rafting, bicycling, hiking
Finding the campground: From I-5 in Burlington take exit 230 and drive east on WA 20 (North Cascades Highway) for 38 miles to the town of Rockport. Turn right (south) onto WA 530 and continue 3 blocks. The campground is on the right.
The campground: This is a nice wooded and grassy site on the north bank of the Skagit River, a designated Wild and Scenic River. This is steelhead country, and the fishing is reputed to be good here. The park is home to the Skagit River Interpretive Center and the Bald Eagle Awareness Team. Annual events include the Bald Eagle Festival, guest speakers, guided walks, and educational programs. Reservations can be made up to 10 months in advance; call (360) 853-8808 or e-mail hmsp@fidalgo.net.

82 Hutchinson Creek

Location: 24 miles northeast of Burlington on Hutchinson Creek
GPS: N48 42.390' / W122 10.726'
Elevation: 150 feet
Season: Year-round
Sites: 11 sites for tents or self-contained RVs
Facilities: Tent pads, picnic tables, fire grills, vault toilets; no drinking water
Fee per night: None
Management: Washington Department of Natural Resources, Northwest Region, (360) 856-3500
Activities: Fishing, hiking
Finding the campground: From I-5 in Burlington take exit 230 and head east on WA 20 (North Cascades Highway). Drive 6 miles, passing through Sedro Woolley, and turn left (north) onto WA 9. Continue 15 miles to Acme and cross the Nooksack River Bridge just north of town. Turn right onto Mosquito Lake Road; continue for 2.4 miles and turn right at the campground sign onto a gravel one-lane access road that ends in 0.4 mile at the campground.
The campground: This campground on Hutchinson Creek is one of just a few DNR campgrounds in rural Whatcom County. It is enveloped in a forest of evergreens, alders, and cottonwoods. The creek is purported to offer good cutthroat fishing. The campsites are a bit close together, but rarely are more than a few of them occupied. There is a grocery store in nearby Acme.

83 Kayak Point County Park

Location: 14 miles northwest of Marysville on Port Susan Bay
GPS: N48 08.333' / W122 21.517'
Elevation: Sea level
Season: May to late Sept
Sites: 28 standard sites for tents or RVs with partial hookups, 1 cabin, 10 yurts
Facilities: Drinking water, picnic tables, restrooms, firewood, boat docks, boat ramps
Fee per night: $$$$
Management: Snohomish County Parks, (360) 652-7992
Activities: Kayaking, boating, swimming, hiking, fishing, clam digging
Finding the campground: From I-5 in Marysville take exit 199 and go west on Tulalip Road/ Marine Drive for 14 miles through the Tulalip Indian Reservation. The park entrance is on the left.
The campground: This 428-acre county park comes pretty close to being camping heaven. It is mostly wooded and has a 3,300-foot beach, so there is plenty of room to roam. It is on the southern end of Port Susan Bay, which is one of the most productive estuaries on Puget Sound, lush in its mix of organic matter on which intertidal animals thrive. The park has a 300-foot fishing pier. Keep an eye out for gray whales, which sometimes come within 100 feet of the pier. There are also seals and sea lions. Do not forget your kayak, and try your hand at clam digging. There is an eighteen-hole golf course nearby. For reservations visit www.reserveamerica.com.

84 Larrabee State Park

Location: About 5 miles south of Bellingham on Samish Bay
GPS: N48 39.504' / W122 28.596'
Elevation: Sea level
Season: Open year-round
Sites: 51 tent sites, 26 sites with full hookups for RVs no longer than 60 feet, 8 primitive tent sites, 1 group site for up to 40 people
Facilities: Drinking water, picnic tables, fire grills, restrooms, dump station, coin-operated showers, firewood, band shell, boat ramp
Fee per night: $$-$$$$
Management: Washington State Parks and Recreation Commission, (360) 902-8844 (information); (360) 676-2093 (park office)
Activities: Hiking, boating, fresh- and saltwater fishing, clam digging, mountain biking, waterskiing, crabbing, beachcombing, scuba diving
Finding the campground: From I-5 in Bellingham take exit 250 and drive west on Old Fairhaven Parkway (WA 11) for just over 1 mile to the third traffic signal. Turn left (south) at the light onto 12th Street, which in 1 block becomes Chuckanut Drive. Follow it for about 5 miles to the park entrance on your right.
The campground: Larrabee was the first state park created in Washington, in 1923. It covers 2,700 acres and features 8,000 feet of saltwater shoreline on Samish Bay and 6,700 feet of

freshwater shoreline on Fragrance and Lost Lakes. A railroad underpass and downhill trail allow access to the beach. The park occupies most of the west side of Chuckanut Mountain in Whatcom and Skagit Counties and stretches from sea level to an elevation of 1,940 feet. The mountain provides good views of the entire park and a whole lot more. A hiking trail leads to the summit. Mountain bike routes, mostly on old logging roads, weave around its flanks. Wildlife you may see here includes black-tailed deer, bald eagles, and raccoons. Sea birds and sea mammals are commonly seen offshore.

Larrabee has a wonderful band shell and grass amphitheater, which feature events as diverse as Air Force Band concerts and the awards ceremony for the 7-mile Chuckanut Foot Race, held each year in July. The 5.5-mile Interurban Trail, once an electric-train route between Bellingham and Sedro Woolley, connects the park with Bellingham. It is used a lot by hikers, bicyclists, and Chuckanut Foot Racers. The park's rocky beach, backed by a sandstone bluff, offers some of the best tidepooling around. Individual campsites can be reserved year-round by visiting https://secure.camis.com/WA/ or calling (888) 226-7688.

The band shell/amphitheater at Larrabee State Park is the site of many concerts and the center for bike and foot race stops and finishes throughout the year.

85 Marble Creek

Location: 55 miles east of Burlington on Marble Creek
GPS: N48 31.760' / W121 16.425'
Elevation: 900 feet
Season: Mid-May to mid-Sept
Sites: 23 sites for tents or self-contained RVs no longer than 22 feet
Facilities: Picnic tables, fire grills, vault toilets; no drinking water
Fee per night: $$
Management: Mount Baker–Snoqualmie National Forest, Mount Baker Ranger District, (360) 599-2714
Activities: Hiking, fishing
Finding the campground: From I-5 in Burlington take exit 230; drive east on WA 20 (North Cascades Highway) for 46 miles to Marblemount. Where the North Cascades Highway jogs left in Marblemount, turn right onto Cascade Road and cross the bridge over the Skagit River. Follow Cascade Road for 8 miles and then turn right (south) onto unpaved FR 1530. Drive another 1 mile to the campground.
The campground: This campground is very primitive but in a beautiful wilderness setting. It is just inside the Mount Baker–Snoqualmie National Forest and not far from the trailhead for the Cascade Pass hiking trail. North Cascades National Park is less than 1 mile to the north. For a minimal fee you can make reservations by contacting the National Recreation Reservation Service at www.recreation.gov or (877) 444-6777.

86 Mineral Park

Location: About 62 miles east of Burlington on the Cascade River
GPS: N48 27.798' / W121 09.691'
Elevation: 1,400 feet
Season: Mid-May to mid-Sept
Sites: 7 tent/trailer sites (Mineral Park West has 14 tent/trailer sites.)
Facilities: Picnic tables, fire rings, vault toilets; no drinking water
Fee per night: $$
Management: Mount Baker–Snoqualmie National Forest, Mount Baker Ranger District, (360) 599-2714
Activities: Hiking, fishing
Finding the campground: From I-5 in Burlington take exit 230; head east on WA 20 for 46.6 miles. Turn east onto Cascade Road (CR 3528) and drive 15 miles to the campground.
The campground: Mineral Park is very small and very primitive, but those qualities make it very appealing. It is situated among the trees in Mount Baker–Snoqualmie National Forest, next to the Cascade River, which has fair fishing. Nearby trails lead into the Glacier Peak Wilderness. For a minimal fee you can make reservations by contacting the National Recreation Reservation Service at www.recreation.gov or (877) 444-6777.

87 Money Creek

Location: 4 miles west of Skykomish on the Skykomish River
GPS: N47 43.748' / W121 27.446'
Elevation: 820 feet
Season: May 1 through Sept 30
Sites: 6 tent sites, 11 sites for tents or RVs no longer than 21 feet
Facilities: Drinking water, picnic tables, vault toilets
Fee per night: $$$
Management: Mount Baker-Snoqualmie National Forest, Skykomish Ranger District, (360) 677-2414
Activities: Hiking, fishing, swimming
Finding the campground: From the town of Skykomish, drive 4 miles west on US 2 to the campground.
The campground: Situated in the Mount Baker–Snoqualmie National Forest, across the Skykomish River from the highway and 46 miles east of Everett, this 13-acre campground is heavily forested with old-growth Douglas fir. Freight trains run close by. The fishing is not bad, and the camp is a good base from which to hike the Cascade foothills. For a minimal fee you can make reservations by contacting the National Recreation Reservation Service at www.recreation.gov or (877) 444-6777.

88 North Cascades National Park: Colonial Creek

Location: 65 miles east of Sedro Woolley, on Diablo Lake in North Cascades National Park
GPS: N48 41.908' / W121 05.657'
Elevation: 1,200 feet
Season: Late May to late Sept
Sites: 142 sites for tents or self-contained RVs no longer than 32 feet
Facilities: Drinking water, restrooms, dump station, boat ramp
Fee per night: $$
Management: North Cascades National Park, (360) 854-7200
Activities: Fishing, boat launch, hiking, summer nature programs
Finding the campground: The campground is located 65 miles east of Sedro Woolley and 10 miles east of Newhalem on WA 20, the North Cascades Highway.
The campground: Colonial Creek Campground occupies 28 acres on the south end of 5-mile-long Diablo Lake in the Ross Lake National Recreation Area, which is part of North Cascades National Park. Diablo is sandwiched between Ross and Gorge Lakes; all three lakes were created by hydroelectric dams operated by Seattle City Light. The campground is very pleasant, and the sites are set far enough from the highway that road noise is not a problem. The area is wooded and hilly, and some people swim a bit in the frigid water.

89 North Cascades National Park: Goodell Creek

Location: 55 miles east of Sedro Woolley, on the Skagit River in North Cascades National Park
GPS: N48 40.400' / W121 15.950'
Elevation: 600 feet
Season: Year-round; no services during winter
Sites: 21 sites for tents or self-contained RVs no longer than 22 feet
Facilities: Drinking water, picnic tables, fire grills, vault toilets
Fee per night: $
Management: North Cascades National Park, (360) 854-7200
Activities: Fishing, river rafting
Finding the campground: From Everett head north on I-5 and take exit 230. Drive northeast on WA 20 (North Cascades Highway) for 5 miles to Sedro Woolley and then continue east on WA 20 for another 55 miles. You will reach the campground just before the town of Newhalem.
The campground: This 4-acre campground in the Ross Lake National Recreation Area and North Cascades National Park is at the confluence of Goodell Creek and the Wild and Scenic Skagit River. It is pristine yet close to Newhalem and groceries. The easy river access makes this a popular site for river rafters.

90 North Cascades National Park: Hozomeen

Location: 1 mile south of the Canadian border on Ross Lake in North Cascades National Park; accessible only from Canada.
GPS: N48 59.076' / W121 04.272'
Elevation: 1,600 feet
Season: Late May to late Oct; no services in Oct
Sites: 75 sites for tents or self-contained RVs no longer than 22 feet, other camping areas
Facilities: Drinking water, picnic tables, fireplaces, vault toilets, boat ramp
Fee per night: None
Management: North Cascades National Park, (360) 854-7200
Activities: Fishing, boating, hiking
Finding the campground: From the town of Hope, British Columbia, on the Trans-Canada Highway (Canada Highway 1), drive 40 miles south on Silver Skagit Road to the campground. Part of the drive goes through British Columbia's Manning Provincial Park. The road is dirt much of the way.
The campground: This 4-acre campground is in the Ross Lake National Recreation Area and North Cascades National Park. Ross Lake itself extends into British Columbia. This is an area of great natural beauty, and since the road ends just 1 mile beyond the campground, there is very little traffic. Only people who are serious about camping travel this far to enjoy it. Fishing and boating are the main attractions.

91 North Cascades National Park: Newhalem Creek

Location: About 60 miles east of Burlington in North Cascades National Park
GPS: N48 40.188' / W121 15.738'
Elevation: 980 feet
Season: Mid-May to mid-Sept
Sites: 128 sites for tents or self-contained RVs up to 32 feet long
Facilities: Drinking water, picnic tables, fire grills, restrooms, dump station
Fee per night: $$$$
Management: North Cascades National Park, (360) 854-7200
Activities: Fishing, hiking, summer campfire programs
Finding the campground: From I-5 in Burlington take exit 230; drive east on WA 20 (North Cascades Highway) for 60 miles toward the town of Newhalem. The campground entrance is just before Newhalem; follow the campground signs beginning at milepost 120.
The campground: This is a nice, relatively new campground in the Ross Lake National Recreation Area, which is part of North Cascades National Park. It is also near the Wild and Scenic Skagit River. An outstanding park visitor center is a short walk from the campground.

92 Panorama Point

Location: About 16 miles north of Concrete on Baker Lake
GPS: N48 43.443' / W121 40.363'
Elevation: 730 feet
Season: May to mid-Sept
Sites: 15 sites for tents or self-contained RVs up to 21 feet long
Facilities: Drinking water, picnic tables, vault toilets
Fee per night: $$$
Management: Mount Baker-Snoqualmie National Forest, Mount Baker Ranger District, (360) 599-2714
Activities: Hiking, fishing, boating, sailing, waterskiing, mountain biking
Finding the campground: From the town of Concrete on WA 20, drive 9.5 miles north on CR 25 (Baker River Road). Cross the Upper Baker Dam, and then drive a bit over 1 mile on FR 1106 to its intersection with FR 11 (Baker Lake Road). Turn right onto Baker Lake Road and drive just over 4 miles. The campground entrance is on the right.
The campground: This national forest campground sits on a lovely point on the western shore of Baker Lake. The fishing is very good, with kokanee salmon, Dolly Varden trout, and cutthroat trout among the possibilities. The views of Mount Baker are outstanding, and the campground is neat and pleasant. For a minimal fee you can make reservations by contacting the National Recreation Reservation Service at www.recreation.gov or (877) 444-6777.

South End Campground campsites on Cascade Lake in Moran State Park are popular with families, who return year after year for warm reunions, evening fire circles, and lots of fond memories.

93 Park Creek

Location: About 17 miles north of Concrete near Baker Lake
GPS: N48 44.138' / W121 39.951'
Elevation: 800 feet
Season: Mid-May to early Sept
Sites: 12 sites for tents or self-contained RVs no longer than 22 feet
Facilities: Picnic tables, vault toilets, boat ramp (fee), docks; no drinking water
Fee per night: $$
Management: Mount Baker–Snoqualmie National Forest, Mount Baker Ranger District, (360) 599-2714
Activities: Hiking, fishing, boating
Finding the campground: From the town of Concrete on WA 20, drive 9.5 miles north on CR 25 (Baker River Road). Cross the Upper Baker Dam, and then drive a bit over 1 mile on FR 1106 to its intersection with FR 11 (Baker Lake Road). Turn right onto Baker Lake Road and drive 6 miles to the campground.
The campground: This 9-acre campground is on Park Creek, not far from the western shore of Baker Lake. The camping is primitive, but the area is nice and woodsy. Reservations are required, and you can make them, for a minimal fee, by contacting the National Recreation Reservation Service at www.recreation.gov or (877) 444-6777.

94 Rasar State Park

Location: 25 miles east of Burlington on the Skagit River, near Concrete
GPS: N48 32.363' / W121 51.214'
Elevation: 180 feet
Season: Year-round
Sites: 18 standard sites, 20 RV sites for vehicles up to 40 feet, 8 walk-in tent sites (including 2 four-person Adirondack shelters), 3 reservable group sites
Facilities: Drinking water, picnic tables, restrooms, dump station
Fee per night: $$–$$$$
Management: Washington State Parks and Recreation Commission, (360) 902-8844 (information); (360) 826-3942 (park office)
Activities: Hiking, fishing
Finding the campground: From I-5 in Burlington take exit 230; drive east on WA 20 (North Cascades Highway) for 23 miles. Turn right onto Lusk Road; drive 0.5 mile and turn left onto Capehorn Road. Continue 1.5 miles to the park.
The campground: Rasar State Park encompasses 168 acres and fronts the Wild and Scenic Skagit River for nearly 1 mile. The state acquired most of the land in 1986 through a donation from the Rasar family. The acreage north of Capehorn Road was acquired from the Washington Department of Natural Resources in 1990. A wheelchair-accessible trail leads from the day-use area to the river, and there are interpretive trails through the park. Individual campsites can be reserved year-round by visiting https://secure.camis.com/WA/ or calling (888) 226-7688.

95 Red Bridge

Location: About 32 miles east of Everett on the South Fork Stillaguamish River
GPS: N48 04.233' / W121 39.115'
Elevation: 1,300 feet
Season: Late May to early Sept
Sites: 16 sites for tents or self-contained RVs no longer than 31 feet
Facilities: Picnic tables, flush toilets, firewood; no drinking water
Fee per night: $$
Management: Mount Baker–Snoqualmie National Forest, Darrington Ranger District, (360) 691-7791
Activities: Hiking, fishing, swimming
Finding the campground: From I-5 in Everett take exit 194; go east for 2 miles on US 2. Stay in the left lane over the causeway that crosses Ebey Island and go left onto WA 204 toward Lake Stevens. In another 2 miles, at WA 9, turn north and drive 2 more miles to WA 92 (Mountain Loop Highway). Turn right onto WA 92 and continue for 8 miles to the town of Granite Falls. Drive north out of town and then east on what is now the Mountain Loop Highway (CR 92/FR 7). Continue 18 miles to the campground, which is on the right (south) side of the road.
The campground: The Verlot Public Service Center, 11 miles east of Granite Falls, is a good place to get local maps and check road conditions and campsite availability. You can also learn about

nearby remnants of the gold and silver mining that took place in this area at the turn of the twentieth century: ghost towns, old mine tunnels, and overgrown railroad grades. The 6-acre campground is very popular, with its sunny patches between the trees. It offers access to the South Fork Stillaguamish River from both sides of its namesake bridge. A lot of people taking the scenic Mountain Loop Highway stop here to enjoy the river. For a minimal fee you can make reservations by contacting the National Recreation Reservation Service at www.recreation.gov or (877) 444-6777.

96 Silver Fir

Location: About 44 miles east of Bellingham on the North Fork Nooksack River, near Glacier
GPS: N48 54.282' / W121 41.803'
Elevation: 600 feet
Season: May through Sept
Sites: 20 sites for tents or self-contained RVs no longer than 31 feet
Facilities: Drinking water, picnic tables, fire grills, vault toilets
Fee per night: $$$
Management: Mount Baker–Snoqualmie National Forest, Mount Baker Ranger District, (360) 599-2714
Activities: Hiking, cross-country skiing
Finding the campground: From I-5 in Bellingham drive 31 miles northeast on WA 542 to Glacier. Continue another 12.5 miles east to the campground.
The campground: This campground is mostly known as a day-use area for cross-country skiers in winter, but in summer it is a very pleasant wooded campground on the North Fork Nooksack River. Galena Creek feeds into the river nearby. Silver Fir is on the Mount Baker Scenic Byway, which continues on to the Mount Baker Ski Area and beyond to Artist Point. The road is paved the whole way, and there are some major trailheads at the end of it. For a minimal fee you can make reservations by contacting the National Recreation Reservation Service at www.recreation.gov or (877) 444-6777.

97 Silver Lake Park

Location: 30 miles northeast of Bellingham on Silver Lake, near the town of Maple Falls
GPS: N48 58.708' / W122 04.142'
Elevation: 820 feet
Season: Year-round
Sites: 90 tent/RV sites, 30 RV water and electric hookup sites in the group camp, 28-site horse camp with services
Facilities: Drinking water, flush toilets, bunkhouse, overnight lodge, rental cabins, group shelters, day lodge, boat ramp, boat rentals
Fee per night: $$–$$$
Management: Whatcom County Parks, (360) 733-2900; (360) 599-2776 (park office)
Activities: Boating, fishing, swimming, picnicking, horseback riding

Finding the campground: From I-5 in Bellingham take exit 255; head northeast on WA 542 (Mount Baker Highway). Drive 27 miles to the town of Maple Falls; turn left onto Silver Lake Road and drive 3 miles to the park entrance.

The campground: This is a wonderful, out-of-the-way county park used mainly by locals. The lake is stocked with rainbow and cutthroat trout, and the fishing is great. Each April, Silver Lake Park holds a 1-hour fishing derby for anglers of all ages. There is no entry fee. Registration is on derby day from 5 to 9 a.m., and prizes are awarded at 10 a.m. There is also a pancake breakfast from 6:30 a.m. to noon. For reservations call the park office at (360) 599-2776.

98 Squire Creek County Park

Location: 44 miles northeast of Everett on Squire Creek, near Darrington
GPS: N48 17.816' / W121 33.634'
Elevation: 400 feet
Season: Year-round
Sites: 33 sites with no hookups for tents or RVs no longer than 25 feet
Facilities: Drinking water, picnic tables, restrooms, dump station, firewood, 2 large shelters with cook stoves
Fee per night: $$$-$$$$
Management: Snohomish County Parks, (425) 388-6600; (360) 435-3441 (park office)
Activities: Fishing, hiking
Finding the campground: From Everett drive north on I-5 for 15 miles. Take exit 208 and drive east on WA 530 for 29 miles through Arlington to the park, which is on the north (left) side of the highway just 3 miles before you reach Darrington.

The campground: This Snohomish County park near Darrington occupies 28 acres in an old-growth forest on Squire Creek. The summer camping and fishing are good. Just 3 miles away in the Mount Baker–Snoqualmie National Forest, the 49,000-acre Boulder River Wilderness lies in a low-elevation valley that has never been logged. It is fairly rugged, but there are about 25 miles of trails. For reservations visit www.reserveamerica.com.

99 Turlo

Location: 24 miles east of Everett on the South Fork Stillaguamish River, near Granite Falls
GPS: N48 05.552' / W121 47.013'
Elevation: 900 feet
Season: Mid-May to late Sept
Sites: 18 sites for tents or self-contained RVs no longer than 31 feet
Facilities: Drinking water, picnic tables, flush toilets, firewood
Fee per night: $$$
Management: Mount Baker–Snoqualmie National Forest, Darrington Ranger District, (360) 691-7791

A traveler gets directions, good maps, and enlightening information at one of the national forests' well-staffed visitor centers.

Activities: Hiking, fishing, swimming

Finding the campground: From I-5 in Everett take exit 194; go east for 2 miles on US 2. Stay in the left lane over the causeway that crosses Ebey Island and go left onto WA 204 toward Lake Stevens. In another 2 miles, at WA 9, turn north for 2 more miles to WA 92 (Mountain Loop Highway). Turn right onto WA 92 and continue for 8 miles to the town of Granite Falls. Drive north out of town and then east on what is now the Mountain Loop Highway (CR 92/FR 7). Continue 10 miles to the campground.

The campground: The Verlot Public Service Center, 11 miles east of Granite Falls, is a good place to get local maps and information on road conditions and campsite availability. You can camp right on the river at Turlo, and there are hiking trails nearby. Late summer is a good time to visit, before the fall and winter rains start. This region gets 140 inches of rain a year. For a minimal fee you can make reservations by contacting the National Recreation Reservation Service at www.rec reation.gov or (877) 444-6777.

100 **Verlot**

Location: 26 miles east of Everett on the South Fork Stillaguamish River, near Granite Falls
GPS: N48 05.410' / W121 46.548'
Elevation: 900 feet
Season: Mid-May to late Sept

Sites: 26 sites for tents or self-contained RVs up to 31 feet long
Facilities: Drinking water, picnic tables, flush toilets, firewood
Fee per night: $$$
Management: Mount Baker–Snoqualmie National Forest, Darrington Ranger District, (360) 691-7791
Activities: Hiking, fishing, swimming
Finding the campground: From I-5 in Everett take exit 194; go east for 2 miles on US 2. Stay in the left lane over the causeway that crosses Ebey Island and go left onto WA 204 toward Lake Stevens. In another 2 miles, at WA 9, turn north for 2 more miles to WA 92 (Mountain Loop Highway). Turn right onto WA 92 and continue for 8 miles to the town of Granite Falls. Drive north out of town and then east on what is now the Mountain Loop Highway (CR 92/FR 7). Continue 11 miles to the campground.
The campground: The Verlot Public Service Center is right next to this campground. It is a good place to get local maps and check road conditions and campsite availability. The shady, 6-acre campground sits nicely on the "Stilly," as the locals call the river, in the Mount Baker–Snoqualmie National Forest. Grocery shopping is available nearby. For a minimal fee you can make reservations by contacting the National Recreation Reservation Service at www.recreation.gov or (877) 444-6777.

101 Wallace Falls State Park

Location: About 28 miles east of Everett on the Wallace River, near Gold Bar
GPS: N47 52.233' / W121 39.233'
Elevation: 160 feet
Season: Year-round
Sites: 2 walk-in tent sites and 5 reservable cabins (1 is pet-friendly)
Facilities: Drinking water, picnic tables, fire grills, restrooms
Fee per night: $$-$$$$
Management: Washington State Parks and Recreation Commission, (360) 902-8844 (information); (360) 793-0420 (park office)
Activities: Hiking, fishing, berry picking, mushrooming, mountain biking
Finding the campground: From I-5 in Everett take exit 194 (City Center/Stevens Pass) onto US 2 and drive 27 miles southeast to Gold Bar. Turn left onto First Street and go about 0.5 mile to McKenzie (Ley) Road. Turn right (east) and follow the signs to the park.
The campground: The park has good hiking trails and primitive but adequate campsites. One fun trail is actually a former railway abandoned by a logging company. A 7-mile loop trail leads to the spectacular falls, which cascade 265 feet over a series of cliffs and ledges. The 1,400-acre park also features 6,300 feet of freshwater shoreline on the Wallace River and Wallace Lake. The name Wallace is actually an anglicized version of a Skykomish Indian name, Kwayaylsh. Joe and Sarah Kwayaylsh, members of the Skykomish tribe, homesteaded near the present town of Startup (which was also named Wallace until 1901). Gold Bar, the town nearest the park, was named for the gravel bars in the Skykomish River, on which Chinese railroad workers used to pan for gold. To reserve a cabin visit https://secure.camis.com/WA/ or call (888) 226-7688.

102 Washington Park

Location: About 21 miles west of Burlington on Rosario Strait, near Anacortes
GPS: N48 29.934' / W122 37.631'
Elevation: Sea level
Season: Year-round
Sites: 70 sites for tents or RVs up to 70 feet long, including 46 with full (including cable TV) or water and electrical hookups
Facilities: Drinking water, restrooms, showers, public phone, playground, recreation field, dump station, laundry room, boat ramp
Fee per night: $$$$
Management: City of Anacortes, (360) 293-1918 (parks office); (360) 293-1927 (campground availability); reservations for locals only
Activities: Bicycling, boating, fishing, hiking
Finding the campground: From I-5 in Burlington, take exit 230 onto WA 20; drive west for 18 miles to Anacortes, following signs for the ferries. At 12th Street turn left; drive about 2 miles. Stay left on 12th Street at the ferry terminal and continue about 0.5 mile to the park.
The campground: This 22-acre camp is on Fidalgo Head, 0.5 mile past the Washington State Ferries terminal. The wooded sites are small but neat. The park features a 3.5-mile loop trail, part of which is along the shoreline. The beach is good for collecting little treasures and watching boat traffic coming and going.

Western Region: San Juan Islands and Island County

	Group Sites	RV Sites	Total # of sites	Max RV Length	Hookups	Toilets	Showers	Drinking water	Dump station	Pets	Wheelchair	Recreation	Fee	Season	Can reserve	Stay limit
103 Camano Island State Park	•	•	94	30		F	•	•	•	•	•	HFB	$$-$$$$	year-round		10
104 Deception Pass State Park	•	•	316	60		F	•	•	•	•	•	HFBS	$-$$	year-round	•	10
105 Fort Casey State Park		•	38	40		F	•	•		•	•	HFB	$$-$$$$	year-round		10
106 Fort Ebey State Park	•	•	52	70		F	•	•	•	•	•	HF	$$-$$$$	year-round	•	10
107 Moran State Park		•	151	45		F	•	•		•	•	HFBS	$$-$$$$	year-round	•	10
108 Oak Harbor City Beach Park		•	86		WE	F	•	•	•	•		FSB	$$-$$$$	year-round		
109 Odlin County Park		•	30	35		P		•		•		FSB	$$$$	year-round	•	
110 San Juan County Park		•	20	25	WES	F		•		•		HFB	$$$$	year-round	•	
111 South Whidbey State Park	•	•	55	50		F	•	•	•	•	•	HFB	$$-$$$$	Mar 15-Oct 15		10
112 Spencer Spit State Park	•	•	45	20		F	•		•	•	•	F	$$-$$$$	Mar-Oct	•	10

Hookups: W=Water E=Electric S=Sewer
Toilets: F=Flush V=Vault P=Pit
Recreation: C = Bicycling/Mountain Biking H=Hiking S=Swimming F=Fishing B=Boating
O=Off-highway driving R=Horseback Riding
Maximum Trailer/RV Length given in feet. Stay Limit given in days.
Fee $ = less than $10; $$ = $10–$15; $$$ = $16–20; $$$$ = more than $20.
If no entry under Fee, camping is free.

103 Camano Island State Park

Location: 34 miles northwest of Everett on Camano Island
GPS: N48 07.956' / W122 30.234'
Elevation: Sea level
Season: Year-round
Sites: 88 sites for tents or self-contained RVs up to 30 feet long, 5 reservable cabins, 1 group site for up to 100 people
Facilities: Drinking water, picnic tables, fire grills, restrooms, coin-operated showers, dump station, playground, boat ramps, underwater park
Fee per night: $$-$$$$
Management: Washington State Parks and Recreation Commission, (360) 902-8844 (information); (360) 387-3031 (park office)
Activities: Hiking, boating, fishing, clam digging, nature study, scuba diving, birding, rock collecting

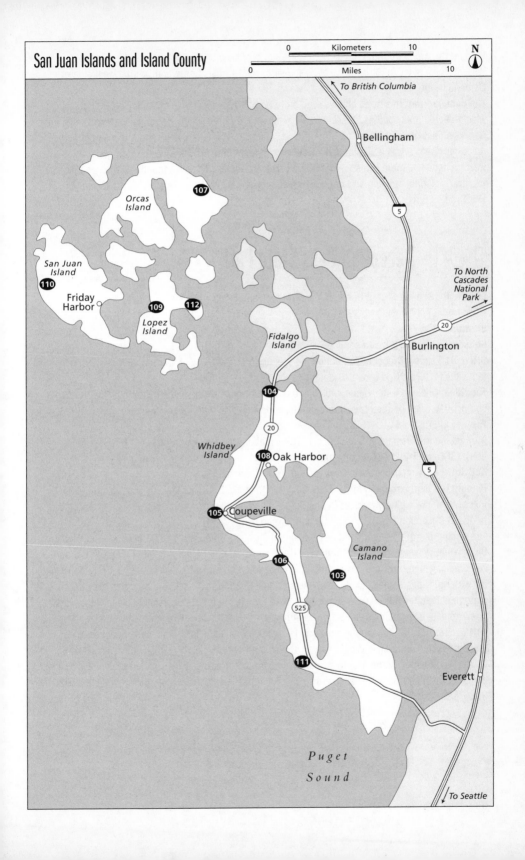

San Juan Islands and Island County

0 — Kilometers — 10
0 — Miles — 10

N

To British Columbia

Bellingham

5

To North
Cascades
National
Park

20

Burlington

Orcas
Island

107

San Juan
Island

110

Friday
Harbor

109   112

Lopez
Island

Fidalgo
Island

104

20

Whidbey
Island

108 Oak Harbor

105 Coupeville

106

Camano
Island

103

525

5

111

Everett

Puget

Sound

To Seattle

Finding the campground: From I-5, 15 miles north of Everett, take exit 212 and go west on WA 532 for 5 miles to Stanwood. Follow the signs for 14 miles to the park, on the west side of Camano Island.

The campground: This quiet and wooded state park is 10 miles south of the town of Utsalady, which means "many berries." It covers 134 acres and features 6,700 feet of saltwater frontage on Saratoga Passage and Elger Bay. There are 4.5 miles of good hiking trails and 1.3 miles of beach. A 0.5-mile nature trail leads though an old-growth forest that includes western red cedar and western hemlock. There is also a stand of old-growth Douglas firs. On some trails, bridges take you over seasonal streams and deep ravines. To reserve a cabin call Camano Beach State Park at (360) 387-1550.

104 **Deception Pass State Park**

Location: 18 miles west of Burlington on Whidbey and Fidalgo Islands
GPS: N48 17.374' / W122 39.471'
Elevation: Sea level
Season: Year-round; limited services in winter
Sites: 310 sites for tents or self-contained RVs up to 60 feet long (143 have utilities), 5 primitive tent sites for hikers and bikers, 1 group site for up to 50 people
Facilities: Drinking water, picnic tables, fire pits, restrooms, showers, dump station, concession stand, boat ramp, boat rentals, buoys, floats, underwater park at Rosario Beach
Fee per night: $–$$
Management: Washington State Parks and Recreation Commission, (360) 902-8844 (information); (360) 675-2417 (park office)
Activities: Fishing, hiking, swimming, scuba diving, boating
Finding the campground: From I-5 in Burlington take exit 230 onto WA 20; drive west for 12 miles. When the highway forks at Deans Corner, head south on WA 20; drive 6 miles, crossing the bridge at Deception Pass, to reach the park on the right.
The campground: This park straddles Deception Pass, encompassing 4,128 acres on the northern tip of Whidbey Island (in Island County) and the southern tip of Fidalgo Island (in Skagit County). The tide surges through the pass too swiftly for paddlers to navigate against the tide, but the rushing water provides a spectacle for onlookers on the 182-foot-high bridge that spans the pass. The state park features a few lakes, some old-growth Douglas fir forests, marshland, sand dunes, and a few smaller islands. There are 35 miles of hiking trails and a 1.5-mile interpretive trail, as well as 15 miles of saltwater shoreline with rocky bluffs, coves, tidal flats, and sandy beaches. Black-tailed deer are common, and bald eagles nest in the treetops. US Navy jets from nearby Naval Air Station Whidbey Island may fly over the campground at any time for several hours. Individual campsites can be reserved year-round by visiting https://secure.camis.com/WA/ or calling (888) 226-7688.

105 Fort Casey State Park

Location: About 38 miles southwest of Burlington on Whidbey Island
GPS: N48 10.403' / W122 40.396'
Elevation: Sea level
Season: Year-round
Sites: 35 sites (14 with utilities) for tents or self-contained RVs no longer than 40 feet, 3 primitive tent sites
Facilities: Drinking water, picnic tables, fire grills, restrooms, flush toilets, coin-operated showers, lighthouse/interpretive center, historic bunkers, 2 boat ramps with grounding floats, underwater park
Fee per night: $$–$$$$
Management: Washington State Parks and Recreation Commission, (360) 902-8844 (information); (360) 678-4519 (park office); no reservations.
Activities: Boating, fishing, scuba diving, hiking, driftwood collecting, clam digging
Finding the campground: From I-5 in Burlington take exit 230. Drive west on WA 20 for about 38 miles, through Coupeville, to the park.
The campground: Fort Casey State Park (including Keystone Spit) encompasses 411 acres and offers 7,000 feet of freshwater frontage on Crockett Lake and 10,810 feet of saltwater shoreline on Admiralty Inlet. Established in the late 1890s as a US Coast Guard artillery fort, Fort Casey was incorporated into Ebey's Landing National Historical Reserve by the National Park Service in 1980. Old gunnery fortifications are still in place. The beach on the west side of the campground is fine for walks and exploring. Occasionally you can see whales from both Fort Casey and Ebey's Landing. Pods of orcas that stray from their usual waters around the San Juan Islands are the most fun to see, but there are plenty of river otters, harbor seals, and California sea lions as well. Dolphins, minke whales, and humpback whales are less commonly sighted. In late spring and early summer you can see gray whales migrating from California to the Arctic. You can walk north along the beach for 4 miles to Fort Ebey (see below).

106 Fort Ebey State Park

Location: About 10 miles southwest of Oak Harbor on Whidbey Island
GPS: N48 14.628' / W122 44.688'
Elevation: Sea level
Season: Year-round
Sites: 50 sites (11 with utilities) for tents or self-contained RVs up to 70 feet long, 1 kayaker site, 1 group site for up to 60 people
Facilities: Drinking water, picnic tables, fire grills, restroom, coin-operated showers, dump station
Fee per night: $$–$$$$
Management: Washington State Parks and Recreation Commission, (360) 902-8844 (information); (360) 678-4636 (park office)
Activities: Hiking, fishing, beachcombing

Finding the campground: From Oak Harbor on Whidbey Island, drive 8 miles south on WA 20 to its intersection with Libbey Road. Turn right (west) onto Libbey Road; drive 1.2 miles and turn left (south) onto Fort Ebey Road. Proceed for 0.25 mile on Fort Ebey Road to the park.

The campground: You will find Fort Ebey on the bluffs high above the Strait of Juan de Fuca, where the strait flows into Admiralty Inlet. There are 24 picnic sites in the day-use area. The 645-acre park offers 3 miles of bluff trails and 1.5 miles of beach trails. Follow the curving boardwalk over the driftwood-strewn beach and look for Japanese glass fishing floats. Gun batteries and bunkers remain from the days when the fort was operational, and they are fun to explore. The park is a stop on the Cascadia Marine Trail. It features 8,000 feet of saltwater shoreline on Admiralty Inlet and 1,000 feet of freshwater frontage on Lake Pondilla. Individual campsites can be reserved year-round up to 9 months in advance by visiting https://secure.camis.com/WA/ or calling (888) 226-7688.

107 Moran State Park

Location: 15 miles from the ferry landing on Orcas Island in the San Juan Islands
GPS: N48 39.390' / W122 49.056'
Elevation: 800 feet
Season: Year-round
Sites: 136 sites for tents or self-contained RVs up to 45 feet long, 15 primitive hike-in/bike-in tent sites, all spread over 4 campgrounds
Facilities: Drinking water, picnic tables, fire grills, restrooms, showers, firewood, boat docks, fishing supplies, launching facilities (fee), boat rentals, environmental learning center
Fee per night: $$–$$$$
Management: Washington State Parks and Recreation Commission, (360) 902-8844 (information); (360) 376-2326 (park office)
Activities: Hiking, fishing, swimming, boating, picnicking
Finding the campground: From the ferry landing on Orcas Island, take an immediate left onto Orcas to Olga Road; drive 15 miles around East Sound to the park.

The campground: In 1920 Robert Moran, a shipbuilder and former mayor of Seattle, donated 2,600 acres on Orcas Island to the state for use as a park. Moran State Park has since grown to more than 5,000 acres, and it now includes 5 lakes, 30 miles of foot trails, and 300 acres of old-growth forest. Most trails run through the woods, but you will find some paths with views of nearby islands. Among Moran's greatest attractions are the views from Mount Constitution (2,409 feet) and Little Summit Lookout (2,039 feet). You can drive, bike, or hike to either. A 52-foot tower at the top of Mount Constitution was patterned after watchtowers built in the Caucasus Mountains of Eastern Europe in the twelfth century.

Cold Springs is a particularly pleasant picnic spot. Dogs must be on a leash (8 feet in length or less) at all times, and they must be prevented from annoying other park visitors. Cleaning up after your pet is also required. You will find campsites on and across the road from Cascade Lake and at Mountain Lake. The latter is a reservoir, so swimming is not allowed. Fishing is permitted. The park is busiest on summer weekends. Individual campsites can be reserved year-round by visiting https://secure.camis.com/WA/ or calling (888) 226-7688.

108 Oak Harbor City Beach Park (also called Sailaway RV Park)

Location: In Oak Harbor on Whidbey Island
GPS: N48 18.906' / W122 38.246'
Elevation: Sea level
Season: Year-round
Sites: 56 RV sites with water and electrical hookups, 30 non-service sites
Facilities: Drinking water, picnic tables, restrooms, coin-operated showers, dump station, playground, beach
Fee per night: $$-$$$$
Management: City of Oak Harbor, (360) 279-4756; no reservations
Activities: Fishing, swimming, boating
Finding the campground: Head south through the town of Oak Harbor on WA 20 and cross West Pioneer Way onto the continuation of 80 Southwest Street. The campground is on the left in 1 block.
The campground: The swimming beach is the real attraction of this RV-only park. The campground is very pleasant and pretty busy throughout the summer.

109 Odlin County Park

Location: 1 mile from the ferry landing on Lopez Island in the San Juan Islands
GPS: N48 33.456' / W122 53.427'
Elevation: Sea level
Season: Year-round
Sites: 30 sites for tents or self-contained RVs up to 35 feet long
Facilities: Drinking water, pit toilets, pier, float, boat ramp, mooring buoys, ball parks, covered cook shack
Fee per night: $$$$
Management: San Juan County Parks, (360) 378-8420
Activities: Fishing, boating, swimming
Finding the campground: The park is 1 mile south of the ferry landing, via Ferry Road, at the northwest end of Lopez Island.
The campground: A stopping point on the Cascadia Marine Trail system, Odlin Park offers 80 acres of relaxation in a natural setting, as well as 1 mile of sandy beach on Upright Channel. You do not find many sandy beaches in the Northwest, and this is a nice one. Swim if you dare—at 50 degrees Fahrenheit, the water feels mighty cold to most. Showers are available in nearby Lopez Village. You can make reservations for April through October 5 to 90 days in advance by visiting www.sanjuanco.com/parks.

110 San Juan County Park

Location: 11 miles west of the Friday Harbor ferry landing on San Juan Island
GPS: N48 32.573' / W123 09.644'
Elevation: Sea level
Season: Year-round
Sites: 20 sites, including 8 with full hookups for RVs no longer than 25 feet
Facilities: Drinking water, flush toilets, boat ramp
Fee per night: $$$$
Management: San Juan County Parks, (360) 378-8420
Activities: Hiking, whale watching, fishing, boating
Finding the campground: From the Washington State Ferries terminal at Friday Harbor, head southeast on Front Street. In 2 blocks turn right (southwest) onto Spring Street. Near the western city limits, Spring Street becomes San Juan Valley Road. Turn left (south) onto Wold Road and then right (west) onto Bailer Hill Road, which becomes Westside Road and continues north up the coast. Once you pass Lime Kiln Point State Park, look for San Juan County Park Road and follow it into the park.
The campground: This is the only county park on San Juan Island. It is located on Smallpox Bay on the west-central shore of the island. The campground is basic but pristine, and the views are outstanding. There are plenty of eagles and orcas to watch. You can make reservations 5 to 90 days in advance in summer by visiting https://sanjuanco.com/CAMP/parkreservations/.

111 South Whidbey State Park

Location: About 5 miles south of Greenbank on Whidbey Island
GPS: N48 01.239' / W122 35.470'
Elevation: Sea level
Season: Mar 15 to Oct 15; day use only in winter
Sites: 54 sites for tents or self-contained RVs (including 8 utility sites) no longer than 50 feet, 1 group site for up to 60 people
Facilities: Drinking water, picnic tables, fire grills, restrooms, coin-operated showers, dump station, firewood (fee), amphitheater
Fee per night: $$-$$$$
Management: Washington State Parks and Recreation Commission, (360) 902-8844 (information); (360) 331-4559 (park office)
Activities: Hiking, saltwater fishing, boating, scuba diving, beachcombing, rock collecting, clam digging, birding, crabbing, driftwood collecting
Finding the campground: From WA 525, almost 1 mile north of Greenbank, take Smugglers Cove Road west and south for about 4.5 miles to the campground on the right.
The campground: This campground is a favorite. The 347-acre park has 4,500 feet of saltwater shoreline on Admiralty Inlet on the western shore of Whidbey Island. It offers a sandy beach and views of Puget Sound and the Olympic Mountains. There is a good loop trail through an old-growth cluster of western red cedar and Douglas fir. Some of the trees are more than 250 years old.

Individual campsites can be reserved in summer only by visiting https://secure.camis.com/WA/ or calling (888) 226-7688.

112 Spencer Spit State Park

Location: 3 miles south of the ferry landing on Lopez Island in the San Juan Islands
GPS: N48 32.184' / W122 51.726'
Elevation: Sea level
Season: Mar through Oct
Sites: 37 sites for tents or self-contained RVs no longer than 20 feet, including 10 walk-in sites; 7 hiker/biker sites, some kayaker sites, 1 Adirondack shelter, 1 group site for up to 24 people
Facilities: Drinking water, picnic tables, fire grills, restrooms, dump station, 16 offshore moorage buoys
Fee per night: $$–$$$$
Management: Washington State Parks and Recreation Commission, (360) 902-8844 (information); (360) 468-2251 (park office)
Activities: Saltwater fishing, clam digging, beachcombing, bird watching
Finding the campground: From the ferry landing on Upright Head, on the north end of the island, go south on Ferry Road for just over 1 mile. Turn left (east) onto Port Stanley Road and continue nearly 2 miles around Swifts Bay to the park.
The campground: Beach parks are a rarity on the rocky coast of Washington, especially in the "banana belt" San Juan Islands. This is an exceptionally nice one. The 130-acre park has 7,840 feet of saltwater shoreline on Lopez Sound. The park's main feature is a 0.25-mile-long sand spit that contains a saltwater lagoon. The park also contains a midden—archaeological remains of an early Coast Salish campsite. The area is frequented by migratory birds, great blue herons, geese, and kingfishers. There are plenty of rabbits, deer, and raccoons. Individual campsites can be reserved in summer only by visiting https://secure.camis.com/WA/ or calling (888) 226-7688.

Western Region: South Puget Sound

	Group Sites	RV Sites	Total # of sites	Max RV Length	Hookups	Toilets	Showers	Drinking water	Dump station	Pets	Wheelchair	Recreation	Fee	Season	Can reserve	Stay limit
113 Adams Fork		•	22	22		V		•		•		HFS	$	May–late Oct	•	14
114 Alder Lake		•	173	25		F		•		•		FBS	$$$$	see entry	•	14
115 Battle Ground State Park	•	•	51	35		F	•	•	•	•	•	HFBSR	$$–$$$$	year-round	•	10
116 Beacon Rock State Park		•	31	40		F	•	•	•	•		HFBRC	$$–$$$$	summer		10
117 Beaver		•	23	25		P		•		•	•	HFS	$$$	mid May–late Sept	•	14
118 Cat Creek		•	5	16		P				•		HF	$	mid May–late Oct		14
119 Cold Creek		•	6			V		•		•		HFC		year-round		7
120 Corral Pass			20			V				•		HR		July–late Sept		14
121 Council Lake		•	9	16		P				•		HFSB	$	July–mid Sept		14
122 Cultus Creek		•	50	32		V		•		•	•	H	$$	June–Sept	•	14
123 The Dalles		•	45	21		V		•		•		HF	$–$$	mid May–late Sept	•	14
124 Dash Point State Park	•	•	142	40	WE	F	•	•	•	•	•	HFS	$$–$$$$	year-round	•	10
125 Dougan Creek		•	7			V		•		•		HF		mid May–mid Sept		7
126 Elbe Hills ORV Trailhead		•	3			P				•		O		year-round	•	7
127 Evans Creek			23			V		•		•		HFO		mid Jun–late Sept		14
128 Fall Creek		•	8			V				•		HRC		Apr–Nov		7
129 Falls Creek-Crest Horse Camp		•	4	15		P				•		HR		mid June–late Sept		14
130 Goose Lake		•	19	18		V				•		HFS	$$	mid June–late Sept	•	14
131 Horseshoe Lake		•	10	16		P				•		HFBS	$$	mid June–late Sept		14
132 Ike Kinswa State Park		•	103	60	WES	F	•	•	•	•	•	HFSB	$$–$$$$	year-round	•	10
133 Iron Creek		•	98	42		P		•		•		HF	$$$	mid May–late Oct	•	14
134 Kanaskat-Palmer State Park	•	•	51	50	E	F	•	•		•		HFB	$$–$$$$	year-round	•	10

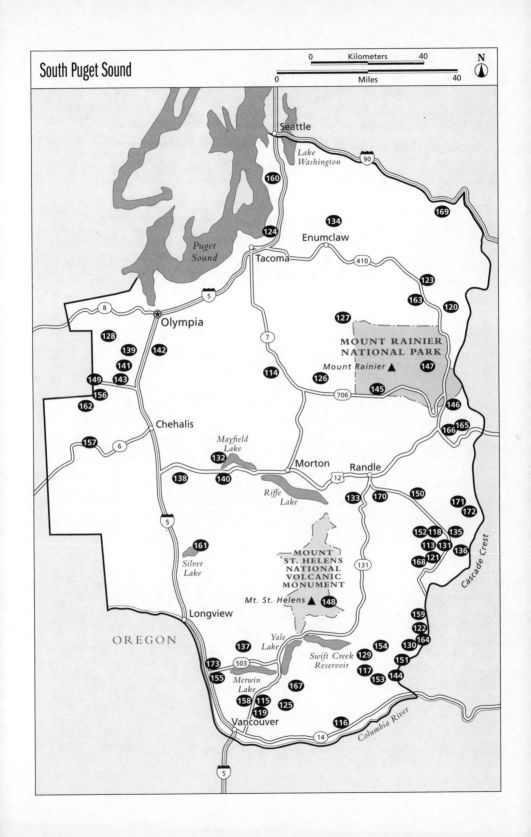

South Puget Sound

Kilometers 0 — 40

Miles 0 — 40

N

Seattle

Lake Washington

90

169

Puget Sound

160

134

Enumclaw

124

Tacoma

410

123

5

163

120

8

Olympia

127

128

139

142

7

MOUNT RAINIER NATIONAL PARK

Mount Rainier ▲

147

141

114

126

706

145

149

143

146

156

162

166

165

Chehalis

Mayfield Lake

157

6

132

Morton

Randle

138

140

12

Riffe Lake

133

170

150

171

172

5

152 118 135

161

113 131

Silver Lake

MOUNT ST. HELENS NATIONAL VOLCANIC MONUMENT

131

168 121

136

Mt. St. Helens ▲

148

159

Longview

122

OREGON

Yale Lake

137

154

130 164

129

151

Swift Creek Reservoir

173

503

155

117

153

144

Merwin Lake

167

158 115

125

119

Vancouver

116

Columbia River

14

5

	Group Sites	RV Sites	Total # of sites	Max RV Length	Hookups	Toilets	Showers	Drinking water	Dump station	Pets	Wheelchair	Recreation	Fee	Season	Can reserve	Stay limit
135 Keene's Horse Camp		•	13	21		V				•		HR	$$	July–late Sept		14
136 Killen Creek		•	9	22		P				•		HR		July–late Sept		14
137 Lake Merrill			11			V		•				HFB		May–Sept		7
138 Lewis and Clark State Park	•	•	42	60		F		•		•		HFR	$$–$$$$	June–Oct		10
139 Margaret McKenny		•	32			P				•		HRC		Apr–Nov		14
140 Mayfield Lake Park	•	•	56	40		F	•	•	•	•	•	FBS	$$$$	Apr 15–Oct 15	•	14
141 Middle Waddell		•	24			V				•		OC		Apr–Nov		14
142 Millersylvania State Park	•	•	169	35		F	•	•	•	•	•	HFBSC	$$–$$$$	year-round	•	10
143 Mima Falls Trailhead		•	5			P		•		•		HRC		Apr–Nov		14
144 Moss Creek		•	16	32		P		•		•		F	$$$	mid May–late Sept	•	14
145 Mount Rainier National Park: Cougar Rock	•	•	178	30		F		•	•	•	•	HF	$$	late May–early Oct	•	14
146 Mount Rainier National Park: Ohanapecosh	•	•	190	32		F	•	•	•	•		H	$$	late May–early Oct	•	14
147 Mount Rainier National Park: White River		•	112	20		F		•	•	•	•	HFR	$$	late June–late Sept		14
148 MSHNVM: Lower Falls RA		•	43	60		V		•		•	•	HR	$$	May–Oct		14
149 North Creek		•	5			V		•		•		HC		Apr–Nov		14
150 North Fork		•	30	32		V		•		•		HFC	$$$	mid May–late Sept	•	14
151 Oklahoma		•	22	22		P		•		•	•	F	$$$–$$$$	mid May–mid Oct	•	14
152 Olallie Lake		•	5	22		P				•		FSB	$$	July–late Sept	•	14
153 Panther Creek		•	84	25		P		•		•		HF	$$$–$$$$	mid May–mid Oct	•	14
154 Paradise Creek		•	42	25		V		•		•	•	HF	$$$	mid May–mid Oct	•	14
155 Paradise Point State Park		•	85	40		F	•	•	•	•	•	HFB	$$–$$$$	year-round	•	10
156 Porter Creek		•	14			V				•		HRCO		Apr–Nov		14
157 Rainbow Falls State Park	•	•	46	60		F	•	•	•	•	•	HFSB	$$–$$$$	Apr–Aug		10
158 Rock Creek		•	19			V		•		•	•	HFR		year-round		7
159 Saddle			12			P				•		HF		mid June–late Sept		14

	Group Sites	RV Sites	Total # of sites	Max RV Length	Hookups	Toilets	Showers	Drinking water	Dump station	Pets	Wheelchair	Recreation	Fee	Season	Can reserve	Stay limit
160 Saltwater State Park		•	48	50		F	•	•	•	•	•	HFS	$$–$$$$	mid May–mid Sept		10
161 Seaquest State Park	•	•	94	50	WES	F	•	•	•	•	•	HF	$–$$$	year-round	•	10
162 Sherman Valley	•		8			V		•		•		HC		Apr–Nov		14
163 Silver Springs	•	•	57	21		V		•		•		HF	$$$	mid May–late Sept	•	14
164 Smokey Creek	•		3	22		P			•			H		June–late Sept		14
165 Soda Springs			6			V			•			H		mid June–early Sept		14
166 Summit Creek	•		6			P			•			H		mid June–early Sept		14
167 Sunset	•		18	22		P		•		•		HF	$$	year-round		14
168 Takhlakh	•		53	22		V		•		•		HFB	$$$	mid June–late Sept	•	14
169 Tinkham	•		47	21		V		•		•	•	HF	$$–$$$$	mid May–mid Sept	•	14
170 Tower Rock	•		22	22		V		•		•		F	$$$	mid May–late Sept	•	14
171 Walupt Horse Camp	•		6	18		V		•		•		FHR	$$$	Jun–Sept	•	14
172 Walupt Lake	•		44	22		V		•		•		HFSB	$$$	mid Jun–early Sept	•	14
173 Woodland	•		10			V		•		•	•			May–Sept		7

Hookups: W=Water E=Electric S=Sewer
Toilets: F=Flush V=Vault P=Pit
Recreation: C=Bicycling/Mountain Biking H=Hiking S=Swimming F=Fishing B=Boating
O=Off-highway driving R=Horseback Riding
Maximum Trailer/RV Length given in feet. Stay Limit given in days.
Fee $ = less than $10; $$ = $10–$15; $$$ = $16–20; $$$$ = more than $20.
If no entry under Fee, camping is free.

113 Adams Fork

Location: About 117 miles southeast of Olympia in the Randle Recreation Area on the Cispus River
GPS: N46 20.355' / W121 38.729'
Elevation: 2,600 feet
Season: May to late Oct
Sites: 22 sites for tents or self-contained RVs no longer than 22 feet
Facilities: Drinking water, picnic tables, vault toilets
Fee per night: $
Management: Gifford Pinchot National Forest, Cowlitz Valley Ranger District, (360) 497-1100
Activities: Hiking, fishing, swimming

Finding the campground: From I-5, 45 miles south of Olympia, take exit 68; head east on US 12. Drive 48 miles to the town of Randle and turn south onto WA 131. Drive 1 mile, turn left (southeast) onto FR 23 (Cispus Road), and drive 18 miles. Take the left fork, turning east onto FR 21, and drive 5 miles. Turn right (southeast) onto FR 56 and drive 0.1 mile to the campground.

The campground: This campground on the Upper Cispus River is in an inspiring location: about 12 miles from the summit of Mount Adams. It is a fine place to kick back and refresh yourself, and there are plenty of trails for walking or hiking. For a minimal fee you can make reservations by contacting the National Recreation Reservation Service at www.recreation.gov or (877) 444-6777.

114 Alder Lake

Location: 30 miles southeast of Tacoma on Alder Lake, near Eatonville
GPS: N46 45.806' / W122 15.440'
Elevation: 1,100 feet
Season: Year-round except closed Dec 20 through Jan 1; limited facilities in winter
Sites: 173 sites at 4 campgrounds for tents or self-contained RVs no longer than 25 feet
Facilities: Drinking water, picnic tables, fire grills, tent pads, flush toilets, 2 boat ramps, dock
Fee per night: $$$$
Management: Tacoma Power, (360) 569-2778 (park office)
Activities: Fishing, boating, waterskiing, swimming
Finding the campground: From I-5 in Tacoma take exit 134 and head south on WA 7. Drive 30 miles to the campground. From Eatonville the campground is 6 miles south via WA 161 and WA 7.
The campground: This 231-acre lakeshore campground is wooded and relatively peaceful but for the water-skiers, who start early in the morning. For reservations visit https://secure.camis.com/WA/AlderLake-TacomaPowerPark or call (888) 226-7688.

115 Battle Ground State Park

Location: About 19 miles northeast of Vancouver on Battle Ground Lake
GPS: N45 48.232' / W122 29.448'
Elevation: 450 feet
Season: Year-round
Sites: 15 hike-in (0.25 to 0.5 mile) primitive tent sites, 25 sites for tents or self-contained RVs no longer than 35 feet, 6 hookup sites, 4 cabins, 1 tents-only group site (minimum 25 people)
Facilities: Drinking water, fire grills, picnic tables, flush toilets, showers, dump station, store, firewood, restaurant, playground, unguarded swimming beach, boat ramp, boat rentals
Fee per night: $$-$$$$
Management: Washington State Parks and Recreation Commission, (360) 902-8844 (information); (360) 687-4621 (park office)
Activities: Hiking, swimming, boating, fishing, scuba diving, horseback riding, horseshoe pit, sports field, marina

Finding the campground: From I-5 in Vancouver take exit 2 onto WA 500; drive east for almost 5 miles. Turn north onto WA 503 and drive north for 9.5 miles to the town of Battle Ground. From there follow the signs for 3 miles to the park.

The campground: Battle Ground covers 280 acres and has 4,100 feet of freshwater shoreline on 28-acre Battle Ground Lake. The park is very popular because of its easy access to the lake. However, no motorboats are allowed. The campground is a nice mix of primitive and RV sites. There are 5 miles of horse trails for equestrians. Individual campsites can be reserved year-round by visiting https://secure.camis.com/WA/ or calling (888) 226-7688.

116 Beacon Rock State Park

Location: 35 miles east of Vancouver on the Columbia River
GPS: N45 38.470' / W121 59.260'
Elevation: Sea level
Season: Summer only; Woodard Creek, year-round
Sites: 26 sites for tents or self-contained RVs no longer than 20 feet (open summer only). The Woodard Creek Campground (open year round) has 5 utility sites. Follow signs near milepost 34 to the watercraft launch area and then to the RV campsites, maximum length 40 feet.
Facilities: Drinking water, picnic tables, fire grills, flush toilets, dump station, coin-operated showers, firewood (fee), playground, 2 boat ramps, dock
Fee per night: $$–$$$$
Management: Washington State Parks and Recreation Commission, (360) 902-8844 (information); (509) 427-8265 (park office)
Activities: Hiking, fishing, boating, rock climbing, horseback riding, mountain biking
Finding the campground: From I-5 in Vancouver drive east on WA 14 for 35 miles.
The campground: Just 1 mile east of the town of Skamania, Beacon Rock looms over the highway like a monolith from outer space. In fact, it is one of the largest monoliths in the nation. Serious hikers can take the steep 1-mile trail to the top of the rock (elevation 848 feet) for a fine view of this part of the Columbia Gorge. The trail has a handrail, but people who suffer from vertigo will want to forego the climb. The remains of an ancient volcano, the rock was named by Lewis and Clark in 1805. It marks the last of the rapids on the Columbia River and the beginning of tidal influence from the Pacific Ocean, 150 miles away. The park covers 4,500 acres on both sides of the highway, including 1.8 miles of shoreline on the Columbia River. There are 14 miles of hiking trails, 7 of them shared with equestrians and mountain bikers. Several creeks offer excellent fishing. Individual campsites can be reserved by visiting https://secure.camis.com/WA/ or calling (888) 226-7688.

117 Beaver

Location: 59 miles northeast of Vancouver on the Wind River
GPS: N45 51.370' / W121 57.417'

Elevation: 1,100 feet

Season: Mid-May to late Sept

Sites: 23 sites for tents or self-contained RVs no longer than 25 feet

Facilities: Drinking water, fire grills, picnic tables, pit toilets

Fee per night: $$$

Management: Gifford Pinchot National Forest, Mount Adams Ranger District, (509) 395-3400

Activities: Hiking, fishing, swimming, berry and mushroom picking

Finding the campground: From I-5 in Vancouver take exit 1 and head east on WA 14 for 47 miles to the town of Carson. Turn left (north) onto Wind River Road and drive 12 miles to the campground.

The campground: This campground is remote yet easy to reach. It is shady, comfortable, cool, and right beside the Wind River. It is open from mid-May to late September. For a minimal fee you can make reservations by contacting the National Recreation Reservation Service at www.recreation .gov or (877) 444-6777.

118 Cat Creek

Location: 119 miles southeast of Olympia on the Cispus River, near Randle.

GPS: N46 20.912' / W121 37.418'

Elevation: 3,000 feet

Season: Mid-May to late Oct

Sites: 5 sites for tents or self-contained RVs no longer than 16 feet

Facilities: Picnic tables, fire grills, pit toilets, firewood; no drinking water

Fee per night: $

Management: Gifford Pinchot National Forest, Cowlitz Valley Ranger District, (360) 497-1100; no reservations

Activities: Fishing, hiking

Finding the campground: From I-5, 45 miles south of Olympia, take exit 68; head east on US 12 for 48 miles to the town of Randle. Turn right (south) onto WA 131, drive 1 mile; turn left (southeast) onto FR 23 (Cispus Road) and drive 18 miles. Take the left fork and go east for 7 miles on FR 21 to the campground.

The campground: Located in Gifford Pinchot National Forest, this camp is only 12 miles from Mount Adams; Mount St. Helens is to the west behind Blue Lake Ridge. The small, primitive campground is at the confluence of Cat Creek and the Cispus River.

119 Cold Creek

Location: About 25 miles northeast of Vancouver on Cold Creek

GPS: N45 45.690' / W122 20.454'

Elevation: 640 feet

Season: Year-round

Campers set up at a favorite site on the shore of Cascade Lake.

Sites: 6 sites for tents or self-contained RVs
Facilities: Drinking water, picnic tables, fire grills, tent pads, vault toilets, horse-loading ramp
Fee per night: None
Management: Washington Department of Natural Resources, South Puget Sound Region, (360) 825-1631
Activities: Hiking, fishing, mountain biking
Finding the campground: From I-5, 5 miles north of Vancouver, take exit 9; drive east on Northeast 179th Street for 5.5 miles. Turn right (south) onto WA 503 and drive 1.5 miles. Turn left (east) onto Northeast 159th Street and drive 2.5 miles. At a Y junction bear left onto Rawson Road. At 2 miles the pavement ends and the road becomes the L-1400 Road. Continue on it for 4 more miles; turn left onto L-1000 Road and drive for 3.2 miles. Turn left onto L-1300 Road and go 0.8 mile to the campground.
The campground: Situated in the Green Mountain State Forest, this basic DNR campground is wooded and not heavily used. Hiking and mountain biking are the main attractions, and there are plenty of hills to climb.

120 Corral Pass

Location: 37 miles southeast of Enumclaw
GPS: N47 00.978' / W121 27.150'
Elevation: 5,700 feet
Season: July to late Sept
Sites: 20 tent sites
Facilities: Picnic tables, fire grills, vault toilets, firewood, horse-loading ramp; no drinking water
Fee per night: None
Management: Mount Baker-Snoqualmie National Forest, Snoqualmie Ranger District, (425) 888-1421
Activities: Hiking, horse packing
Finding the campground: From Enumclaw, just east of Tacoma, drive 31 miles southeast on WA 410. Turn left (east) onto FR 7174 and drive 6 miles to the campground. The last 6 miles are on a winding dirt road that may be difficult for trailers and big RVs to negotiate.
The campground: This 15-acre camp is both high and remote. It is near the western boundary of the Norse Peak Wilderness. The campground is quite rustic, but it is well suited as a base camp for explorations on foot or hoof. Trails head north and east from camp.

121 Council Lake

Location: 126 miles southeast of Olympia on Council Lake, near Randle
GPS: N46 15.792' / W121 37.908'
Elevation: 4,300 feet
Season: July to mid-Sept
Sites: 9 sites for tents or self-contained RVs no longer than 16 feet
Facilities: Picnic tables, pit toilets; no drinking water
Fee per night: $
Management: Gifford Pinchot National Forest, Cowlitz Valley Ranger District, (360) 497-1100; no reservations.
Activities: Hiking, fishing, swimming, boating
Finding the campground: From I-5, 45 miles south of Olympia, take exit 68; head east on US 12. Drive 48 miles to the town of Randle and take WA 131 south. In 1 mile turn southeast onto FR 23 (Cispus Road) and drive 31 miles. Take the right fork, going west on FR 2334, and drive 1 mile to the campground.
The campground: This campground is so close to Mount Adams that it is actually on the mountain's northern apron. It sits at the edge of Council Lake with easy access to hiking trails. It is a bit rustic but comfortable.

122 Cultus Creek

Location: 109 miles northeast of Vancouver on Cultus Creek, near the town of Trout Lake
GPS: N46 03.665' / W121 58.260'
Elevation: 4,000 feet
Season: June through Sept
Sites: 39 single sites for tents or self-contained RVs no longer than 32 feet, 11 double sites
Facilities: Drinking water, picnic tables, fire rings, vault toilets
Fee per night: $$
Management: Gifford Pinchot National Forest, Mount Adams Ranger District, (509) 395-3400; no reservations
Activities: Hiking, berry picking, evening nature programs
Finding the campground: From I-5 in Vancouver take exit 1; head east on WA 14 for 66 miles. At Bingen turn left (north) onto WA 141 and drive 25 miles to the town of Trout Lake. Continue through Trout Lake on WA 141 for 5.5 miles. The route becomes FR 24 at the Skamania County line. Continue on FR 24 for 12.5 miles to the campground.
The campground: Busiest during huckleberry season, this campground is located near both the Pacific Crest National Scenic Trail and the Indian Heaven Wilderness. The Big Lava Bed is a few miles to the south. This is high and dry country, so the forests are largely composed of pines. The campground is very pleasant and relaxing. Campground hosts are on site. For a minimal fee you can make reservations by contacting the National Recreation Reservation Service at www .recreation.gov or (877) 444-6777.

123 The Dalles

Location: 25 miles southeast of Enumclaw on Minnehaha Creek
GPS: N47 04.700' / W121 34.984'
Elevation: 2,400 feet
Season: Mid-May to late Sept
Sites: 19 tent sites, 26 sites for tents or self-contained RVs no longer than 21 feet
Facilities: Drinking water, picnic tables, fire grills, vault toilets, firewood
Fee per night: $-$$
Management: Mount Baker–Snoqualmie National Forest, Snoqualmie Ranger District, (425) 888-1421
Activities: Hiking, fishing, hunting
Finding the campground: From Enumclaw, just east of Tacoma, drive 25 miles southeast on WA 410 to the campground.
The campground: This is a good-size camp for being relatively primitive. Part of its appeal is the beauty of this valley along the White River and the stands of old-growth forest. The campground is nestled between Dalles and Huckleberry Ridges on the main entrance road to the east side of Mount Rainier National Park. The White River is just across the highway. For a minimal fee you can make reservations by contacting the National Recreation Reservation Service at www.recreation .gov or (877) 444-6777.

124 Dash Point State Park

Location: About 8 miles north of Tacoma on Puget Sound
GPS: N47 18.956' / W122 24.440'
Elevation: Sea level
Season: Year-round
Sites: 114 tent sites, 27 sites with water and electrical hookups for RVs no longer than 40 feet, group site for up to 96 people
Facilities: Drinking water, picnic tables, flush toilets, showers, dump station, playground
Fee per night: $$–$$$$
Management: Washington State Parks and Recreation Commission, (360) 902-8844 (information); (253) 661-4955 (park office)
Activities: Fishing, hiking, beachcombing, swimming, sailboarding, kayaking, marine-life study
Finding the campground: From I-5 in Tacoma take exit 136 and drive north for 2 blocks, passing WA 99 (Pacific Highway). Turn right onto WA 509 (East-West Road) and drive 8 miles to the park.
The campground: Dash Point State Park straddles the line between King and Pierce Counties, which separates Tacoma from Federal Way. It covers 400 acres and has 3,300 feet of shoreline on Puget Sound's East Passage, plus 7.4 miles of hiking and mountain biking trails. The beach is a very popular place to walk and enjoy the views of Puget Sound. However, the water has been somewhat polluted by nearby industries, so clam digging is not recommended. This is basically an urban state park and therefore very well used. Individual campsites can be reserved year-round by visiting https://secure.camis.com/WA/ or calling (888) 226-7688.

125 Dougan Creek

Location: About 32 miles east of Washougal on Dougan Creek and the Washougal River
GPS: N45 40.407' / W122 09.355'
Elevation: 720 feet
Season: Mid-May to mid-Sept
Sites: 7 sites for tents or self-contained RVs
Facilities: Drinking water, picnic tables, tent pads, fire grills, vault toilets
Fee per night: None
Management: Washington Department of Natural Resources, Pacific Cascade Region, (360) 577-2025
Activities: Hiking, fishing
Finding the campground: From I-5 in Vancouver take exit 1 and head east on WA 14 for 16 miles to Washougal. Turn north onto Washougal River Road and follow it for 16.4 miles to the campground.
The campground: This camp, located at the confluence of Dougan Creek and the Washougal River, has a volunteer campground host on site. The campsites are nicely spaced within sight of the river.

126 Elbe Hills ORV Trailhead

Location: About 103 miles southeast of Olympia, near Elbe
GPS: N46 46.953' / W122 04.810'
Elevation: 2,200 feet
Season: Year-round
Sites: 3 primitive sites for tents or self-contained RVs
Facilities: Picnic tables, tent pads, fire grills, pit toilets, group shelter; no drinking water
Fee per night: None
Management: Washington Department of Natural Resources, South Puget Sound Region, (360) 825-1631; reservations required
Activities: Off-road driving
Finding the campground: From I-5, 45 miles south of Olympia, take exit 68 and drive 31 miles east on US 12 to the town of Morton. Then take WA 7 north for 17 miles to the town of Elbe. Turn right (east) at Elbe onto WA 706 and drive 6.3 miles. Turn left onto Stoner Road and drive 3.1 miles. Keep right and continue 0.6 mile. Turn left for 0.1 mile to the campground.
The campground: This camp is pretty basic, but its main purpose is to provide a base for accessing the 8 miles of trails maintained by the DNR for off-road-vehicle use.

127 Evans Creek

Location: About 30 miles southeast of Tacoma on Evans Creek, near Buckley
GPS: N46 56.384' / W121 56.250'
Elevation: 3,400 feet
Season: Mid-June to late Sept
Sites: 23 tent/trailer sites
Facilities: Drinking water, picnic tables, fire grills, vault toilets, firewood
Fee per night: None
Management: Mount Baker–Snoqualmie National Forest, Snoqualmie Ranger District, (425) 888-1421; no reservations.
Activities: Hiking, fishing, off-road driving
Finding the campground: From I-5 in Tacoma take exit 135 and drive east on WA 167 for 9 miles to Sumner. Then continue east for 12 miles on WA 410 to Buckley. From there take WA 165 south for 19 miles. Turn left onto FR 7920 and drive 1.5 miles to the campground.
The campground: This is a rustic, 6-acre creekside campground in the Mount Baker–Snoqualmie National Forest. It is well into the foothills of Mount Rainier and offers plenty of opportunities for hiking and fishing. There are 40 miles of trails for off-road driving nearby, so it is not entirely quiet.

128 Fall Creek

Location: About 20 miles southwest of Olympia on Fall Creek
GPS: N46 56.556' / W123 07.709'
Elevation: 900 feet
Season: Apr through Nov
Sites: 8 primitive sites for tents or self-contained RVs
Facilities: Picnic tables, tent pads, fire grills, vault toilets, horse-loading ramp; no drinking water
Fee per night: None
Management: Washington Department of Natural Resources, Pacific Cascade Region, (360) 577-2025
Activities: Hiking, horseback riding, mountain biking
Finding the campground: From I-5, just 1 mile south of Olympia, take exit 104 and drive north-west on US 101 for 4 miles. Turn south onto Delphi Road Southwest and drive for 6 miles, to the point where it becomes Waddell Creek Road Southwest. Continue for another 3 miles. At the inter-section with Noschka Road, take C-line Road west for 3.3 miles. Turn south onto D-3000 Road and drive 2.4 miles. The site is on the right. Some of the road is unpaved.
The campground: This is a nice, small, primitive campground on Fall Creek in the Black Hills southwest of Olympia. It is quieter than some of the other campgrounds in the vicinity because motorized vehicles are not allowed on the nearby trails.

129 Falls Creek–Crest Horse Camp

Location: 68 miles east of Vancouver
GPS: N45 57.991' / W121 50.681'
Elevation: 3,497 feet
Season: Mid-June to late Sept
Sites: 4 sites for tents or self-contained RVs no longer than 15 feet
Facilities: Picnic tables, fire grills, pit toilets; no drinking water
Fee per night: None
Management: Gifford Pinchot National Forest, Mount Adams Ranger District, (509) 395-3400; no reservations
Activities: Hiking, horseback riding
Finding the campground: From I-5 in Vancouver take exit 1 and head east on WA 14 for 47 miles to Carson. Turn left (north) onto the Wind River Road and drive 6 miles. Turn right onto FR 65 (Pan-ther Creek Road) and drive 15 miles to the campground.
The campground: This camp for equestrians is close to the Pacific Crest National Scenic Trail and the Indian Heaven Wilderness in the Gifford Pinchot National Forest.

130 Goose Lake

Location: About 105 miles northeast of Vancouver on Goose Lake, near the town of Trout Lake
GPS: N45 56.447' / W121 45.513'
Elevation: 3,143 feet
Season: Mid-June to late Sept
Sites: 18 tent sites, 1 site for a tent or self-contained RV no longer than 18 feet
Facilities: Picnic tables, fire rings, vault toilets; no drinking water
Fee per night: $$
Management: Gifford Pinchot National Forest, Mount Adams Ranger District, (509) 395-3400; no reservations
Activities: Hiking, fishing, swimming, berry picking
Finding the campground: From I-5 in Vancouver take exit 1 and head east on WA 14 for 66 miles to Bingen. At Bingen turn north onto WA 141 and drive 25 miles to the town of Trout Lake. Continue through Trout Lake on WA 141 for 5.5 miles. WA 141 becomes FR 24 at the Skamania County line. Continue on FR 24 even as it becomes FR 60, and drive west to Goose Lake. The distance from Trout Lake to Goose Lake is about 14 miles.
The campground: This campground is set on the northern edge of the Big Lava Bed in Gifford Pinchot National Forest. It is a good, relaxed site at the edge of Goose Lake; the fishing is fair.

131 Horseshoe Lake

Location: About 133 miles southeast of Olympia on Horseshoe Lake
GPS: N46 18.601' / W121 33.928'
Elevation: 4,150 feet
Season: Mid-June to late Sept
Sites: 10 sites for tents or self-contained RVs no longer than 16 feet
Facilities: Picnic tables, pit toilets; no drinking water
Fee per night: $$
Management: Gifford Pinchot National Forest, Cowlitz Valley Ranger District, (360) 497-1100; no reservations
Activities: Hiking, fishing, boating (no gas motors), swimming, berry picking
Finding the campground: From I-5, 45 miles south of Olympia, take exit 68 and drive east on US 12 for 48 miles to the town of Randle. From there take WA 131 south for 1 mile. Turn left (east) onto FR 23 (Cispus Road) and drive 30 miles. At Takhlakh Lake take a sharp left and head north on FR 2329. The road goes nearly all the way around Takhlakh Lake, but you should turn left (west) onto FR 78 after 7 miles. Drive 1.5 miles to the campground.
The campground: This small, mid-altitude campground is very appealing, even though it is primitive. It sits right on the lakeshore, and trails from camp lead to nearby mountains, including Mount Adams.

132 Ike Kinswa State Park

Location: 64 miles southeast of Olympia on Mayfield Lake, near Mossyrock
GPS: N46 33.360' / W122 31.819'
Elevation: 1,300 feet
Season: Year-round
Sites: 31 developed tent sites, 31 sites with water and electric, 41 sites with full hookups for RVs no longer than 60 feet
Facilities: Drinking water, picnic tables, fire grills, flush toilets, showers, dump station, store, cafe, playground, boat ramp
Fee per night: $$–$$$$
Management: Washington State Parks and Recreation Commission, (360) 902-8844 (information); (360) 983-3402 (park office)
Activities: Hiking, fishing, swimming, boating, waterskiing
Finding the campground: From I-5, 45 miles south of Olympia, take exit 68 and drive east on US 12 for 15 miles. Then turn left onto WA 122 and drive 4 miles to the campground.
The campground: This campground offers 454 acres of fine scenery along Mayfield Lake and the Cowlitz and Tilton Rivers. In all, there are 8.7 miles of freshwater shoreline, including 400 feet of unguarded swimming beach. There are also 6 miles of hiking trails. Motorboat and ski traffic is heavy on Mayfield Lake, but the shore still attracts ospreys and eagles that nest in the Douglas firs. The fishing is good too. There are two fish hatcheries nearby. Paddlers can enjoy the quieter waters of the Tilton River, which flows through a gorge and features several small waterfalls. Individual campsites can be reserved year-round by visiting https://secure.camis.com/WA/ or calling (888) 226-7688.

133 Iron Creek

Location: About 102 miles southeast of Olympia on the Cispus River, near Randle
GPS: N46 25.857' / W121 59.045'
Elevation: 1,083 feet
Season: Mid-May to late Oct
Sites: 98 sites for tents or self-contained RVs no longer than 42 feet
Facilities: Drinking water, pit toilets
Fee per night: $$$
Management: Gifford Pinchot National Forest, Cowlitz Valley Ranger District, (360) 497-1100
Activities: Hiking, fishing
Finding the campground: From I- 5, 45 miles south of Olympia, take exit 68 and head east on US 12 for 48 miles to the town of Randle. From there go south on WA 131 (Woods Creek Road). In about 1 mile it becomes FR 25. Stay on FR 25 for 7.5 miles to the campground entrance on the left.
The campground: This 32-acre campground is very popular because of its proximity to the east side of Mount St. Helens and its easy RV access. A forest service visitor center is nearby. For a

minimal fee you can make reservations by contacting the National Recreation Reservation Service at www.recreation.gov or (877) 444-6777.

134 Kanaskat-Palmer State Park

Location: 36 miles east of Tacoma on the Green River, near Enumclaw
GPS: N46 33.360' / W122 31.819'
Elevation: 885 feet
Season: Year-round
Sites: 25 tent sites, 19 drive-through sites with electrical hookups for RVs no longer than 50 feet, 6 yurts, 1 group site for up to 80 people
Facilities: Drinking water, picnic tables, flush toilets, coin-operated showers, dump station
Fee per night: $$-$$$$
Management: Washington State Parks and Recreation Commission, (360) 902-8844 (information); (360) 886-0148 (park office)
Activities: Fishing, hiking, rafting, kayaking, nature study
Finding the campground: From I-5 in Tacoma take exit 135; drive east on WA 167 for 9 miles to Sumner. From there take WA 410 east for 16 miles to Enumclaw. Turn north onto Farman Road and drive 11 miles to the park on the left.
The campground: Located in the Green River Gorge Recreation Area, Kanaskat-Palmer covers nearly 300 acres and has 2.5 miles of river frontage. The Green River is known for its winter steelhead fishing (one of the state's top ten), as well as for summer rafting and kayaking. It also offers 3 miles of hiking trails. The campground has an on-site host. Individual campsites can be reserved year-round by visiting https://secure.camis.com/WA/ or calling (888) 226-7688.

135 Keene's Horse Camp

Location: About 132 miles southeast of Olympia on South Fork Spring Creek, near Randle
GPS: N46 18.624' / W121 32.688'
Elevation: 4,400 feet
Season: July to late Sept
Sites: 13 sites for tents or RVs no longer than 21 feet
Facilities: Picnic tables, fire grills, vault toilets, horse corrals; no drinking water
Fee per night: $$
Management: Gifford Pinchot National Forest, Cowlitz Valley Ranger District, (360) 497-1100; no reservations
Activities: Hiking, horse packing
Finding the campground: From I-5, 45 miles south of Olympia, take exit 68 and head east on US 12 for 48 miles to Randle. From there head south on WA 131 for 1 mile. Turn left (southeast) onto FR 23 (Cispus Road) and drive 30 miles. At Takhlakh Lake turn left onto FR 2329 and drive 8 miles. Then turn west onto FR 82 and drive 100 yards to the campground.

The campground: Horse packers appreciate the accessibility of this campground in Gifford Pinchot National Forest. Trails lead right out of camp into the backcountry and high country. The Pacific Crest National Scenic Trail passes within a couple of miles of camp, which is located on South Fork Spring Creek on the northwest flank of Mount Adams.

136 Killen Creek

Location: About 130 miles southeast of Olympia, near Randle
GPS: N46 17.678' / W121 32.896'
Elevation: 4,449 feet
Season: July to late Sept
Sites: 9 sites for tents or self-contained RVs no longer than 22 feet
Facilities: Picnic tables, pit toilets; no drinking water
Fee per night: None
Management: Gifford Pinchot National Forest, Cowlitz Valley Ranger District, (360) 497-1100; no reservations
Activities: Hiking, berry picking, horse packing
Finding the campground: From I-5, 45 miles south of Olympia, take exit 68 and head east on US 12 for 48 miles to Randle. From there take WA 131 south for 1 mile. Turn left (southeast) onto FR 23 (Cispus Road) and drive 30 miles. At Takhlakh Lake make a sharp left and drive north on FR 2329 for 6 miles. The campground entrance is on the left.
The campground: This very basic campground is a 3-mile hike from the Pacific Crest National Scenic Trail, which runs across the northwestern flank of Mount Adams. In fact, the campground sits practically on the border of the Mount Adams Wilderness.

137 Lake Merrill

Location: About 34 miles northeast of Woodland on Merrill Lake
GPS: N46 05.673' / W122 18.723'
Elevation: 1,640 feet
Season: May through Sept
Sites: 11 tent sites
Facilities: Drinking water, picnic tables, tent pads, fire grills, vault toilets, boat ramp
Fee per night: None
Management: Washington Department of Natural Resources, Pacific Cascade Region, (360) 577-2025
Activities: Hiking, fishing, boating
Finding the campground: From I-5 in Woodland take exit 21 and drive east on WA 503 for 23 miles. Turn left (north) onto Cougar Road (FR 81) and go 5.5 miles to the campground on the left.
The campground: The campground is pretty basic, but it is also usually pretty quiet. It sits in the woods on the shores of 2-mile-long Lake Merrill.

138 Lewis and Clark State Park

Location: About 13 miles southeast of Chehalis
GPS: N46 31.179' / W122 49.149'
Elevation: 196 feet
Season: June through Oct
Sites: 25 sites for tents or self-contained RVs no longer than 60 feet, 9 utility sites, 5 primitive equestrian sites, 1 hiker/biker site, 2 group camps
Facilities: Drinking water, picnic tables, fire grills, flush toilets, horseshoe pits, playground, corral/horseback riding area with stalls, loading ramps
Fee per night: $$–$$$$
Management: Washington State Parks and Recreation Commission, (360) 902-8844 (information); (360) 864-2643 (park office); no reservations.
Activities: Hiking, fishing for children, nature program, wading, horseback riding
Finding the campground: From Chehalis drive 8 miles south on I-5 and take exit 68. Drive east on US 12 for almost 3 miles and then turn right (south) onto Jackson Highway 99. The park is on your right in 1.5 miles.
The campground: The Mount St. Helens crater is visible from this 620-acre park, which contains one of the last stands of lowland old-growth forest in western Washington. A 1.5-mile interpretive trail and a 3.5-mile equestrian trail cut through the forest, and the park features a Mount St. Helens visitor center. A children's fishing pond is stocked with trout, and there is a natural wading pool. The park contains the first known home built by a white settler north of the Columbia River (in 1845), the John R. Jackson log cabin. The north spur of the Oregon Trail from Cowlitz River Landing to Tumwater passed through the park. Cooling lava from Mount Rainier formed underground caverns here several thousand years ago. El Paso Natural Gas Company now uses these to store natural gas.

139 Margaret McKenny

Location: About 17 miles southwest of Olympia on Waddell Creek
GPS: N46 55.506' / W123 03.692'
Elevation: 80 feet
Season: Apr through Nov
Sites: 25 primitive sites for tents or self-contained RV sites, 7 walk-in sites
Facilities: Picnic tables, tent pads, pit toilets, campfire circle, horse-loading ramp; no drinking water
Fee per night: None
Management: Washington Department of Natural Resources, Pacific Cascade Region, (360) 577-2025
Activities: Hiking, horseback riding, mountain biking
Finding the campground: From I-5, 10 miles south of Olympia, take exit 95 and head west on WA 121 for 3 miles to Littlerock. Continue west for 1 mile and turn right onto Waddell Creek Road Southwest. Drive 2.5 miles, turn left, and drive 0.2 mile to the campground.

The campground: Close to the Mima Mounds Natural Area Preserve, this primitive, forested campground sits on the bank of Waddell Creek in Capitol State Forest. There are several inviting trails nearby.

140 Mayfield Lake Park

Location: 25 miles southeast of Centralia on Mayfield Lake
GPS: N46 31.912' / W122 33.422'
Elevation: 215 feet
Season: Apr 15 to Oct 15
Sites: 55 sites with water and electric hookups for tents or self-contained RVs no longer than 40 feet, 1 12-unit group camp
Facilities: Drinking water, restrooms, showers, dump station
Fee per night: $$$$
Management: Tacoma Power, (360) 985-2364 (park office)
Activities: Fishing, swimming, boating, waterskiing
Finding the campground: From I-5, 14 miles south of Centralia, take exit 68 and head east on US 12 for 11 miles to the campground.
The campground: Though slightly primitive, this lakeside campground is popular. Reservations are recommended. The sites are wooded and cool, and access to the lake is easy. For reservations visit https://secure.camis.com/WA/ or call (888) 226-7688.

141 Middle Waddell

Location: About 17 miles southwest of Olympia on Waddell Creek
GPS: N46 56.340' / W123 04.674'
Elevation: 75 feet
Season: Apr through Nov
Sites: 24 sites for tents or self-contained RVs
Facilities: Picnic tables, fire grills, tent pads, vault toilets; no drinking water
Fee per night: None
Management: Washington Department of Natural Resources, Pacific Cascade Region, (360) 577-2025
Activities: Mountain biking, motorbiking
Finding the campground: From I-5, 10 miles south of Olympia, take exit 95 and drive west on WA 121 for 3 miles to Littlerock. Continue west for 1 mile and turn right onto Waddell Creek Road Southwest. Drive 3 miles, turn left, and drive 0.1 mile to the campground.
The campground: If the noise of motorcycles does not bother you, or if you are a motorcycle enthusiast yourself, then this wooded campground in Capitol State Forest will suit you just fine.

142 Millersylvania State Park

Location: About 10 miles south of Olympia on Deep Lake
GPS: N46 54.756' / W122 54.658'
Elevation: 210 feet
Season: Year-round
Sites: 120 tent sites, 48 sites for RVs no longer than 35 feet, 1 group site for 20–40 people
Facilities: Drinking water, picnic tables, fire grills, flush toilets, showers, playground, dump station, boat ramp, environmental learning center
Fee per night: $$–$$$$
Management: Washington State Parks and Recreation Commission, (360) 902-8844 (information)
Activities: Hiking, fishing, boating, swimming, mountain biking
Finding the campground: From I-5, 6 miles south of Olympia, take exit 99 and head east on 93rd Avenue for just over 1 mile to Tilley Road Southwest. Turn right onto Tilley Road Southwest and drive about 3 miles to the park entrance on the right.
The campground: It is hard to believe that this 842-acre park, which features 3,300 feet of frontage on Deep Lake, was acquired for a total cost of $251. The state purchased it in five parcels, the first in 1921 and the last in 1952. The property was once owned by John H. Miller, a former general in the Austrian army and a bodyguard of the Austrian emperor. The Miller family stipulated that the land should go to the state for use as a park upon the death of the last remaining family member. The park was developed by the Civilian Conservation Corps in the mid-1930s.

This excellent park is big and uncrowded. It features old-growth forest crisscrossed by 6.6 miles of hiking trails, including a wheelchair-accessible fitness trail. Some old buildings constructed by the CCC of logs and Tenino sandstone lend the park some real charm. Wildlife you may see here includes foxes, black-tailed deer, coyotes, red-tailed hawks, wood ducks, and porcupines. The raccoons can be clever in their pursuit of an easy meal, so seal your food containers and do not leave food lying around. Individual campsites can be reserved in summer only by visiting https://secure.camis.com/WA/ or calling (888) 226-7688.

143 Mima Falls Trailhead

Location: About 18 miles southwest of Olympia, near Littlerock
GPS: N46 54.673' / W123 05.275'
Elevation: 80 feet
Season: Apr through Nov
Sites: 5 primitive sites for tents or self-contained RVs
Facilities: Drinking water, picnic tables, fire grills, tent pads, pit toilets, horse-loading ramp
Fee per night: None
Management: Washington Department of Natural Resources, Pacific Cascade Region, (360) 577-2025.
Activities: Hiking, horseback riding, mountain biking

Finding the campground: From Olympia drive south on I-5 for 11 miles. Take exit 95 and drive west on WA 121 for 3 miles to Littlerock. Continue on WA 121 for 1 mile; turn left onto Gate Mima Road Southwest and drive for 1.5 miles to Bordeaux Road Southwest. Turn right and drive for 0.75 mile to Marksman Street Southwest, where you turn right and drive for 0.66 mile. Turn left and go about 200 yards to the campground.

The campground: This is a very quiet and peaceful site. The Mima Mounds Natural Area Preserve is about 1 mile to the northwest, and the trail to it is excellent.

144 Moss Creek

Location: 58 miles east of Vancouver on the White Salmon River
GPS: N45 47.691' / W121 37.976'
Elevation: 1,300 feet
Season: Mid-May to late Sept
Sites: 16 sites for tents or self-contained RVs no longer than 32 feet
Facilities: Drinking water, fire rings, picnic tables, pit toilets
Fee per night: $$$
Management: Gifford Pinchot National Forest, Mount Adams Ranger District, (509) 395-3400
Activities: Fishing
Finding the campground: From I-5 in Vancouver take exit 1; drive east on WA 14 for 50 miles to Cook. Turn left (north) onto Cook-Underwood Road (CR 1800) and drive 8 miles to the campground. The name of the route changes to Willard Road and then Oklahoma Road along the way.
The campground: This wooded 7-acre campground in Gifford Pinchot National Forest is rarely full. It sits on the White Salmon River, not far from the Big Lava Bed, which can be reached via FR 66. For a minimal fee you can make reservations by contacting the National Recreation Reservation Service at www.recreation.gov or (877) 444-6777.

145 Mount Rainier National Park: Cougar Rock

Location: About 115 miles southeast of Olympia in Mount Rainier National Park
GPS: N46 46.033' / W121 47.667'
Elevation: 3,180 feet
Season: Late May to early Oct
Sites: 173 sites for tents or self-contained RVs no longer than 30 feet, 5 group sites
Facilities: Drinking water, picnic tables, flush toilets, dump station
Fee per night: $$
Management: Mount Rainier National Park, (360) 569-2211
Activities: Recreation program, hiking, trout fishing
Finding the campground: From I-5, 45 miles south of Olympia, take exit 68 and head east on US 12 for 31 miles to Morton. Take WA 7 north for 17 miles to the town of Elbe. Turn east at Elbe onto WA 706 and drive 14 miles to the park's southwest entrance. The campground is about 8 miles inside the park. Part of the drive is on gravel road.

The campground: This is a fine, rustic, mid-altitude campground, and it is easier to get to than most camps in the park. It is not far from the Paradise Visitor Center. It packs a lot of campsites onto 60 acres, but they are nicely laid out. Besides, the main appeal is to have a place to park your gear while you go hiking. For reservations visit www.recreation.gov.

146 Mount Rainier National Park: Ohanapecosh

Location: 121 miles southeast of Olympia on the Ohanapecosh River in Mount Rainier National Park
GPS: N46 43.854' / W121 34.290'
Elevation: 1,914 feet
Season: Late May to early Oct
Sites: 188 sites for tents or self-contained RVs no longer than 32 feet, 2 group sites
Facilities: Drinking water, picnic tables, flush toilets, dump station, interpretive center
Fee per night: $$
Management: Mount Rainier National Park, (360) 569-2211
Activities: Hiking
Finding the campground: From I-5, 45 miles south of Olympia, take exit 68 and drive east on US 12 for 72 miles to WA 123. Turn left (north) onto WA 123 and drive 4 miles to the campground's entrance. The park's through road begins 1 mile farther north.
The campground: Hiking is the main appeal of Ohanapecosh, with arguably the best day hikes in the state right outside the tent flap or RV door. You can walk among 1,000-year-old western red cedars and Douglas firs, over a thundering gorge, and to the base of a giant waterfall. The campground itself is huge and is one of the best in Washington despite its size. The shady sites are spaced to give campers plenty of room. The river is relatively noisy, so you may not want to camp right next to it. Reservations can be made by visiting www.recreation.gov.

The park encompasses 378 square miles. The hiking trails are generally accessible beginning in mid- to late June or early July, depending on snow depths. Saddle and pack stock are permitted on more than 100 miles of trails. However, bicycles are not permitted on any park trails, and the park roads are uncomfortably narrow for bicycling. All locations and facilities in Mount Rainier National Park are open from July 1 through Labor Day. Most locations are accessible from Memorial Day to July and from Labor Day into October. From November or December through May, snow limits vehicle access to the 18-mile stretch of road between the Nisqually entrance and Paradise.

147 Mount Rainier National Park: White River

Location: 48 miles southeast of Enumclaw on the White River in Mount Rainier National Park
GPS: N46 54.156' / W121 38.472'
Elevation: 4,400 feet
Season: Late June to late Sept
Sites: 112 sites for tents or self-contained RVs no longer than 20 feet
Facilities: Drinking water, picnic tables, fire grills, flush toilets, dump station

Fee per night: $$

Management: Mount Rainier National Park, (360) 569-2211

Activities: Hiking, backpacking, campfire and evening interpretive programs, interpretive walks, fishing, horseback riding

Finding the campground: From Enumclaw take WA 410 east for 43 miles to the park's northeast entrance. The campground is 5 miles beyond the entrance.

The campground: This campground is in a beautiful setting on the White River. It is large and comfortable, with reasonable privacy from other sites. But it is often crowded with climbers and backpackers, because the campground is a trailhead for the backcountry. No bicycles are allowed on park trails, and the park roads are uncomfortably narrow for bicycling.

148 Mount St. Helens National Volcanic Monument: Lower Falls Recreation Area in Gifford Pinchot National Forest

Location: 53 miles east of Woodland on the Lewis River in Mount St. Helens National Volcanic Monument

GPS: N46 09.398' / W121 52.707'

Elevation: 1,700 feet

Season: May through Oct

Sites: 43 sites for tents or self-contained RVs no longer than 60 feet

Facilities: Drinking water (hand pump), composting toilets

Fee per night: $$

Management: Mount St. Helens National Volcanic Monument, (360) 449-7800; no reservations

Activities: Hiking, horseback riding

Finding the campground: From I-5 in Woodland take exit 21; drive east on WA 503 for 32 miles. WA 503 becomes FR 90 at the Skamania County line. Continue east on FR 90 for 21 miles to the campground.

The campground: This campground is nestled in tall firs on the Lewis River in the Gifford Pinchot National Forest. It is close to three very beautiful waterfalls. They are accessible via the Lewis River Trail, which includes a wheelchair-accessible loop. The area is sometimes incorrectly referred to as Lower Lewis River Falls Recreation Area. Several other trails pass nearby as they crisscross the east flank of Mount St. Helens.

149 North Creek

Location: About 43 miles southwest of Olympia on Cedar Creek

GPS: N46 53.388' / W123 12.210'

Elevation: 276 feet

Season: Apr through Nov

One of Moran State Park's (Campground 107) most sought after campsites, is #17, at the South End Campground on the shores of Cascade Lake. Who would want to ever leave?

Sites: 5 primitive sites for tents or self-contained RVs
Facilities: Drinking water, picnic tables, fire grills, tent pads, vault toilets
Fee per night: None
Management: Washington Department of Natural Resources, Pacific Cascade Region, (360) 577-2025
Activities: Hiking, mountain biking
Finding the campground: From I-5, 25 miles south of Olympia, take exit 88 and drive west on US 12 for 12 miles to Oakville. Continue for another 2.5 miles west on US 12 to Cedar Creek Road (D-Line Road). Turn right (east) and drive for 3.9 miles. The campground is on the right.
The campground: This small, rustic DNR campground sits at the confluence of Cedar and North Creeks, well shaded by the forest canopy. There are plenty of trails for hiking and mountain biking.

150 North Fork

Location: 105 miles southeast of Olympia on the Cispus River
GPS: N46 27.081' / W121 47.135'
Elevation: 1,400 feet

Season: Mid-May to late Sept
Sites: 30 sites for tents or self-contained RVs no longer than 32 feet
Facilities: Drinking water, picnic tables, vault toilets
Fee per night: $$$
Management: Gifford Pinchot National Forest, Cowlitz Valley Ranger District, (360) 497-1100
Activities: Hiking, fishing, mountain biking
Finding the campground: From I-5, 45 miles south of Olympia, take exit 68 and head east on US 12 for 48 miles to Randle. From there take WA 131 south for 1 mile. Turn left (southeast) onto FR 23 (Cispus Road) and drive 11 miles to the campground.
The campground: The backcountry is easy to reach from this riverside campground in Gifford Pinchot National Forest. The campsites are reasonably spaced, and there is plenty to do given the hiking trails and bike paths. The fishing is rumored to be OK too. For a minimal fee you can make reservations by contacting the National Recreation Reservation Service at www.recreation.gov or (877) 444-6777.

151 Oklahoma

Location: 64 miles east of Vancouver on the Little White Salmon River
GPS: N45 52.291' / W121 37.385'
Elevation: 1,700 feet.
Season: Mid-May to mid-Oct
Sites: 22 sites for tents or self-contained RVs no longer than 22 feet
Facilities: Drinking water, fire rings, picnic tables, pit toilets
Fee per night: $$$–$$$$
Management: Gifford Pinchot National Forest, Mount Adams Ranger District, (509) 395-3400
Activities: Fishing
Finding the campground: From I-5 in Vancouver take exit 1 and drive east on WA 14 for 50 miles to Cook. Turn left (north) onto Cook-Underwood Road (CR 1800) and drive 14 miles to the campground. The name of the route changes to Willard Road and then Oklahoma Road along the way.
The campground: This 12-acre campground on the upper reaches of the Little White Salmon River in Gifford Pinchot National Forest is a bit rustic, but its shady riverbank location makes up for a lot. For a minimal fee you can make reservations by contacting the National Recreation Reservation Service at www.recreation.gov or (877) 444-6777.

152 Olallie Lake

Location: About 126 miles southeast of Olympia on Olallie Lake
GPS: N46 17.357' / W121 37.155'
Elevation: 4,200 feet
Season: July to late Sept
Sites: 5 sites for tents or self-contained RVs no longer than 22 feet
Facilities: Picnic tables, pit toilets; no drinking water

Fee per night: $$
Management: Gifford Pinchot National Forest, Cowlitz Valley Ranger District, (360) 497-1100.
Activities: Fishing, boating, swimming
Finding the campground: From I-5, 45 miles south of Olympia, take exit 68 and head east on US 12 for 48 miles to the town of Randle. From there head south on WA 131. In 1 mile turn left (southeast) onto FR 23 (Cispus Road) and drive 30 miles. At Takhlakh Lake take a sharp left and head north on FR 2329 for 1 mile. Then continue north on FR 5601 for 0.5 mile to the campground.
The campground: This campground is especially quiet because gas-powered motors are prohibited on Olallie Lake. This is an alpine lake, fed by glacial streams from Mount Adams. The campground is rustic but very nicely situated in Gifford Pinchot National Forest. For a minimal fee you can make reservations by contacting the National Recreation Reservation Service at www .recreation.gov or (877) 444-6777.

153 Panther Creek

Location: About 58 miles east of Vancouver on Panther Creek, near Carson
GPS: N45 49.231' / W121 52.579'
Elevation: 1,000 feet
Season: Mid-May to mid-Oct
Sites: 32 sites for tents, 52 sites for self-contained RVs no longer than 25 feet
Facilities: Drinking water, picnic tables, pit toilets
Fee per night: $$$–$$$$
Management: Gifford Pinchot National Forest, Mount Adams Ranger District, (509) 395-3400
Activities: Hiking, fishing, berry and mushroom picking
Finding the campground: From I-5 in Vancouver, take exit 1 and head east on WA 14 for 47 miles to Carson. Turn left (north) onto the Wind River Road and drive 9 miles. Then turn right onto FR 6517. Drive 1.5 miles to FR 65 (Panther Creek Road) and turn left (north) to the campground just ahead.
The campground: Just a hair's breadth away from the Pacific Crest National Scenic Trail, this campground in Gifford Pinchot National Forest is a nice fishing camp on Panther Creek. For a minimal fee you can make reservations by contacting the National Recreation Reservation Service at www.recreation.gov or (877) 444-6777.

154 Paradise Creek

Location: 67 miles east of Vancouver on the Wind River
GPS: N45 56.960' / W121 56.030'
Elevation: 1,500 feet
Season: Mid-May to mid-Oct
Sites: 42 sites for tents or self-contained RVs no longer than 25 feet
Facilities: Drinking water, picnic tables, fire grills, vault toilets

Fee per night: $$$
Management: Gifford Pinchot National Forest, Mount Adams Ranger District, (509) 395-3400
Activities: Hiking, fishing
Finding the campground: From I-5 in Vancouver, take exit 1 and head east on WA 14 for 47 miles to Carson. Turn left (north) onto the Wind River Road and drive 20 miles to the camp.
The campground: This campground is in the deep, thick woods of Gifford Pinchot National Forest, at the confluence of Paradise Creek and the Wind River. Several trails lead out of the campground, one of which climbs to the scenic Lava Butte. For a minimal fee you can make reservations by contacting the National Recreation Reservation Service at www.recreation.gov or (877) 444-6777.

155 Paradise Point State Park

Location: About 15 miles north of Vancouver on the East Fork Lewis River, near Woodland
GPS: N45 51.919' / W122 42.261'
Elevation: 40 feet
Season: Year-round
Sites: 76 sites for tents or self-contained RVs (18 with utilities) no longer than 40 feet, 9 primitive tent sites in the woods
Facilities: Drinking water, fire grills, picnic tables, flush toilets, showers, dump station, primitive boat ramp
Fee per night: $$–$$$$
Management: Washington State Parks and Recreation Commission, (360) 902-8844 (information); (360) 263-2350 (park office)
Activities: Hiking, fishing, boating
Finding the campground: From Vancouver drive 15 miles north on I-5. Take the Paradise Point State Park exit and follow the signs to the campground. The park is adjacent to the freeway.
The campground: This 88-acre campground has more than a mile of freshwater shoreline on the East Fork Lewis River. The fishing is good, and the river access is easy. Two hiking trails pass through camp. This is mainly a layover for I-5 travelers, but it is a comfortable camp. Individual campsites can be reserved year-round by visiting https://secure.camis.com/WA/ or calling (888) 226-7688.

156 Porter Creek

Location: 50 miles southwest of Olympia on Porter Creek
GPS: N46 58.956' / W123 14.742'
Elevation: 170 feet
Season: Apr through Nov
Sites: 14 primitive sites for tents or self-contained RVs
Facilities: Picnic tables, fire grills, tent pads, vault toilets, horse-loading ramps; no drinking water
Fee per night: None

Management: Washington Department of Natural Resources, Pacific Cascade Region, (360) 577-2025

Activities: Hiking, horseback riding, trail biking, motorbiking

Finding the campground: From I-5, 25 miles south of Olympia, take exit 88 and head west on US 12 west for 21 miles to Porter. Turn right (northeast) onto Porter Creek Road and drive for 3.4 miles. At a four-way intersection continue straight on B-line Road for 0.6 mile to the campground on the left.

The campground: Capitol State Forest is rife with trails, and several connect with this campground, which is within the state forest boundary. The camp, on the bank of Porter Creek, is pretty rustic but shady and comfortable.

157 Rainbow Falls State Park

Location: 17 miles west of Chehalis on the Chehalis River

GPS: N46 37.848' / W123 14.159'

Elevation: 290 feet

Season: Apr through Aug

Sites: 45 sites for tents or self-contained RVs no longer than 60 feet (3 saved for hikers/bikers and 3 for horse campers), 1 group site with 14 camping units for up to 60 people (call park office to reserve group site, 360-291-3767)

Facilities: Drinking water, picnic tables, flush toilets, showers, dump station, playground, recreation field

Fee per night: $$–$$$$

Management: Washington State Parks and Recreation Commission, (360) 902-8844 (information); (360) 291-3767 (park office); no reservations

Activities: Hiking, fishing, swimming, kayaking

Finding the campground: From I-5 in Chehalis take exit 77 and drive 17 miles west on WA 6 to the park entrance.

The campground: This 850-acre state park has 3,400 feet of shoreline on the Chehalis River. There are plenty of hiking trails, some through old-growth forest, and the pool beneath the falls is a delight for both swimmers and anglers. Bear, elk, deer, and grouse live in the surrounding area.

158 Rock Creek

Location: About 24 miles northeast of Vancouver on Rock Creek

GPS: N48 24.376' / W119 45.537'

Elevation: 1,050 feet

Season: Year-round

Sites: 19 sites for tents or self-contained RVs

Facilities: Drinking water, picnic tables, fire grills, tent pads, vault toilets, horse-loading ramp

Fee per night: None

Management: Washington Department of Natural Resources, Pacific Cascade Region, (360) 577-2025

Activities: Hiking, fishing, horseback riding

Finding the campground: From I-5, 5 miles north of Vancouver, take exit 9 and drive east on Northeast 179th Street for 5.5 miles. Turn right onto WA 503 and drive 1.5 miles. Turn left onto Northeast 159th Street. Drive 2.5 miles and then, at a Y junction, take the left turn onto Rawson Road. After 2 miles the pavement ends and the route becomes the L-1400 Road. Continue on it for another 4 miles; turn left onto L-1000 Road and drive for 3.7 miles. Turn left onto L-1200 Road and go 0.2 mile to the camp entrance on the right.

The campground: Situated in the Yacolt Burn State Forest, this basic DNR campground is wooded and not heavily used. Hiking and trail riding are the main activities, and there are plenty of hills to climb. There is a campground host on site.

159 Saddle

Location: About 115 miles northeast of Vancouver near the Mosquito Lakes

GPS: N46 07.095' / W121 45.745'

Elevation: 4,200 feet

Season: Mid-June to late Sept

Sites: 12 tent sites

Facilities: Picnic tables, fire rings, pit toilets; no drinking water

Fee per night: None

Management: Gifford Pinchot National Forest, Mount Adams Ranger District, (509) 395-3400; no reservations

Activities: Hiking, fishing, huckleberry picking

Finding the campground: From I-5 in Vancouver take exit 1 and head east on WA 14 for 66 miles. At Bingen turn north onto WA 141 and drive 25 miles to the town of Trout Lake. Continue through town on WA 141 for 5.5 miles. The route becomes FR 24 at the Skamania County line. Continue on FR 24 for 18 miles to the campground.

The campground: This primitive campground is way out there in Gifford Pinchot National Forest, but it is worth the drive. It is on the Pacific Crest National Scenic Trail. Forest roads in this area are good, and the scenery is magnificent. The region is dotted with lakes. Mosquitoes are a problem though—Mosquito Creek feeds nearby Big Mosquito Lake. Carry your DEET and Skin So Soft.

160 Saltwater State Park

Location: 19 miles south of downtown Seattle on East Passage, near Des Moines

GPS: N47 22.513' / W122 19.105'

Elevation: Sea level

Season: Mid-May to mid-Sept

Sites: 47 sites for tents or self-contained RVs no longer than 50 feet, 1 primitive site

Facilities: Drinking water, picnic tables, fire grills, flush toilets, dump station, showers, playground, firewood, scuba rinse station, 3 buoys
Fee per night: $$–$$$$
Management: Washington State Parks and Recreation Commission, (360) 902-8844 (information); (253) 661-4956 (park office)
Activities: Hiking, scuba diving, clam digging
Finding the campground: From I-5, 15 miles south of downtown Seattle, take exit 149 and head west on WA 516 for 2 miles. Turn south onto WA 509 (Marine View Drive) and go 2 more miles to the park at Eighth Place South.
The campground: Because of the unusual underwater park, which features a sunken barge and a tire reef, this campground is a favorite of scuba divers. On shore the park covers 90 acres, including 0.25 mile of shoreline and 150 feet of unguarded beach. There are 2 miles of hiking trails, with some good views of the Olympic Mountains and the islands in Puget Sound. The original park facilities were built by the Civilian Conservation Corps in the 1930s. Later, the bed of McSorely Creek was actually moved north to enlarge the parking area and extend the beach.

161 Seaquest State Park

Location: 62 miles south of Olympia, near Silver Lake
GPS: N46 17.742' / W122 49.056'
Elevation: 485 feet
Season: Year-round
Sites: 55 standard campsites, 33 sites (with full hookups) for RVs no longer than 50 feet, 5 yurts, 1 group site for up to 25 people
Facilities: Drinking water, picnic tables, flush toilets, showers, playground, horseshoe pits, ball field, dump station
Fee per night: $–$$$
Management: Washington State Parks and Recreation Commission, (360) 902-8844 (information); (360) 274-8633 (park office)
Activities: Hiking, horseshoes, fishing
Finding the campground: From I-5 in Castle Rock, 57 miles south of Olympia, take exit 49 and head east on WA 504 for 5 miles to the park.
The campground: Seaquest State Park, which is nowhere near the sea, encompasses 475 acres, including more than 1 mile of shoreline on freshwater Silver Lake and 116 acres of wetland. The Mount St. Helens National Volcanic Monument Interpretive Center is located across WA 504 from the entrance to Seaquest. The state park is lovely and offers all the amenities, including 8 miles of hiking trails. It is used mostly as a base camp for people visiting Mount St. Helens. Area wildlife includes marmots, pikas, red-tailed hawks, Steller's jays, whiskey jacks, black-tailed deer, and sometimes a black bear. Trout, salmon, and spiny-ray fish await anglers. The campground is just across the highway from Silver Lake. Individual campsites can be reserved in summer only by visiting https://secure.camis.com/WA/ or calling (888) 226-7688.

162 Sherman Valley

Location: About 46 miles southwest of Olympia on Cedar Creek
GPS: N46 53.806' / W123 09.409'
Elevation: 384 feet
Season: Apr through Nov
Sites: 5 primitive sites for tents or self-contained RVs, 3 walk-in sites
Facilities: Drinking water, picnic tables, fire grills, tent pads, vault toilets
Fee per night: None
Management: Washington Department of Natural Resources, Pacific Cascade Region, (360) 577-2025
Activities: Hiking, mountain biking
Finding the campground: From I-5, 25 miles south of Olympia, take exit 88 and head west on US 12 for 12 miles to Oakville. Go another 2.5 miles west on US 12 to Cedar Creek Road (D-Line Road). Turn right (east) and continue for 1.6 miles. Then take the fork on the right. Continue 4.5 miles to the campground on the right.
The campground: This rustic campground along Porter Creek in Capitol State Forest is mainly a hiking and mountain biking destination. Horses are not permitted on the trails. The campground is very peaceful, shady, and small.

163 Silver Springs

Location: 32 miles southeast of Enumclaw on the White River
GPS: N46 59.649' / W121 31.879'
Elevation: 2,600 feet
Season: Mid-May to late Sept
Sites: 16 tent sites, 40 sites for tents or self-contained RVs no longer than 21 feet, 1 group site for 20–50 people
Facilities: Drinking water, picnic tables, fire grills, vault toilets, firewood, grocery store
Fee per night: $$$
Management: Mount Baker-Snoqualmie National Forest, Snoqualmie Ranger District, (425) 888-1421
Activities: Hiking, fishing
Finding the campground: From Enumclaw, east of Tacoma, head southeast on WA 410 and drive 32 miles to the campground.
The campground: This 25-acre campground in old-growth forest is on the White River just a few miles north of Mount Rainier National Park. It is on the east side of the Sourdough Mountains, just a bit over 5 miles from the park's northeast entrance to Sunrise. A good trail leads from camp to Crystal Mountain, a popular ski area, and to the Pacific Crest National Scenic Trail. For a minimal fee you can make reservations by contacting the National Recreation Reservation Service at www .recreation.gov or (877) 444-6777.

164 Smokey Creek

Location: About 104 miles northeast of Vancouver on Smokey Creek
GPS: N46 01.879' / W121 41.295'
Elevation: 3,700 feet
Season: June to late Sept
Sites: 3 sites for tents or self-contained RVs no longer than 22 feet
Facilities: Picnic tables, pit toilets; no drinking water
Fee per night: None
Management: Gifford Pinchot National Forest, Mount Adams Ranger District, (509) 395-3400; no reservations
Activities: Hiking, berry picking
Finding the campground: From I-5 in Vancouver, take exit 1 and head east on WA 14 for 66 miles to Bingen. Turn left (north) onto WA 141 and drive 25 miles to the town of Trout Lake. Continue through town on WA 141 for 5.5 miles to the Skamania County line, where the route becomes FR 24. Continue on FR 24 for 7 miles to the campground.
The campground: This campground is near the Indian Heaven Wilderness in Gifford Pinchot National Forest. It is really small, and since it is not used much, you will probably have it all to yourself. Hiking trails in the area are good, and the campground is next to Smokey Creek.

165 Soda Springs

Location: About 127 miles southeast of Olympia on Summit Creek
GPS: N45 53.491' / W121 06.888'
Elevation: 3,200 feet
Season: Mid-June to early Sept
Sites: 6 primitive tent sites
Facilities: Picnic tables, vault toilets; no drinking water
Fee per night: None
Management: Gifford Pinchot National Forest, Cowlitz Valley Ranger District, (360) 497-1100; no reservations
Activities: Hiking
Finding the campground: From I-5, 45 miles south of Olympia, take exit 68 and head east on US 12. Drive 75 miles and turn left (north) onto FR 45 (10 miles past Packwood). In a bit less than 0.5 mile, FR 4510 takes off to the left (north). Take it, and continue for 7 miles to the campground at the end of the road.
The campground: Soda Springs is used mainly as a base camp for backpacking and hiking into the William O. Douglas Wilderness. Horses are not allowed in the wilderness area. The camp is primitive, but it sits alongside Summit Creek in Gifford Pinchot National Forest.

166 Summit Creek

Location: About 123 miles southeast of Olympia on Summit Creek
GPS: N46 42.623' / W121 32.205'
Elevation: 2,400 feet
Season: Mid-June to early Sept
Sites: 6 primitive sites for tents or self-contained RVs
Facilities: Picnic tables, pit toilets; no drinking water
Fee per night: None
Management: Gifford Pinchot National Forest, Cowlitz Valley Ranger District, (360) 497-1100; no reservations
Activities: Hiking
Finding the campground: From I-5, 45 miles south of Olympia, take exit 68 and head east on US 12. Drive 75 miles and turn left (north) onto FR 45 (10 miles past Packwood). In a bit less than 0.5 mile, FR 4510 takes off to the left (north). Take it, and continue for 3 miles to the campground.
The campground: This campground is attractive and rustic at the same time. It sits next to Summit Creek in Gifford Pinchot National Forest and is used mainly as a base camp for hikers and backpackers.

167 Sunset

Location: About 32 miles northeast of Vancouver on the East Fork Lewis River
GPS: N45 49.124' / W122 15.011'
Elevation: 1,000 feet
Season: Year-round
Sites: 18 sites for tents or self-contained RVs no longer than 22 feet
Facilities: Drinking water, picnic tables, pit toilets
Fee per night: $$
Management: Gifford Pinchot National Forest, Mount St. Helens National Volcanic Monument, (360) 449-7800; no reservations
Activities: Hiking, fishing, huckleberry picking
Finding the campground: From I-5, 5 miles north of Vancouver, take exit 9 and drive north and then east on WA 502 for 8 miles to the town of Battle Ground. Turn left (north) onto WA 503 and drive for 5.2 miles. Then turn right (east) onto Lucia Falls Road. Follow it as it goes south for 1 mile and east for 6 miles to Moulton. At Moulton turn right (southeast) onto CR 12 and follow it for 7 miles to the campground.
The campground: The campground is worth the drive. It is just inside the western boundary of Gifford Pinchot National Forest, right beside the East Fork Lewis River. Jack Mountain is 1 mile to the north, and the drainage rivers and creeks east of the campground offer some good hikes and fishing.

168 Takhlakh Lake

Location: 126 miles southeast of Olympia on Takhlakh Lake
GPS: N46 16.668' / W121 35.937'
Elevation: 4,500 feet
Season: Mid-June to late Sept
Sites: 53 sites for tents or self-contained RVs no longer than 22 feet
Facilities: Drinking water, picnic tables, vault toilets, boat ramp
Fee per night: $$$
Management: Gifford Pinchot National Forest, Cowlitz Valley Ranger District, (360) 497-1100
Activities: Hiking, canoeing, fishing, berry picking
Finding the campground: From I-5, 45 miles south of Olympia, take exit 68 and head east on US 12. Drive 48 miles to the town of Randle and take WA 131 south. In 1 mile turn left (southeast) onto FR 23 (Cispus Road) and drive for 30 miles. Turn left (northeast) onto FR 2329 and drive 2 miles to the campground.
The campground: This shoreside campground in Gifford Pinchot National Forest is well designed, pleasant, and quiet due to a prohibition of boats with gas motors. There are great views of Mount Adams. For a minimal fee you can make reservations by contacting the National Recreation Reservation Service at www.recreation.gov or (877) 444-6777.

169 Tinkham

Location: About 44 miles southeast of Seattle on the Snoqualmie River
GPS: N47 24.181' / W121 33.964'
Elevation: 1,300 feet
Season: Mid-May to mid-Sept
Sites: 47 sites for tents or self-contained RVs no longer than 21 feet
Facilities: Drinking water, picnic tables, vault toilets, firewood
Fee per night: $$–$$$
Management: Mount Baker-Snoqualmie National Forest, Snoqualmie Ranger District, (425) 888-1421
Activities: Hiking, fishing
Finding the campground: From I-5 in Seattle head east on I-90; drive 42 miles and take exit 42. Turn right onto FR 55 and drive 1.5 miles southeast to the campground.
The campground: This riverside campground is pleasant enough, except it sits close to the interstate. The hiking is terrific though. The very popular Alpine Lakes Wilderness starts just north of the highway. For a minimal fee you can make reservations by contacting the National Recreation Reservation Service at www.recreation.gov or (877) 444-6777.

170 Tower Rock

Location: 104 miles southeast of Olympia on the Cispus River
GPS: N46 26.760' / W121 51.966'
Elevation: 1,100 feet
Season: Mid-May to late Sept
Sites: 22 sites for tents or self-contained RVs no longer than 22 feet
Facilities: Drinking water, picnic tables, vault toilets
Fee per night: $$$
Management: Gifford Pinchot National Forest, Cowlitz Valley Ranger District, (360) 497-1100
Activities: Fishing
Finding the campground: From I-5, 45 miles south of Olympia, take exit 68 and head east on US 12. Drive 48 miles to the town of Randle and take WA 131 south. In 1 mile turn (left) southeast onto FR 23 (Cispus Road) and drive for 6.5 miles. Turn right (south) onto FR 28 and drive 1.5 miles to FR 76. Turn left (west) and drive 2 miles to the campground.
The campground: This is a good size campground on the Cispus River, with more room than most. Fishing is the primary activity here. For a minimal fee you can make reservations by contacting the National Recreation Reservation Service at www.recreation.gov or (877) 444-6777.

171 Walupt Horse Camp

Location: About 128 miles southeast of Olympia, near Walupt Lake
GPS: N46 25.381' / W121 28.418'
Elevation: 3,930 feet
Season: June through Sept
Sites: 6 sites for tents or self-contained RVs no longer than 18 feet
Facilities: Drinking water, picnic tables, vault toilets
Fee per night: $$$
Management: Gifford Pinchot National Forest, Cowlitz Valley Ranger District, (360) 497-1100; no reservations
Activities: Fishing, horse packing, hiking
Finding the campground: From I-5, 45 miles south of Olympia, take exit 68 and head east on US 12. Drive 62.5 miles to FR 21, which you reach 2.5 miles before you get to Packwood. Turn right (southeast) onto FR 21 and drive 16.5 miles. Then turn left (east) onto FR 2160 and drive 3.5 miles to the campground. For about the last 20 miles, the road is gravel.
The campground: This campground, located in Gifford Pinchot National Forest, is very popular with equestrians because of its close proximity to trails that lead into the nearby Goat Rocks Wilderness. There are 85 miles of pack trails.

172 Walupt Lake

Location: 128 miles southeast of Olympia on Walupt Lake
GPS: N46 25.425' / W121 28.361'
Elevation: 3,900 feet
Season: Mid-June to early Sept
Sites: 8 tent sites, 36 sites for tents or self-contained RVs no longer than 22 feet
Facilities: Drinking water, picnic tables, vault toilets, boat ramp
Fee per night: $$$
Management: Gifford Pinchot National Forest, Cowlitz Valley Ranger District, (360) 497-1100
Activities: Hiking, fishing, swimming, canoeing, boating (trolling motors only)
Finding the campground: From I-5, 45 miles south of Olympia, take exit 68 and head east on US 12. Drive 62.5 miles to FR 21, which you reach 2.5 miles before you get to Packwood. Turn right (southeast) onto FR 21 and drive 16.5 miles. Then turn left (east) onto FR 2160 and drive 4 miles to the campground. About the last 20 miles is on gravel road.
The campground: Walupt Lake may seem tough to reach, but it is well worth it. The campground is on the lakeshore, and access to the water is easy. Lots of hikers stay here because of the nearby trails. One trail begins in the campground and leads to the Goat Rocks Wilderness. For a minimal fee you can make reservations by contacting the National Recreation Reservation Service at www .recreation.gov or (877) 444-6777.

173 Woodland (Bratton Canyon Property)

Location: About 24 miles north of Vancouver, just outside Woodland
GPS: N45 53.929' / W122 44.236'
Elevation: 160 feet
Season: May to Sept
Sites: 10 sites for tents or self-contained RVs
Facilities: Drinking water, picnic tables, fire grills, tent pads, vault toilets, firewood, playground
Fee per night: None
Management: Vancouver-Clark Parks and Recreation, (360) 397-2446; permit required
Activities: Children's play, horseshoe pits
Finding the campground: From I-5 in Woodland take exit 21 and drive east on WA 503 for 1 block. Turn right onto East CC Street and cross the bridge over the Lewis River. Just south of the bridge, turn right onto CR 1 and drive 0.3 mile. Turn left onto CR 38 and drive 2.5 miles to the campground on the left.
The campground: This is a cozy campground close to I-5, with a playground for the kids. There is not much to do here, but it is a good stopover for through travelers. To secure a permit visit www .emailmeform.com/builder/form/9BSePcne2U or call (360) 487-8311.

Eastern Region

The part of Washington east of Wenatchee is getting popular both for desert camping and lake sports between Wenatchee and Spokane and for mountain sports up north in the Colville National Forest. Be sure to take your own camping and sports gear to eastern Washington. Amenities such as bike shops, ski rentals, and outfitters are still few and far between.

The Columbia River winds through this region like a dropped bootlace, flowing in all directions of the compass. Because of all the hydroelectric dams, vast sections of the river are actually lakes.

Chief Joseph Dam holds back the mighty Columbia near Brewster (campground 271).

Southeastern Washington, including the Palouse Hills south of Spokane, actually makes up the northern end of the Great Basin. Its surface was formed by vast lava flows. No trees have grown in the region for several million years. The average annual rainfall is less than 12 inches, but it adds up quickly to form the mighty Columbia River, whose drainage basin blankets 260,000 square miles that range over 10 degrees of latitude. In the extreme southeast are the relatively modest Blue Mountains. The Columbia Plateau extends eastward across the southern two-thirds of the state from the volcanic Cascade Mountains to and beyond the border with Idaho. Plateau tribes lived as hunters and gatherers for 10,000 years in this land of strong contrasts. Their encyclopedic knowledge of the different environments was their main survival tool.

Eastern Region: North Cascades

	Group Sites	RV Sites	Total # of sites	Max RV Length	Hookups	Toilets	Showers	Drinking water	Dump station	Pets	Wheelchair	Recreation	Fee	Season	Can reserve	Stay limit
174 Alta Lake State Park	•	•	125	38	W	F	•	•	•	•	•	HFSB	$$-$$$$	Apr-Oct	•	10
175 Ballard			7	28		V				•		HF	$	June-Sept or Oct		14
176 Beverly		•	10	21		P				•		HF	$	Jun-mid Nov		14
177 Blackpine Creek Horse Camp		•	10	60		V		•		•		HR	$$	mid May-late Oct		14
178 Bridge Creek	•		7	19		V	•		•			HF	$$	mid Apr-late Oct	•	14
179 Camp Four			5			V				•		HFR	$	June-late Sept		14
180 Chatter Creek	•	•	13	21		V		•		•		HF	$$	May-late Oct	•	14
181 Chewuch		•	16	35		V				•		HFRC	$$	June-late Sept		14
182 Chopaka Lake		•	8			V		•		•		HFBRC		year-round		14
183 Conconully State Park		•	70	60	W	F	•	•	•	•		HFBS	$$-$$$$	year-round		10
184 Cottonwood		•	25	20		P	•			•		HF	$$	June-Sept		14
185 Early Winters		•	12	24		V	•			•		HFC	$	June-Sept or Oct		14
186 Eightmile	•	•	46	50		V	•			•		HF	$$$	mid Apr-late Oct	•	14
187 Falls Creek		•	7	18		V	•			•		HFSR	$	June-late Sept		14
188 Fish Lake			5			V				•		HFB		July-Oct		14
189 Flat		•	12	15		V	•			•		HF	$	June-late Sept		14
190 Foggy Dew		•	12	25		V				•		HFC	$	late May-early Sept		14
191 Fox Creek			16	25		V				•		HFC	$$	May-mid Oct		14
192 Glacier View			23			P	•			•		HFBS	$$	May-Sept		14
193 Honeymoon		•	5	18		V				•		HF	$	June-late Sept		14
194 Ida Creek		•	10	30		V	•			•		HF	$$	May-late Oct		14
195 Indian Camp		•	9			P				•		HF		year-round		7
196 Johnny Creek		•	65	50		V	•			•		HF	$$	May-late Oct		14
197 JR		•	6	16		V				•		HFC	$	late May-early Sept		14
198 Kachess	•	•	153	32		P	•	•	•	•	•	HFSBC	$$$	late May-mid Sept	•	14
199 Klipchuck		•	46	34		FV	•					HFC	$$	June-late Sept		14
200 Lake Chelan State Park		•	144	30	WES	F	•	•	•	•	•	HFBS	$$-$$$$	Mar-Oct	•	10

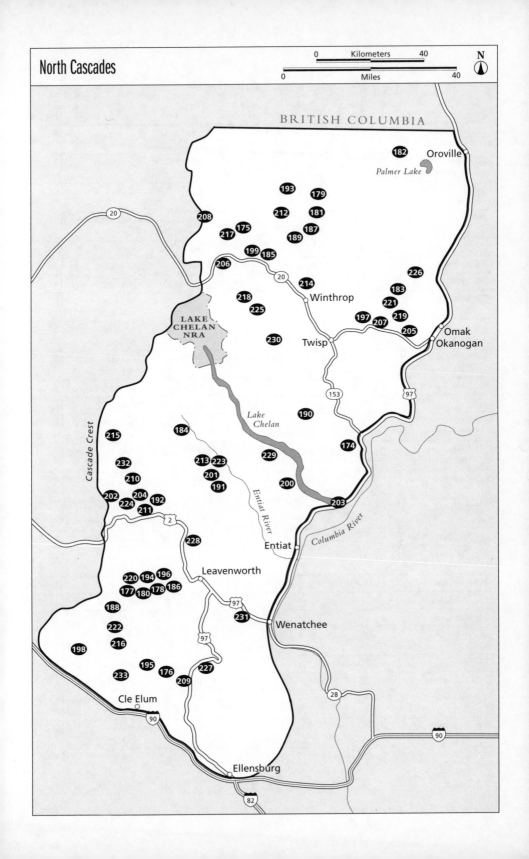

North Cascades

	Group Sites	RV Sites	Total # of sites	Max RV Length	Hookups	Toilets	Showers	Drinking water	Dump station	Pets	Wheelchair	Recreation	Fee	Season	Can reserve	Stay limit
201 Lake Creek (Entiat River)		•	18	30		V		•		•		HF	$$	May–mid Oct		14
202 Lake Creek (Little Wenatchee River)			8			P				•		HF		May–early Nov		14
203 Lakeshore RV Park		•	174		WES	F	•	•		•		FBS	$$$$	year-round	•	
204 Lake Wenatchee State Park	•	•	200	60		F	•	•	•	•	•	HFBSCR	$$–$$$$	May–Sept	•	10
205 Leader Lake		•	16			P				•		HF		year-round		7
206 Lone Fir		•	27	36		V		•		•		HF	$	June–late Sept		14
207 Loup Loup		•	25	21		V		•		•		HFC	$	May–Sept		14
208 Meadows			14			V				•		H	$	mid July–late Sept		14
209 Mineral Springs	•	•	7	21		V				•		HF	$$$	late May–early Sept	•	14
210 Napeequa Crossing		•	5	30		P				•		HF		mid May–late Oct		14
211 Nason Creek		•	73	31		F		•		•		HFSB	$$$	May–late Oct		14
212 Nice		•	3	35		V				•		HF	$	Jun–late Sept		14
213 North Fork			8			P		•		•		HF	$$	mid May–late Sept		14
214 Pearrygin Lake State Park	•	•	133	60	WES	F	•	•	•	•		HFSB	$$–$$$$	Apr–Oct	•	10
215 Phelps Creek		•	13	30		P				•		HFR		mid June–mid Oct		14
216 Red Mountain		•	10	30		P				•		HF	$$	mid May–mid Nov		14
217 River Bend		•	5	30		V				•		HFR	$	June–late Sept		14
218 Roads End		•	4	16		V				•		HF	$	late May–early Sept		14
219 Rock Creek		•	6			V		•		•		HF		year-round		7
220 Rock Island			22			V		•		•		HF	$$	May–late Oct		14
221 Rock Lakes		•	8			V				•		HF		year-round		7
222 Salmon La Sac		•	69	21		F		•		•		HFR	$$$	late May–late Sept	•	14
223 Silver Falls		•	29	30		V		•		•		HF	$$	Mem Day–Sept	•	14
224 Soda Springs			26			P				•		HF		May–late Oct		14
225 South Creek		•	4	30		V				•		HFR	$	late May–early Sept		14
226 Sugarloaf			4			V				•		FB	$	mid May–mid Sept		14
227 Swauk		•	22	21		P				•		HF	$$$	mid Apr–late Sept		14
228 Tumwater	•	•	85	30		F		•		•		HF	$$$	May–mid Oct	•	14

	Group Sites	RV Sites	Total # ofsites	Max RV Length	Hookups	Toilets	Showers	Drinking water	Dump station	Pets	Wheelchair	Recreation	Fee	Season	Can reserve	Stay limit
229 Twenty-five Mile Creek State Park	•	•	68	30	WES	F	•	•	•	•		HFSBC	$$–$$$$	early Apr–early Oct	•	10
230 War Creek		•	11	21		V		•	•			HF	$	May–Sept		14
231 Wenatchee River County Park		•	79		WES	F	•	•	•	•		F	$$$$	Apr–Oct	•	
232 White River Falls			5			P				•		HF		June–mid Oct		14
233 Wish Poosh		•	39	21		F		•	•			HFSB	$$$–$$$$	mid May–mid Sept	•	14

Hookups: W = Water E = Electric S = Sewer
Toilets: F = Flush V = Vault P = Pit
Recreation: C = Bicycling/Mountain Biking H = Hiking S = Swimming F = Fishing B = Boating
O = Off-highway driving R = Horseback Riding
Maximum Trailer/RV Length given in feet. Stay Limit given in days.
Fee $ = less than $10; $$ = $10–$15; $$$ = $16–20; $$$$ = more than $20.
If no entry under Fee, camping is free.

174 Alta Lake State Park

Location: About 65 miles northeast of Wenatchee on Alta Lake, near Chelan
GPS: N48 01.382' / W119 56.463'
Elevation: 1,150 feet
Season: Apr through Oct
Sites: 91 tent sites, 32 RV sites with water and electrical hookups, 2 group sites for up to 45 and 85 people, respectively
Facilities: Drinking water, picnic tables, fire grills, flush toilets, coin-operated showers, 2 boat ramps, bathhouse, boat dock, dump station
Fee per night: $$–$$$$
Management: Washington State Parks and Recreation Commission, (360) 902-8844 (information); (509) 923-2473 (park office)
Activities: Hiking, fishing, swimming, scuba diving, boating, waterskiing, birding, snowmobiling, cross-country skiing
Finding the campground: From WA 285, 2 miles north of Wenatchee, head north on US 97 (or use US 97A—the two routes converge after following opposite banks of the Columbia River) for 58 miles to its junction with WA 153. Turn left (northwest) onto WA 153 and drive 2 miles to Alta Lake Road. Then turn left (southwest) and drive 2.5 miles to the park.
The campground: This 180-acre state park lies in a pine forest at the eastern edge of the Okanogan-Wenatchee National Forest. It offers most of the usual amenities as well as 300 feet of beach and a 0.6-mile hiking trail. There is even a golf course nearby. Individual campsites can be reserved in summer (April through October) by visiting https://secure.camis.com/WA/ or calling (888) 226-7688.

175 Ballard

Location: 22 miles northwest of Winthrop near the Methow River
GPS: N48 39.288' / W120 32.958'
Elevation: 2,521 feet
Season: June through Sept or Oct, depending on the weather
Sites: 7 tent/RV sites, 28-foot length limit
Facilities: Picnic tables, fire grills, vault toilets; no drinking water
Fee per night: $
Management: Okanogan-Wenatchee National Forest, Methow Valley Ranger District, (509) 996-4003; no reservations
Activities: Hiking, fishing
Finding the campground: From Winthrop drive west for 13 miles on WA 20 to the Mazama turn-off on your right. At Mazama, 0.5 mile from the turnoff, turn left (northwest) onto Mazama Road toward Harts Pass and drive 8 miles to the campground on the left.
The campground: Hiking trails abound here, and the river is close by for trout fishing. This campground in Okanogan-Wenatchee National Forest borders on primitive, but it is serviceable.

176 Beverly

Location: About 108 miles southeast of Seattle on the North Fork Teanaway River, near Cle Elum
GPS: N47 22.644' / W120 52.980'
Elevation: 3,200 feet
Season: June to mid-Nov
Sites: 10 sites for tents or self-contained RVs no longer than 21 feet
Facilities: Picnic tables, fire grills, pit toilets; no drinking water.
Fee per night: $
Management: Okanogan-Wenatchee National Forest, Cle Elum Ranger District, (509) 852-1100; no reservations
Activities: Hiking, fishing
Finding the campground: From I-5 in Seattle take exit 164 and drive east on I-90 for 85 miles. Take exit 85 and cross the freeway to Cle Elum and WA 970. Turn right (east) onto WA 970 and continue 7 miles to Teanaway Road. Turn left (north) onto Teanaway Road and drive for about 7 miles along the Teanaway River. At Casland turn north onto North Fork Teanaway Road, which becomes FR 9737. Follow FR 9737 to the campground, about 9 miles from Casland. The last 9 miles are unpaved.
The campground: This is a good base camp for hikers, because trails lead from here into the Alpine Lakes Wilderness. The 5-acre campground is primitive but peaceful, and it offers good fishing opportunities.

177　Blackpine Creek Horse Camp

Location: 18 miles west of Leavenworth on Icicle Creek
GPS: N47 36.546' / W120 56.700'
Elevation: 3,000 feet
Season: Mid-May to late Oct
Sites: 10 sites for tents or self-contained RVs no longer than 60 feet
Facilities: Drinking water, fire grills, picnic tables, vault toilets, firewood, riding facilities
Fee per night: $$
Management: Okanogan-Wenatchee National Forest, Wenatchee River Ranger District, (509) 548-2550; no reservations
Activities: Horseback riding, hiking
Finding the campground: From US 2 at the west end of Leavenworth, turn south onto Icicle Road and drive 18 miles south and west to the campground. The last mile is unpaved.
The campground: Blackpine sits at the confluence of Blackpine Creek and Icicle Creek, at the end of Icicle Road in the Okanogan-Wenatchee National Forest. Since this rustic camp is close to the boundary of the Alpine Lakes Wilderness and has facilities for horses, it serves well as a base camp for pack trips.

178　Bridge Creek

Location: 9 miles west of Leavenworth on Icicle Creek
GPS: N47 33.834' / W120 46.920'
Elevation: 1,900 feet
Season: Mid-Apr to late Oct
Sites: 6 sites for tents or self-contained RVs no longer than 19 feet, 1 group site
Facilities: Drinking water, fire grills, picnic tables, vault toilets, firewood
Fee per night: $$
Management: Okanogan-Wenatchee National Forest, Wenatchee River Ranger District, (509) 548-2550
Activities: Hiking, fishing
Finding the campground: From US 2 at the west end of Leavenworth, turn south onto Icicle Road and drive 9 miles to the campground.
The campground: This small, primitive camp is nestled in the shady canyon formed by Icicle Creek in the Okanogan-Wenatchee National Forest. It is close to some hiking trails that access the Alpine Lakes Wilderness. For a minimal fee you can make reservations by contacting the National Recreation Reservation Service at www.recreation.gov or (877) 444-6777.

179 Camp Four

Location: 17 miles north of Winthrop on the Chewuch River
GPS: N48 42.914' / W120 07.519'
Elevation: 2,384 feet
Season: June to late Sept
Sites: 5 tent sites
Facilities: Picnic tables, fire grills, vault toilets; no drinking water
Fee per night: $
Management: Okanogan-Wenatchee National Forest, Methow Valley Ranger District, (509) 996-4003; no reservations
Activities: Hiking, fishing, horse packing
Finding the campground: Drive 6 miles north out of Winthrop on Eastside Chewuch Road. At the junction with West Chewuch Road (FR 51), turn right (north) and drive 11 miles to the campground.
The campground: Camp Four is actually the third camp along this stretch of the Chewuch River. It is smaller than the other two (Falls Creek and Chewuch; see below) and a bit more rustic. The fourth is Thirtymile, about 11 miles farther at the end of the road. Between the two are trailheads for trails leading into the Pasayten Wilderness. There are amenities for horses at the trailheads, including corrals, hitching rails, truck docks, and watering troughs.

180 Chatter Creek

Location: 15 miles west of Leavenworth on Icicle Creek
GPS: N47 36.498' / W120 53.160'
Elevation: 1,500 feet
Season: May to late Oct
Sites: 12 sites for tents or self-contained RVs no longer than 21 feet, 1 group site
Facilities: Drinking water, fire grills, picnic tables, vault toilets
Fee per night: $$
Management: Okanogan-Wenatchee National Forest, Wenatchee River Ranger District, (509) 548-2550
Activities: Hiking, fishing
Finding the campground: From US 2 at the west end of Leavenworth, turn south onto Icicle Road and drive 15 miles south and west to the campground.
The campground: This small campground sits at the confluence of Chatter and Icicle Creeks, slightly downstream from where Trout Creek enters the Icicle. The fishing and hiking possibilities seem infinite here below steep Icicle Ridge, the top of which forms the southern boundary of the of the northern section of the Alpine Lakes Wilderness in the Chiwaukum Mountains. Trails lead north and south from camp into the wilderness area. For a minimal fee you can make reservations by contacting the National Recreation Reservation Service at www.recreation.gov or (877) 444-6777.

181 Chewuch

Location: 14 miles north of Winthrop on the Chewuch River
GPS: N48 40.434' / W120 08.215'
Elevation: 2,278 feet
Season: June to late Sept
Sites: 16 single sites for tents and RVs less than 35 feet
Facilities: Drinking water, picnic tables, fire grills, vault toilets
Fee per night: $$
Management: Okanogan-Wenatchee National Forest, Methow Valley Ranger District, (509) 996-4003; no reservations
Activities: Hiking, fishing, mountain biking, horse packing
Finding the campground: From Winthrop head north on Eastside Chewuch Road for 6 miles. At the junction with West Chewuch Road (FR 51), turn right (north) and drive 8 miles to the campground.
The campground: Chewuch is the second of three campgrounds along this stretch of the Chewuch River. It is rustic here in the ponderosa pine forest, but the fishing is good and some hiking trails lead into the mountains from here. The sites on the river are particularly nice. About 6 miles farther up the road are some trailheads into the Pasayten Wilderness, with horse amenities at the roadside, including corrals, hitching rails, truck docks, and watering troughs.

182 Chopaka Lake

Location: About 57 miles north of Okanogan on Chopaka Lake, near Oroville
GPS: N48 54.843' / W119 42.138'
Elevation: 2,880 feet
Season: Year-round; limited road access in winter
Sites: 8 sites for tents or self-contained RVs
Facilities: Drinking water, picnic shelters, vault toilets, boat ramp
Fee per night: None
Management: Bureau of Land Management, Spokane District, (509) 536-1200
Activities: Hiking, bicycling, boating, climbing, educational programs, fishing, horseback riding
Finding the campground: From Okanogan drive north on US 97 for 24 miles and turn left (north) onto Tonasket-Oroville Westside Road. Drive nearly 11 miles along the Okanogan River, through Tonasket. Bear left (west) on Loomis-Oroville Road and drive 11 miles to Loomis. From the Loomis grocery store, go north for 2.1 miles on Loomis-Oroville Road. Turn left onto Toats Coulee Road; go 1.4 miles, turn right onto a steep one-lane road, and continue 3.4 miles. Stay left and go another 1.7 miles. Turn right and go 2 miles to the campground. This last 2-mile section is unpaved.
The campground: Chopaka Lake and the campground that bears its name are nestled on top of Chopaka Mountain in the rolling, sage-covered Okanogan uplands of eastern Washington. The lake is surrounded by open fields of grass and sagebrush intermixed with dense forests of Douglas fir and ponderosa pine. The campground covers only 10 acres, but the 5,500-acre Chopaka Mountain Wilderness Study Area is right outside your tent flap. Area wildlife includes bears, mountain

goats, and deer. In the basalt canyon of Douglas Creek, songbirds and raptors perch in the cottonwoods, and the road paralleling the creek passes beaver ponds and cascading pools. Only canoes, kayaks, and small boats are permitted on the lake. There are hiking trails in the Chopaka Mountain Wilderness Study Area, but no vehicles, including mountain bikes, are permitted there.

183 Conconully State Park

Location: About 22 miles northwest of Omak on Conconully Lake
GPS: N48 33.903' / W119 43.938'
Elevation: 2,300 feet
Season: Year-round; limited service in winter
Sites: 51 tent sites, 15 sites with water/electric hookups for RVs no longer than 60 feet, 4 cabins
Facilities: Drinking water, fire grills, picnic tables, flush toilets, showers, firewood, dump station, playground, wading pool, gravel boat ramp
Fee per night: $$–$$$$
Management: Washington State Parks and Recreation Commission, (360) 902-8844 (information); (509) 826-0813 (park office); no reservations
Activities: Fishing, boating, swimming, hiking, cross-country skiing, snowmobiling
Finding the campground: From US 97 in Omak drive west on Kermel Road for 6 miles to Conconully Road. Turn right (north) and continue about 16 miles north to the park.
The campground: The 80-acre park is tucked between Conconully Lake and Conconully Reservoir in the eastern foothills of the North Cascades. It has 1 mile of shoreline within its boundaries, providing access to the 4-mile-long lake and large reservoir. Together the bodies of water have a surface area of 760 acres. The name Conconully comes from Conconulp, the Okanogan Indian name for this valley. It meant "money hole" and referred to the valley's large beaver population. Beaver skins were as good as cash at the Fort Okanogan store. This is also the site of the original mining town of Conconully, which was washed out by a flood. It grew back and now has two general stores, a gas station, and several restaurants. The park has a good nature trail; Sinlahekin Road skirts the lake. Anglers will find rainbow trout, cutthroat trout, and smallmouth bass.

184 Cottonwood

Location: 54 miles northwest of Wenatchee on the Entiat River, near Entiat
GPS: N48 01.230' / W120 38.520'
Elevation: 3,100 feet
Season: June through Sept
Sites: 25 sites for tents or self-contained RVs no longer than 20 feet
Facilities: Drinking water, fire grills, picnic tables, pit toilets
Fee per night: $$
Management: Okanogan-Wenatchee National Forest, Entiat Ranger District (509) 784-4700; no reservations
Activities: Hiking, fishing

Finding the campground: From WA 285, 2 miles north of Wenatchee, head north on US 97A for 15 miles. Just before you reach the town of Entiat, turn left (northwest) onto CR 371 (Entiat River Road). Continue 38.5 miles to the campground, making sure you stay on the paved road that becomes FR 51 and then FR 317. The pavement ends at the campground.

The campground: The Entiat River drains both the Chelan and Entiat mountain ranges. Cottonwood Campground sits where Shetipo Creek joins the river from the south. This is about as far into the backcountry as you can get on a paved road, and the 9-acre campground provides good access to the Glacier Peak Wilderness.

185 Early Winters

Location: 15 miles northwest of Winthrop on Early Winters Creek
GPS: N48 35.791' / W120 26.800'
Elevation: 2,130 feet
Season: June through Sept or Oct, depending on the weather
Sites: 12 sites for tents or self-contained RVs no longer than 24 feet
Facilities: Drinking water, picnic tables, fire grills, vault toilets
Fee per night: $
Management: Okanogan-Wenatchee National Forest, Methow Valley Ranger District, (509) 996-4003; no reservations
Activities: Hiking, fishing, mountain biking
Finding the campground: From Winthrop drive northwest on WA 20 for 15 miles to the campground on the left.
The campground: This campground sits at the confluence of Early Winters Creek and the Methow River. It is pretty, comfortable, and spacious—a good place to spend a few days.

186 Eightmile

Location: 8 miles west of Leavenworth on Icicle Creek
GPS: N47 33.048' / W120 46.080'
Elevation: 1,800 feet
Season: Mid-April to late Oct. Access road closed in winter, but walk-in campers are welcome.
Sites: 45 sites for tents or self-contained RVs no longer than 50 feet, 1 group site
Facilities: Drinking water, fire grills, picnic tables, vault toilets
Fee per night: $$$
Management: Okanogan-Wenatchee National Forest, Wenatchee River Ranger District, (509) 548-2550.
Activities: Hiking, fishing
Finding the campground: From US 2 at the west end of Leavenworth, turn south onto Icicle Road and drive 8 miles south and west to the campground.
The campground: This campground on Icicle Creek, the first in a string of seven national forest campgrounds in Icicle Canyon, is the trailhead for some choice backpacking routes south into the

You can test your rock-climbing skills at Peshastin Pinnacles State Park (day use only) near Leavenworth.

Alpine Lakes Wilderness. Nearby Mountaineer Creek was so named for a good reason. The campground nestles at the bottom of a steep canyon, so it is in shade much of the day. For a minimal fee you can make reservations by contacting the National Recreation Reservation Service at www .recreation.gov or (877) 444-6777.

187 Falls Creek

Location: 11 miles north of Winthrop on the Chewuch River
GPS: N48 38.114' / W120 09.335'
Elevation: 2,100 feet
Season: June to late Sept
Sites: 7 sites for tents or self-contained RVs no longer than 18 feet
Facilities: Drinking water, picnic table, vault toilets
Fee per night: $
Management: Okanogan-Wenatchee National Forest, Methow Valley Ranger District, (509) 996-4003; no reservations

Activities: Hiking, fishing, swimming, horse packing

Finding the campground: From Winthrop head north on Eastside Chewuch Road for 6 miles. At the junction with West Chewuch Road (FR 51), turn right (north) and drive 5 miles to the campground.

The campground: Located at the confluence of Falls Creek and the Chewuch River, this campground is fairly good sized; the sites are roomy, shady, and clean. From camp you can hike 0.25 mile to the falls on Falls Creek. About 9 miles farther up the road from camp are some trailheads for trails leading into the Pasayten Wilderness. There are horse amenities beside the road, including corrals, hitching rails, truck docks, and watering troughs.

188 Fish Lake

Location: About 109 miles southeast of Seattle on Tucquala Lake, near Cle Elum
GPS: N47 31.434' / W121 04.380'
Elevation: 3,400 feet
Season: July to Oct
Sites: 5 tent-only sites
Facilities: Picnic tables, fire grills, vault toilets; no drinking water
Fee per night: None
Management: Okanogan-Wenatchee National Forest, Cle Elum Ranger District, (509) 852-1100; no reservations
Activities: Hiking, fishing, boating
Finding the campground: From I-5 in Seattle take exit 164 and head east on I-90 for 80 miles. Take exit 80 (4 miles west of Cle Elum) and go north on Bullfrog Road, which intersects with WA 903 in about 3 miles. Take WA 903 north through Roslyn and Ronald, driving about 5 miles to Salmon la Sac Road (FR 4330) near the southern end of Cle Elum Lake. Take it north along the east side of the lake for 21 miles to the campground. The road is rough and gravel for the last few miles.

The campground: This one is out in the boonies for sure, just 6 miles south of the point at which King, Chelan, and Kittitas Counties intersect and 3 miles east of the Pacific Crest National Scenic Trail. The 2-acre camp is set nicely on the north end of mile-long Tucquala Lake where the Cle Elum River drains into it. The campground is basic and usually used by hikers as a base camp.

189 Flat

Location: 11 miles north of Winthrop on Eightmile Creek
GPS: N48 36.871' / W120 11.701'
Elevation: 2,858 feet
Season: June to late Sept
Sites: 12 sites for tents or self-contained RVs no longer than 15 feet
Facilities: Drinking water, picnic tables, fire grills, vault toilets
Fee per night: $

Management: Okanogan-Wenatchee National Forest, Methow Valley Ranger District, (509) 996-4003; no reservations

Activities: Hiking, fishing

Finding the campground: From Winthrop head north on Eastside Chewuch Road for 6 miles. At the junction with West Chewuch Road (FR 51), turn right (north) and drive 2.5 miles to the intersection with Eightmile Creek Road (FR 5130). Turn left (northwest) and drive 2.5 miles to the campground. The road is paved all the way.

The campground: You can pull a trailer to this camp with no problem. That means it is probably more popular than the camps farther upriver. But it is a nice camp just the same. Eightmile Creek offers some good fishing, and a nearby trail heads up Eightmile Ridge to Lamb Butte.

190 Foggy Dew

Location: 32 miles south of Winthrop on Foggy Dew Creek
GPS: N48 12.340' / W120 11.762'
Elevation: 2,400 feet
Season: Late May to early Sept
Sites: 12 sites for tents or self-contained RVs no longer than 25 feet
Facilities: Picnic tables, fire grills, vault toilets; no drinking water
Fee per night: $
Management: Okanogan-Wenatchee National Forest, Methow Valley Ranger District, (509) 996-4003; no reservations
Activities: Hiking, fishing, mountain biking, trail biking, cross-country skiing, snowmobiling
Finding the campground: From Winthrop, drive south on WA 20 East for 11 miles to the WA 153 turnoff. Take the turnoff to the right and drive 15 miles to Gold Creek Road (Forest Road 4340). Turn right (west) and drive 6 miles to the campground.

The campground: This camp is still about 8 miles shy of Sawtooth Ridge above Lake Chelan, but it feels like it is deep in the wilderness. It is a good-sized campground, though primitive. Foggy Dew Creek flows into the North Fork Gold Creek here, and there are lots of trails nearby that lead to upcountry lakes. In the winter, the area is open to cross-country skiers and snowmobilers during the day.

191 Fox Creek

Location: 42 miles north of Wenatchee on the Entiat River, near Entiat
GPS: N47 55.524' / W120 30.660'
Elevation: 2,000 feet
Season: May to mid-Oct
Sites: 16 sites for tents or self-contained RVs no longer than 25 feet
Facilities: Drinking water, fire grills, picnic tables, vault toilets
Fee per night: $$

Management: Okanogan-Wenatchee National Forest, Entiat Ranger District, (509) 784-4700; no reservations
Activities: Hiking, fishing, mountain biking, cross-country skiing, snowmobiling
Finding the campground: From WA 285, 2 miles north of Wenatchee, head north on US 97A for 15 miles. Just before the town of Entiat, turn left (northwest) onto CR 371 (Entiat River Road). Continue 25 miles to the campground, making sure you stay on the paved road that becomes FR 51.
The campground: Nestled on the west side of the Entiat River, the campground is about halfway between Tommy and Fox Creeks. It is quiet and wooded, like all the forest service campgrounds along the Entiat.

192 Glacier View

Location: About 25 miles northwest of Leavenworth on Lake Wenatchee
GPS: N47 49.446' / W120 48.600'
Elevation: 1,866 feet
Season: May through Sept
Sites: 23 tent sites
Facilities: Drinking water, fire grills, picnic tables, pit toilets, boat ramp
Fee per night: $$
Management: Okanogan-Wenatchee National Forest, Wenatchee River Ranger District, (509) 548-2550; no reservations
Activities: Hiking, fishing, boating, waterskiing, swimming
Finding the campground: From US 2, midway between Stevens Pass (20 miles) and Leavenworth (16 miles), turn north at Coles Corner onto WA 207 and drive 3.5 miles toward Lake Wenatchee. Turn left (west) onto Cedar Brae Road (CR 413/FR 6607) and drive 5 miles to the campground.
The campground: This is a pleasant, sunny little campground, well away from the hubbub of Lake Wenatchee State Park at the other end of the lake. Many of the campsites are walk-ins on the lakeshore.

193 Honeymoon

Location: About 18 miles north of Winthrop on Eightmile Creek
GPS: N48 41.784' / W120 15.850'
Elevation: 3,280 feet
Season: June to late Sept
Sites: 5 single sites for tents or self-contained RVs no longer than 18 feet
Facilities: Picnic tables, fire grills, vault toilets; no drinking water
Fee per night: $
Management: Okanogan-Wenatchee National Forest, Methow Valley Ranger District, (509) 996-4003; no reservations
Activities: Hiking, fishing

Finding the campground: From Winthrop head north on Eastside Chewuch Road for 6 miles. At the junction with West Chewuch Road (FR 51), turn right (north) and drive 2.5 miles to the intersection with Eightmile Creek Road (FR 5130). Turn left (northwest) and drive 9 miles to the campground. The road turns to gravel well before the camp.

The campground: Small and quaint, this campground is the perfect spot for a rustic honeymoon. A forest ranger and his bride thought so too, and that is how the campground got its name.

194 Ida Creek

Location: 13 miles west of Leavenworth on Icicle Creek
GPS: N47 36.408' / W120 50.880'
Elevation: 2,500 feet
Season: May to late Oct
Sites: 10 sites for tents or self-contained RVs no longer than 30 feet
Facilities: Drinking water, fire grills, picnic tables, vault toilets
Fee per night: $$
Management: Okanogan-Wenatchee National Forest, Wenatchee River Ranger District, (509) 548-2550; no reservations
Activities: Hiking, fishing
Finding the campground: From US 2 at the west end of Leavenworth, turn south onto Icicle Road and drive 13 miles south and west to the campground.

The campground: This small camp is on the north side of Icicle Creek, between the confluences of Ida and Big Slide Creeks. It is in the bottom of a canyon, so it is shady much of the day.

195 Indian Camp

Location: About 106 miles southeast of Seattle on the Middle Fork Teanaway River, near Cle Elum
GPS: N47 17.407' / W120 57.438'
Elevation: 2,579 feet
Season: Year-round
Sites: 9 small sites for tents or self-contained RVs
Facilities: Picnic tables, fire grills, pit toilets; no drinking water
Fee per night: None
Management: Washington Department of Natural Resources, Southeast Region, (509) 925-8510
Activities: Hiking, fishing
Finding the campground: From I-5 in Seattle take exit 164 and head east on I-90 for 85 miles. Take exit 85 and cross the freeway to Cle Elum and WA 970. Turn right (east) onto WA 970 and continue 7 miles to Teanaway Road. Turn left (north) onto Teanaway Road and drive about 7 miles along the Teanaway River. In Casland head west on West Fork Teanaway Road for 0.6 mile to Middle Fork Teanaway Road. Turn right (north) and drive 4 miles to the campground on your left. Toward the end the road becomes one-lane gravel.

The campground: This camp is not well known, but it is in a lovely, sunny setting along the Middle Fork Teanaway River. Conditions are primitive.

196 Johnny Creek

Location: 11 miles west of Leavenworth on Icicle Creek
GPS: N47 35.892' / W120 49.020'
Elevation: 2,300 feet
Season: May to late Oct. Access road closed in winter, but walk-in campers are welcome.
Sites: 65 sites for tents or self-contained RVs no longer than 50 feet
Facilities: Drinking water, fire grills, picnic tables, vault toilets
Fee per night: $$
Management: Okanogan-Wenatchee National Forest, Wenatchee River Ranger District, (509) 548-2550; no reservations.
Activities: Hiking, fishing.
Finding the campground: From US 2 at the west end of Leavenworth, turn south onto Icicle Road and drive 11 miles south and west to the campground.
The campground: This camp sits in the bottom of Icicle Canyon where Johnny Creek drains into Icicle Creek from the north and Victoria Creek drains in from the south. It is a large campground compared with others along the creek, and it is close to a few trails into the Alpine Lakes Wilderness.

197 JR

Location: 22 miles east of Winthrop on Frazier Creek
GPS: N48 23.279' / W119 54.038'
Elevation: 3,900 feet
Season: Late May to early Sept
Sites: 6 sites for tents or self-contained RVs no longer than 16 feet
Facilities: Drinking water, picnic tables, vault toilets
Fee per night: $
Management: Okanogan-Wenatchee National Forest, Methow Valley Ranger District, (509) 996-4003; no reservations
Activities: Hiking, fishing, mountain biking, cross-country skiing, snowmobiling
Finding the campground: From Winthrop drive south on WA 20 East for 22 miles to the campground.
The campground: Located in Okanogan-Wenatchee National Forest near the Loup Loup Summit, this rustic campground on Frazier Creek offers a lot of recreational opportunities. Trails head into the forest across the highway, and the Methow Wildlife Area is just 3 miles west.

198 Kachess

Location: 67 miles southeast of Seattle on Kachess Lake, near Cle Elum
GPS: N47 21.432' / W121 14.580'
Elevation: 2,253 feet
Season: Late May to mid-Sept
Sites: 152 sites for tents or self-contained RVs no longer than 32 feet, 1 group site
Facilities: Drinking water, picnic tables, fire grills, pit toilets, dump stations, boat ramp, barrier-free nature trail
Fee per night: $$$
Management: Okanogan-Wenatchee National Forest, Cle Elum Ranger District, (509) 852-1100
Activities: Hiking, fishing, swimming, boating, waterskiing, mountain biking
Finding the campground: From I-5 in Seattle take exit 164 and drive east on I-90 for 62 miles. Take exit 62 off I-90 and turn northeast onto FR 49. Drive 5 miles to the campground.
The campground: This 92-acre campground is immense by forest service standards, and it was certainly well planned with spacious sites. It is very popular with families and with boaters too. Kachess Lake is 10 miles long. Things quiet down by the end of August, and that is also a good time for hiking the many trails in the area. The Alpine Lakes Wilderness is 4 miles northeast of camp via FR 4948. For a minimal fee you can make reservations by contacting the National Recreation Reservation Service at www.recreation.gov or (877) 444-6777.

199 Klipchuck

Location: 19 miles northwest of Winthrop on Early Winters Creek
GPS: N48 35.842' / W120 30.780'
Elevation: 2,900 feet
Season: June to late Sept
Sites: 46 single sites for tents or self-contained RVs no longer than 34 feet
Facilities: Drinking water, picnic tables, flush and vault toilets
Fee per night: $$
Management: Okanogan-Wenatchee National Forest, Methow Valley Ranger District, (509) 996-4003; no reservations.
Activities: Hiking, fishing, mountain biking
Finding the campground: From Winthrop drive west on WA 20 West for 18 miles to FR 300. Turn right (north) and drive 1 mile to the campground.
The campground: This campground is one of the nicest around. Its spacious sites nestle in a pine forest on Early Winters Creek. The trees are majestic. Watch out for rattlesnakes, which are occasionally seen in the area. There are nearby hiking trails for all abilities.

A family sets up camp next to the water at Lake Chelan State Park. Families gravitate to Lake Chelan's shores, especially in the warmer months.

200 Lake Chelan State Park

Location: 39 miles north of Wenatchee on Lake Chelan, near the town of Chelan
GPS: N47 52.017' / W120 10.767'
Elevation: 1,099 feet
Season: Mar through Oct; boat ramp open year-round
Sites: 109 tent sites, 35 sites with full hookups for RVs no longer than 30 feet
Facilities: Drinking water, restrooms, showers, some wheelchair-accessible facilities, playground, bathhouse, boat ramp and dock, water-ski floats, dump station, store, restaurant, ice
Fee per night: $$–$$$$
Management: Washington State Parks and Recreation Commission, (360) 902-8844 (information)
Activities: Hiking, boating, swimming, fishing, waterskiing, sailboarding, personal watercraft, scuba diving, skin diving
Finding the campground: From WA 285, 2 miles north of Wenatchee, head north on US 97A for 31 miles to South Lakeshore Road on Lake Chelan. Turn left (northwest) and drive 6 miles to the campground.

The campground: This state park covers 127 acres and has over 1 mile of waterfront on Lake Chelan, including 300 feet of sandy beach. A lot of recreational boaters and anglers use the park as a base. So if you prefer a quiet setting, look elsewhere. If noise and hubbub do not bother you, this park is ideal for all the activities it affords. Families love it. Reservations—a must here—can be made by visiting https://secure.camis.com/WA/ or calling (888) 226-7688.

201 Lake Creek (Entiat River)

Location: 44 miles north of Wenatchee on the Entiat River, near Entiat
GPS: N47 56.214' / W120 31.020'
Elevation: 2,200 feet
Season: May to mid-Oct
Sites: 18 sites for tents or self-contained RVs no longer than 30 feet
Facilities: Drinking water, picnic tables, fire grills, vault toilets
Fee per night: $$
Management: Okanogan-Wenatchee National Forest, Entiat Ranger District, (509) 784-4700; no reservations
Activities: Hiking, fishing
Finding the campground: From WA 285, 2 miles north of Wenatchee, take US 97A north for 15 miles. Just before you reach the town of Entiat, turn left (northwest) onto CR 371 (Entiat River Road). Continue 27 miles to the campground. Make sure you stay on the paved road that becomes FR 51.
The campground: This is another easy-access campground on the Entiat River. This one is located where Lake Creek empties into the river after descending 4 miles from Pawn Lakes in the Chelan Mountains. Hiking trails here go in all directions. The campground is pretty basic but serviceable.

202 Lake Creek (Little Wenatchee River)

Location: 37 miles northwest of Leavenworth on the Little Wenatchee River
GPS: N47 52.530' / W121 00.780'
Elevation: 2,300 feet
Season: May to early Nov
Sites: 8 tent sites
Facilities: Picnic tables, fire grills, pit toilets; no drinking water
Fee per night: None
Management: Okanogan-Wenatchee National Forest, Wenatchee River Ranger District, (509) 548-2550; no reservations
Activities: Hiking, fishing
Finding the campground: From US 2, midway between Stevens Pass (20 miles) and Leavenworth (16 miles), turn north at Coles Corner onto WA 207 and drive toward Lake Wenatchee. From Coles Corner drive 10.5 miles around the lake on North Shore Drive to FR 6500. Turn left (west) onto FR 6500 and drive for 6.5 miles to the Riverside Campground and the intersection with FR 6701.

Bear left (southwest) on FR 6701 (making sure in less than 0.5 mile to bear right and stay on FR 6701, not FR 6700) and stay on it for 4 miles to the campground.

The campground: This primitive campground is within a few miles of the end of the road, so it is entirely remote and nicely situated on the Little Wenatchee River. This is a good spot for campers who bring their own entertainment. Wenatchee Ridge, to the north, is at the southern end of the Glacier Peak Wilderness.

203 Lakeshore RV Park

Location: 37 miles north of Wenatchee on Lake Chelan, in the town of Chelan.
GPS: N47 51.301' / W120 02.964'
Elevation: 1,099 feet
Season: Year-round
Sites: 165 RV sites with full-service hookups, 9 tent sites

Campers engage in some after-dinner exercise at popular Lakeshore RV Park on Lake Chelan in downtown Chelan. Many families carry their bikes and other toys along to enhance their camping experience.

Facilities: Drinking water, sewer, and electricity at RV sites, water and electricity at tent sites, restrooms, showers, telephones, cable TV, free wireless, tennis courts, adjacent swimming area, 18-hole putting green, bumper boats, go-carts, marina with boat ramp

Fee per night: $$$$

Management: City of Chelan, (509) 682-8023

Activities: Swimming, boating, waterskiing, sailboarding, fishing

Finding the campground: From WA 285, 2 miles north of Wenatchee, take US 97A and drive north for 35 miles to Chelan. The park is on the lake on the north side of town.

The campground: Because of its in-town location, Lakeshore RV Park is for the social set, especially during summer. It is within easy walking distance of shopping and restaurants, and Chelan is very busy during tourist season. It may even be the recreation center of eastern Washington. The attractions are the near-daily sun, water sports, and throngs of like-minded people. Quiet hours are enforced, however, between 11 p.m. and 7 a.m. No dogs are allowed from Memorial Day weekend through Labor Day. You can reserve a campsite up to 9 months in advance by calling (509) 682-8023.

204 Lake Wenatchee State Park

Location: 21 miles northwest of Leavenworth on Lake Wenatchee

GPS: N47 48.683' / W120 43.005'

Elevation: 1,900 feet

Season: May through Sept

Sites: 155 sites for tents, 42 utility sites for RVs no longer than 60 feet, 2 ADA sites, 1 tent-only group site for up to 80 people

Facilities: Drinking water, fire grills, flush toilets, showers, 2 dump stations, bathhouse, amphitheater, playground, boat ramp, dock, boat rentals, horse rentals, food concession

Fee per night: $$–$$$$

Management: Washington State Parks and Recreation Commission, (360) 902-8844 (information); (509) 763-3101 (park office)

Activities: Hiking, fishing, boating, canoeing, swimming, waterskiing, horseback riding, mountain biking, snowmobiling, cross-country skiing, snowshoeing

Finding the campground: From US 2, midway between Stevens Pass (20 miles) and Leavenworth (16 miles), turn north at Coles Corner onto WA 207 toward Lake Wenatchee. Drive for 5 miles to the campground.

The campground: The park covers 490 acres and has more than 2 miles of waterfront on Lake Wenatchee. There are campsites on both sides of the Wenatchee River at the point where it flows out of the lake. Nason Creek skirts the campground. The sites are spacious and pleasant, and all are reasonably close to the lakeshore. American Indian tribes traveling west used to stop at Lake Wenatchee during the sockeye salmon migration, and today's campers happily carry on the tradition of fishing, playing, and relaxing here. This is a very popular family campground, and with good reason. The recreation possibilities—including 3.5 miles of equestrian trails and 7.5 miles of trail for hiking, cross-country skiing, and snowmobiling—could keep you active and happy for a week or two. Individual campsites can be reserved in summer only by visiting https://secure.camis.com/WA/ or calling (888) 226-7688.

205 Leader Lake

Location: 9 miles west of Okanogan on Leader Lake
GPS: N48 21.624' / W119 41.904'
Elevation: 2,273 feet
Season: Year-round
Sites: 16 sites for tents or self-contained RVs of any length
Facilities: Picnic tables, fire grills, tent pads, pit toilets, boat ramp; no drinking water
Fee per night: None
Management: Washington Department of Natural Resources, Northeast Region, (509) 684-7474
Activities: Hiking, fishing
Finding the campground: From US 97 in Okanogan take WA 20 West and drive south and then northwest for 9 miles to Leader Lake Road. Turn right to enter the campground.
The campground: This is a nice little lakeshore campground on the dry side of the Cascade Mountains. It is a bit primitive, but the setting is lovely.

206 Lone Fir

Location: 27 miles northwest of Winthrop on Early Winters Creek
GPS: N48 34.878' / W120 37.440'
Elevation: 3,640 feet
Season: June to late Sept
Sites: 27 sites for tents or self-contained RVs no longer than 36 feet
Facilities: Drinking water, picnic tables, fire grills, vault toilets
Fee per night: $
Management: Okanogan-Wenatchee National Forest, Methow Valley Ranger District, (509) 996-4003; no reservations
Activities: Hiking, fishing
Finding the campground: From Winthrop drive northwest on WA 20 West (North Cascades Highway) for 27 miles to the campground.
The campground: Lone Fir is about 6 miles north of the Washington Pass Overlook on the North Cascades Highway, right beside Early Winters Creek. The sites are small, but the setting cannot be beat for its woodsy comfort and easy access to area hiking trails.

207 Loup Loup

Location: 23 miles southeast of Winthrop
GPS: N48 23.693' / W119 54.126'
Elevation: 4,200 feet
Season: May through Sept, depending on the weather

Sites: 25 sites for tents or self-contained RVs no longer than 21 feet
Facilities: Drinking water, picnic tables, vault toilets
Fee per night: $
Management: Okanogan-Wenatchee National Forest, Methow Valley Ranger District, (509) 996-4003; no reservations
Activities: Hiking, fishing, mountain biking, cross-country skiing, snowmobiling
Finding the campground: From Winthrop drive south and then east on WA 20 East for 22 miles. Turn left (north) onto West Fork Road (FR 42) and drive 1 mile to the campground.
The campground: Right next to the Loup Loup Ski Area, this campground is quiet and removed from the highway. The western larch trees are beautiful here. While not spacious, the sites are certainly comfortable.

208 Meadows

Location: About 34 miles northwest of Winthrop
GPS: N48 42.554' / W120 40.445'
Elevation: 6,200 feet
Season: Mid-July to late Sept
Sites: 14 tent sites
Facilities: Picnic tables, fire grills, vault toilets; no drinking water
Fee per night: $
Management: Okanogan-Wenatchee National Forest, Methow Valley Ranger District, (509) 996-4003; no reservations
Activities: Hiking
Finding the campground: From Winthrop take WA 20 northwest for 13 miles to the Mazama turnoff on your right. At Mazama, 0.5 mile from the turnoff, turn left (northwest) onto Mazama Road toward Harts Pass and drive northwest for about 20 miles to FR 500. At Harts Pass, turn left (south) onto FR 500 and drive 1 mile to the campground.
The campground: This campground's one-lane dirt access road is considered treacherous by some, but regular cars do make the trip. The Pacific Crest National Scenic Trail runs right by camp, so most campers are hikers. Be prepared for seasonal biting flies. The campground is primitive, but the location is stunning.

209 Mineral Springs

Location: About 102 miles southeast of Seattle on Medicine Creek, near Cle Elum
GPS: N47 17.394' / W120 42.000'
Elevation: 2,750 feet
Season: Late May to early Sept
Sites: 6 sites for tents or self-contained RVs no longer than 21 feet, 1 group site
Facilities: Picnic tables, vault toilets; no drinking water
Fee per night: $$$

Management: Okanogan-Wenatchee National Forest, Cle Elum Ranger District, (509) 852-1100

Activities: Hiking, fishing, hunting, snow sports

Finding the campground: From I-5 in Seattle take exit 164 and head east on I-90 for 85 miles. Take exit 85 and cross the freeway to Cle Elum and WA 970. Turn right (east) onto WA 970 and continue 11 miles to US 97. Go north on US 97 for 6 miles to the campground.

The campground: The campground is on the Blewett Pass Highway in mountainous terrain dotted with pines and mixed conifers. The 6-acre camp is nicely situated where Medicine Creek joins Swauk Creek, and the fishing is good. The camp is rather dusty in the dry season, but it makes a great base camp for winter sports activities. There is an on-site snack bar. Mineral Springs Resort, a full-service restaurant and lounge, is just across the highway, within walking distance of the campground. For a minimal fee you can make reservations by contacting the National Recreation Reservation Service at www.recreation.gov or (877) 444-6777.

210 Napeequa Crossing

Location: 33 miles northwest of Leavenworth on the White River

GPS: N47 55.260' / W120 53.760'

Elevation: 2,000 feet

Season: Mid-May to late Oct

Sites: 5 sites for tents or self-contained RVs no longer than 30 feet

Facilities: Picnic tables, fire grills, pit toilets; no drinking water

Fee per night: None

Management: Okanogan-Wenatchee National Forest, Wenatchee River Ranger District, (509) 548-2550; no reservations.

Activities: Hiking, fishing

Finding the campground: From US 2, midway between Stevens Pass (20 miles) and Leavenworth (16 miles), turn north at Coles Corner onto WA 207 and drive 17 miles via WA 207, North Shore Drive, White River Road, and FR 6400 to the campground.

The campground: This rustic forest service campground is small and isolated. It serves as a good base camp for hiking into the Glacier Peak Wilderness.

211 Nason Creek

Location: About 20 miles northwest of Leavenworth on Nason Creek, near Lake Wenatchee

GPS: N47 47.976' / W120 42.960'

Elevation: 1,800 feet

Season: May to late Oct

Sites: 73 sites for tents or self-contained RVs no longer than 31 feet

Facilities: Drinking water, fire grills, picnic tables, flush toilets

Fee per night: $$$

Management: Okanogan-Wenatchee National Forest, Lake Wenatchee Ranger District, (509) 548-2550; no reservations

Activities: Hiking, fishing, swimming, boating, waterskiing

Finding the campground: From US 2, midway between Stevens Pass (20 miles) and Leavenworth (16 miles), turn north at Coles Corner onto WA 207 toward Lake Wenatchee. Drive for 3.5 miles and then turn left (west) onto Cedar Brae Road (CR 413) into the campground.

The campground: While not actually on Lake Wenatchee, this campground is less than a mile away, and the setting is quite nice for such a large campground. It is very popular with boaters and anglers.

212 Nice

Location: About 13 miles north of Winthrop on Eightmile Creek
GPS: N48 37.955' / W120 13.308'
Elevation: 2,728 feet
Season: June to late Sept
Sites: 3 sites for tents or self-contained RVs no longer than 35 feet
Facilities: Picnic tables, fire grills, vault toilets; no drinking water
Fee per night: $
Management: Okanogan-Wenatchee National Forest, Methow Valley Ranger District, (509) 996-4003; no reservations.
Activities: Hiking, fishing
Finding the campground: From Winthrop head north on Eastside Chewuch Road for 6 miles. At the junction with West Chewuch Road (FR 51), turn right (north) and drive 2.5 miles to the intersection with Eightmile Creek Road (FR 5130). Turn left (northwest) and drive 4 miles to the campground. The road is paved all the way.
The campground: Near a beaver pond, this is a good site for group camping. There are only three tent sites, all of them situated at the creek's edge.

213 North Fork

Location: 51 miles north of Wenatchee on the Entiat River, near Entiat
GPS: N47 59.238' / W120 34.860'
Elevation: 2,500 feet
Season: Mid-May to late Sept
Sites: 8 tent sites
Facilities: Drinking water, fire grills, picnic tables, pit toilets
Fee per night: $$
Management: Okanogan-Wenatchee National Forest, Entiat Ranger District, (509) 784-4700; no reservations
Activities: Hiking, fishing
Finding the campground: From WA 285, 2 miles north of Wenatchee, take US 97A north for 15 miles. Just before the town of Entiat, turn left onto CR 371 (Entiat River Road). Drive 34 miles west

and north to the campground, making sure you stay on the paved road that becomes FR 51 and then FR 317.

The campground: This rustic camp is located at the point where the North Fork Entiat River meets the Entiat itself. Entiat Falls are less than 0.5 mile from camp. There are lots of creeks in the area to explore, so be sure to get a forest service map.

214 Pearrygin Lake State Park

Location: About 4 miles northeast of Winthrop on Pearrygin Lake
GPS: N48 29.196' / W120 08.754'
Elevation: 2,100 feet
Season: Apr through Oct
Sites: 76 tent sites, 50 sites with full hookups (electric/water/sewer) for RVs no longer than 60 feet, 2 cabins, 1 vacation house, 2 primitive walk-in sites, 2 group sites for up to 48 and 80 people, respectively
Facilities: Drinking water, picnic tables, fire grills, flush toilets, dump station, showers, firewood, boat ramp, floats
Fee per night: $$–$$$$
Management: Washington State Parks and Recreation Commission, (360) 902-8844 (information); (509) 996-2370 (park office)
Activities: Fishing, boating, swimming, hiking, picnicking, cross-country skiing, snowmobiling, wildlife viewing
Finding the campground: From Winthrop, head north on Eastside Chewuch Road for 1.5 miles. Turn right (east) onto Bear Creek Road and drive 2 miles to the park.
The campground: This easy-to-reach state park bustles with water-skiers on summer weekends. It is just 4 miles away from the fun little western town of Winthrop, which still allows cattle drives down Main Street in late summer. In the 1970s "Old West" facades were added to many of Winthrop's buildings in a successful attempt to attract tourists. Pearrygin State Park covers 580 acres in the rolling, sagebrush-covered foothills of the eastern Cascades. It features 8,200 feet of shoreline on spring-fed, trout-filled Pearrygin Lake, which has a sandy beach. Mountain lions and bears are spotted here from time to time, but deer, groundhogs, and ospreys are the usual wildlife enjoyed by campers. Individual campsites can be reserved by visiting https://secure.camis.com/WA/ or calling (888) 226-7688.

215 Phelps Creek

Location: 44 miles northwest of Leavenworth on the Chiwawa River
GPS: N48 04.182' / W120 50.940'
Elevation: 2,800 feet
Season: Mid-June to mid-Oct
Sites: 13 sites for tents or self-contained RVs no longer than 30 feet
Facilities: Picnic tables, fire grills, pit toilets, horse facilities; no drinking water

Fee per night: None

Management: Okanogan-Wenatchee National Forest, Wenatchee River Ranger District, (509) 548-2550; no reservations

Activities: Hiking, fishing, horse packing

Finding the campground: From US 2, midway between Stevens Pass (20 miles) and Leavenworth (16 miles), turn north at Coles Corner onto WA 207 toward Lake Wenatchee. Drive for 4 miles. Just before Lake Wenatchee State Park, turn right (east) onto Chiwawa Loop Road and drive 1.5 miles. Turn left (north) onto FR 62 (Meadow Creek Road). Stay on FR 62 (which joins Chiwawa River Road in about 3.5 miles) all the way to the campground. The distance from Lake Wenatchee to Phelps Creek Campground is about 24 miles.

The campground: This camp is way out there, nestled between Chiwawa Ridge and the Entiat Mountains, just outside the Glacier Peak Wilderness boundary. The camp is very basic but nicely situated at the confluence of Phelps Creek and the Chiwawa River, with good trail access to the Glacier Peak Wilderness.

216 Red Mountain

Location: 97 miles southeast of Seattle on the Cle Elum River, near Cle Elum
GPS: N47 21.996' / W121 06.120'
Elevation: 2,220 feet
Season: Mid-May to mid-Nov, but not gated in the winter
Sites: 10 sites for tents or self-contained RVs no longer than 30 feet
Facilities: Picnic tables, fire grills, pit toilets, firewood; no drinking water
Fee per night: $$
Management: Okanogan-Wenatchee National Forest, Cle Elum Ranger District, (509) 852-1100; no reservations
Activities: Hiking, fishing, cross-country skiing, snowshoeing
Finding the campground: From I-5 in Seattle take exit 164 and drive 80 miles east on I-90. Take exit 80 (4 miles west of Cle Elum) and go north on Bullfrog Road, which intersects WA 903 in about 3 miles. Take WA 903 north through Roslyn and Ronald, driving about 5 miles to Salmon la Sac Road (FR 4330) near the southern end of Cle Elum Lake. Take Salmon la Sac Road north along the east side of the lake for 9 miles to the campground.

The campground: This rustic 2-acre campground is just about 1 mile above Cle Elum Lake, at the point where Thorp Creek empties into the Cle Elum River. The other camps in the area are better, but this will serve the purpose if the others are full. It is quite popular with snow-sport enthusiasts, who are welcome to stay here (no fee, no services) until snow blocks the access road.

217 River Bend

Location: 22 miles northwest of Winthrop on the Methow River
GPS: N48 39.130' / W120 33.303'
Elevation: 2,600 feet

Season: June to late Sept

Sites: 5 sites for tents or self-contained RVs no longer than 30 feet

Facilities: Picnic tables, fire grills, vault toilets; no drinking water

Fee per night: $

Management: Okanogan-Wenatchee National Forest, Methow Valley Ranger District, (509) 996-4003; no reservations

Activities: Hiking, fishing, horse packing

Finding the campground: From Winthrop drive northwest on WA 20 for 13 miles to the Mazama turnoff on your right. At Mazama, 0.5 mile from the turnoff, turn left (northwest) onto Mazama Road toward Harts Pass and drive another 8.5 miles northwest to FR 54060. Turn left (south) and drive 0.5 mile over rough road to the campground.

The campground: This is quite a primitive campground, but camping on the river makes up for a lot. It is popular with horse packers because of the good trails in the area. The Pasayten Wilderness is within 2 miles.

218 Roads End

Location: 35 miles southwest of Winthrop on the Twisp River

GPS: N48 27.684' / W120 34.678'

Elevation: 3,600 feet

Season: Late May to early Sept

Sites: 4 sites for tents or self-contained RVs no longer than 16 feet

Facilities: Picnic tables, fire grills, vault toilets; no drinking water.

Fee per night: $

Management: Okanogan-Wenatchee National Forest, Methow Valley Ranger District, (509) 996-4003; no reservations

Activities: Hiking, fishing

Finding the campground: From Winthrop drive south on WA 20 East for 9 miles to the town of Twisp. Turn right (west) onto Twisp River Road (CR 9114), which becomes FR 44 and then FR 4440, and drive 26 miles to the campground.

The campground: You would have to hike to get any farther from civilization than this primitive campground. And since it sits 0.25 mile from the Lake Chelan–Sawtooth Wilderness boundary, that would be no problem. The campground is located on the Twisp River near Gilbert Mountain. Good trails head north and west from camp.

219 Rock Creek

Location: 33 miles east of Winthrop on Rock and Loup Loup Creeks

GPS: N48 24.376' / W119 45.537'

Elevation: 2,650 feet

Season: Year-round

Sites: 6 sites for tents or self-contained RVs

Facilities: Drinking water, picnic tables, fire grills, vault toilets, boat launch
Fee per night: None
Management: Washington Department of Natural Resources, Northeast Region, (509) 684-7474
Activities: Hiking, fishing
Finding the campground: From Winthrop drive south and then east on WA 20 East for 29 miles. Turn left (north) onto Loup Loup Canyon Road and drive 4 miles to the camp on the left.
The campground: This rustic campground set at the confluence of Rock and Loup Loup Creeks is pleasant. There are plenty of hiking trails in the area.

220 Rock Island

Location: 17 miles west of Leavenworth on Icicle Creek
GPS: N47 36.504' / W120 55.080'
Elevation: 1,600 feet
Season: May to late Oct
Sites: For tent camping only, 20 single sites, 2 double sites
Facilities: Drinking water, fire grills, picnic tables, vault toilets
Fee per night: $$
Management: Okanogan-Wenatchee National Forest, Wenatchee River Ranger District, (509) 548-2550; no reservations
Activities: Hiking, fishing
Finding the campground: From US 2 at the west end of Leavenworth, turn south onto Icicle Road and drive 17 miles south and west to the campground.
The campground: This is the next to last Okanogan-Wenatchee National Forest campground as you head up Icicle Creek from Leavenworth. It is located on the south side of the creek below Blackjack Ridge. The trail leading to the Alpine Lakes Wilderness is about 1 mile farther downstream at Chatter Creek.

221 Rock Lakes

Location: About 40 miles east of Winthrop on Rock Lakes
GPS: N48 27.159' / W119 47.321'
Elevation: 3,809 feet
Season: Year-round
Sites: 8 sites for tents or self-contained RVs
Facilities: Picnic tables, fire grills, vault toilets; no drinking water
Fee per night: None
Management: Washington Department of Natural Resources, Northeast Region, (509) 684-7474
Activities: Hiking, fishing
Finding the campground: From Winthrop drive south and then east on WA 20 East for 29 miles. Turn left (north) onto Loup Loup Canyon Road and drive 5 miles to Rock Lakes Road. Turn left (west) and drive 6 miles, then turn left and go 0.3 mile to the site.

The campground: This site is favored by anglers for the trout fishing in Rock Lakes. The camp is primitive but nicely situated on the lakeshore.

222 Salmon la Sac

Location: About 100 miles southeast of Seattle on the Cle Elum River, near Cle Elum
GPS: N47 24.072' / W121 06.000'
Elevation: 2,400 feet
Season: Late May to late Sept
Sites: 69 sites for tents or self-contained RVs no longer than 21 feet
Facilities: Drinking water, fire grills, picnic tables, flush toilets, horse camp
Fee per night: $$$
Management: Okanogan-Wenatchee National Forest, Cle Elum Ranger District, (509) 852-1100
Activities: Hiking, fishing, horse packing
Finding the campground: From I-5 in Seattle take exit 164 and drive east on I-90 for 80 miles. Four miles before you reach Cle Elum, take exit 80 and go north on Bullfrog Road. It intersects with WA 903 in about 3 miles. Take WA 903 northwest through Roslyn and Ronald, driving about 5 miles to Salmon la Sac Road (FR 4330) near the southern end of Cle Elum Lake. Take Salmon la Sac Road north along the east side of the lake for 12 miles to the campground.
The campground: Hiking trails head north and east from this 63-acre camp snuggled on the Cle Elum River about 3 miles north of Cle Elum Lake. This is a large and well-developed campground considering how remote it is. There is even a campground host in residence during the summer months. It is a good base camp for hikers and horse packers. For a minimal fee you can make reservations by contacting the National Recreation Reservation Service at www.recreation.gov or (877) 444-6777.

223 Silver Falls

Location: 47 miles north of Wenatchee on the Entiat River, near Entiat
GPS: N47 57.570' / W120 32.340'
Elevation: 2,400 feet
Season: Memorial Day through Sept
Sites: 29 sites for tents or self-contained RVs no longer than 30 feet
Facilities: Drinking water, fire grills, picnic tables, vault toilets
Fee per night: $$
Management: Okanogan-Wenatchee National Forest, Entiat Ranger District, (509) 784-4700
Activities: Hiking, fishing
Finding the campground: From WA 285, 2 miles north of Wenatchee, take US 97A north for 15 miles. Just before you reach the town of Entiat, turn left (northwest) onto CR 371 (Entiat River Road). Continue 30 miles to the campground, making sure you stay on the paved road that becomes FR 51.

The campground: The camp is on the east side of the Entiat River. It is named for Silver Falls, which are an easy 0.5-mile hike up Silver Creek. FR 5900 (Shady Pass Road) heads from here northeast to Shady Pass in the Chelan Mountains and eventually ends at Twenty-five Mile Creek State Park on Lake Chelan, a distance of about 24 miles. For a minimal fee you can make reservations by contacting the National Recreation Reservation Service at www.recreation.gov or (877) 444-6777.

224 Soda Springs

Location: 35 miles northwest of Leavenworth on the Little Wenatchee River
GPS: N47 51.504' / W120 58.200'
Elevation: 2,033 feet
Season: May to late Oct
Sites: 26 tent sites
Facilities: Picnic tables, fire grills, pit toilets; no drinking water
Fee per night: None
Management: Okanogan-Wenatchee National Forest, Wenatchee River Ranger District, (509) 548-2550; no reservations
Activities: Hiking, fishing
Finding the campground: From US 2, midway between Stevens Pass (20 miles) and Leavenworth (16 miles), turn north at Coles Corner onto WA 207 toward Lake Wenatchee. Drive for 10.5 miles along the north shore of Lake Wenatchee via North Shore Drive to its intersection with FR 6500. Turn left (west) onto FR 6500 and drive 8 miles to the campground.
The campground: This is a rustic camp, bordering on primitive, but it is popular as a base camp for backpackers. The riverside setting is nice.

225 South Creek

Location: 32 miles southwest of Winthrop on the Twisp River
GPS: N48 26.311' / W120 31.787'
Elevation: 3,100 feet
Season: Late May to early Sept
Sites: 4 sites for tents or self-contained RVs no longer than 30 feet
Facilities: Picnic tables, fire grills, vault toilets, horse facilities; no drinking water
Fee per night: $
Management: Okanogan-Wenatchee National Forest, Methow Valley Ranger District, (509) 996-4003; no reservations
Activities: Hiking, fishing, horse packing
Finding the campground: From Winthrop drive south on WA 20 East for 9 miles to the town of Twisp. Turn right (west) onto Twisp River Road (CR 9114), which becomes FR 44 and then FR 4440, and drive 23 miles to the campground.

The campground: South Creek flows into the Twisp River at this campground site. The camp is popular with horse packers, who do not seem to care about the primitive conditions. There are several trails near camp that follow creeks into the mountains.

226 Sugarloaf

Location: 23 miles northwest of Okanogan on Sugarloaf Lake
GPS: N48 35.682' / W119 41.820'
Elevation: 2,400 feet
Season: Mid-May to mid-Sept
Sites: 4 tent sites
Facilities: Picnic tables, vault toilets, boat ramp; no drinking water
Fee per night: $
Management: Okanogan-Wenatchee National Forest, Tonasket Ranger District, (509) 486-2186; no reservations
Activities: Fishing, boating
Finding the campground: From Okanogan drive north on CR 9229, which becomes Conconully Road. Drive about 18 miles to Conconully, turn northeast onto CR 4015 (Sinlahekin Road), and drive nearly 5 miles along the lake to the campground.
The campground: This is a mighty small and primitive campground, but it is rarely busy and offers good access to Sugarloaf Lake. It is a good place for a private vacation.

227 Swauk

Location: 107 miles southeast of Seattle on Swauk Creek, near Cle Elum
GPS: N47 19.716' / W120 39.480'
Elevation: 3,200 feet
Season: Mid-April to late Sept
Sites: 22 sites for tents or self-contained RVs no longer than 21 feet
Facilities: Fire grills, picnic tables, pit toilets, firewood; no drinking water
Fee per night: $$$
Management: Okanogan-Wenatchee National Forest, Cle Elum Ranger District, (509) 682-4900; no reservations
Activities: Hiking, fishing, rockhounding, snowmobiling, snow sports
Finding the campground: From I-5 in Seattle take exit 164 and head east on I-90 for 85 miles. Take exit 85 and cross the freeway to Cle Elum and WA 970. Turn right (east) onto WA 970 and continue 11 miles to US 97. Go north on US 97 for 11 miles to the campground.
The campground: The campground, on Swauk Creek, is across the highway from a rockhounding area, and a good hiking trail leads west to Teanaway Ridge. This 130-acre camp is pretty basic, but it is one of the few still open on this stretch of highway between I-90 and US 2. The fishing is rumored to be good, and the camp is a popular day-use area in the winter for snow play.

228 Tumwater

Location: 10 miles northwest of Leavenworth
GPS: N47 40.686' / W120 43.920'
Elevation: 2,050 feet
Season: May to mid-Oct
Sites: 84 sites for tents or self-contained RVs no longer than 30 feet, 1 group site
Facilities: Drinking water, picnic tables, fire grills, flush toilets
Fee per night: $$$
Management: Okanogan-Wenatchee National Forest, Wenatchee River Ranger District, (509) 548-2550
Activities: Hiking, fishing
Finding the campground: From Leavenworth drive west and then north on US 2 West for 10 miles to the campground.
The campground: Hikers heading to the Alpine Lakes Wilderness set their base camp here, but it also makes a good layover for travelers on US 2. The surrounding countryside is stunning. The campground is near the head of Tumwater Canyon, which is steep enough to turn the Wenatchee River into a broiling waterslide. Do not go near the water—just look. For a minimal fee you can make reservations by contacting the National Recreation Reservation Service at www.recreation .gov or (877) 444-6777.

229 Twenty-five Mile Creek State Park

Location: 49 miles north of Wenatchee on Lake Chelan, near Chelan
GPS: N47 59.532' / W120 15.906'
Elevation: 1,098 feet
Season: Early Apr to early Oct
Sites: 46 tent sites, 21 sites with electrical and water hookups (including 13 with sewer) for RVs no longer than 30 feet, 1 group site for up to 50 people
Facilities: Drinking water; picnic tables; restrooms; showers; grocery store; dump station; boat marina with docks, piers, ramp, marine gas pump
Fee per night: $$-$$$$
Management: Washington State Parks and Recreation Commission, (360) 902-8844; (509) 687-3710 (park office)
Activities: Hiking, fishing, swimming, sailboarding, boating, mountain biking
Finding the campground: From WA 285, 2 miles north of Wenatchee, take US 97A north for 31 miles to South Lakeshore Road on Lake Chelan. Turn left (northwest) and drive 16 miles to the campground.
The campground: Creeks flowing into 55-mile-long Lake Chelan were named for their distance up the lake from the town of Chelan—hence Twenty-five Mile Creek's name. The 235-acre park includes 1,500 feet of lakeshore. The camp is used as a base for long backpacking trips into the Chelan Mountains. There are several trailheads in the vicinity. This was originally a lakeside resort,

Boat fueling station on Lake Chelan near Twenty-five Mile Creek State Park. The 55-mile-long lake is drawn down about 15 feet in the fall and allowed to fill again in the spring.

used by early Chelan Valley residents as a place to camp at the end of the road before heading up the lake by boat or horseback. Individual campsites can be reserved by visiting https://secure .camis.com/WA/ or calling (888) 226-7688.

230 War Creek

Location: 24 miles southwest of Winthrop on the Twisp River
GPS: N48 22.057' / W120 23.898'
Elevation: 2,460 feet
Season: May to Sept
Sites: 11 sites for tents or self-contained RVs no longer than 21 feet
Facilities: Drinking water, picnic tables, fire grills, vault toilets
Fee per night: $
Management: Okanogan-Wenatchee National Forest, Methow Valley Ranger District, (509) 996-4003; no reservations
Activities: Hiking, fishing

Finding the campground: From Winthrop drive south on WA 20 East for 9 miles to the town of Twisp. Turn right (west) onto Twisp River Road (CR 9114), which becomes FR 44 and then FR 4440, and drive 15 miles to the campground.

The campground: Located just 2 trail miles from the boundary of the Lake Chelan-Sawtooth Wilderness, this forested camp is popular with hikers and backpackers. The setting is very pleasant.

231 Wenatchee River County Park

Location: About 7 miles northwest of Wenatchee on the Wenatchee River, in Monitor
GPS: N47 29.100' / W120 24.577'
Elevation: 853 feet
Season: Apr through Oct
Sites: 15 tent sites, 64 sites with full hookups for RVs
Facilities: Drinking water, picnic tables, flush toilets, showers, dump station, playground, ping-pong, outdoor workout equipment, free wireless
Fee per night: $$$$
Management: Chelan County, (509) 667-7503
Activities: Fishing
Finding the campground: From WA 285, 2 miles north of Wenatchee, take US 97/2 west for 4.5 miles to Monitor. The campground is close to the highway on the left.
The campground: This is a nice layover park on the Wenatchee River, with all the amenities. For reservations call (509) 667-7503.

232 White River Falls

Location: About 37 miles northwest of Leavenworth on the White River
GPS: N47 57.162' / W120 56.400'
Elevation: 2,100 feet
Season: June to mid-Oct
Sites: 5 tent sites
Facilities: Picnic tables, fire grills, pit toilets; no drinking water
Fee per night: None
Management: Okanogan-Wenatchee National Forest, Wenatchee River Ranger District, (509) 548-2550; no reservations.
Activities: Hiking, fishing
Finding the campground: From US 2, midway between Stevens Pass (20 miles) and Leavenworth (16 miles), turn north at Coles Corner onto WA 207 toward Lake Wenatchee. The campground is about 20.5 miles from this turnoff. WA 207 becomes North Shore Drive, then White River Road, and finally FR 6400 as you make your way around the lake to the campground.
The campground: This isolated campground is just about at the end of the road that runs alongside the White River. It sits below the steep White Mountains in the Glacier Peak Wilderness. There

is a good trail from the nearby falls that leads west to Mount David (elevation 7,420 feet). From the end of the road, trails lead northwest into the wilderness area.

233 Wish Poosh

Location: About 91 miles southeast of Seattle on Cle Elum Lake, near Cle Elum
GPS: N47 16.710' / W121 05.520'
Elevation: 2,400 feet
Season: Mid-May to mid-Sept
Sites: 17 tent sites, 22 sites for tents or self-contained RVs no longer than 21 feet
Facilities: Drinking water, fire grills, picnic tables, flush toilets, firewood, restaurant, grocery store, ice, boat ramp, docks
Fee per night: $$$–$$$$
Management: Okanogan-Wenatchee National Forest, Cle Elum Ranger District, (509) 852-1100
Activities: Hiking, fishing, swimming, boating, sailing, waterskiing, cross-country skiing, snowshoeing
Finding the campground: From I-5 in Seattle take exit 164 and head east on I-90 for 80 miles. Four miles before you reach Cle Elum, take exit 80 and go north on Bullfrog Road, which intersects WA 903 in about 3 miles. Take WA 903 northwest through Roslyn and Ronald, driving about 5 miles to Salmon la Sac Road (FR 4330) near the southern end of Cle Elum Lake. Take Salmon la Sac Road north along the east side of the lake for 2.5 miles to the campground.
The campground: Cle Elum Lake is about 7.5 miles long, and this 100-acre camp is on the east shore, about 2 miles up the lake from the Cle Elum Dam. It is the only campground currently open on the lake. There are several access points to the lake from Salmon la Sac Road, which runs the length of the east shore and into the Wenatchee Mountains beyond. This campground has most of the amenities and is popular with families. For a minimal fee you can make reservations by contacting the National Recreation Reservation Service at www.recreation.gov or (877) 444-6777.

	Group Sites	RV Sites	Total # of sites	Max RV Length	Hookups	Toilets	Showers	Drinking water	Dump station	Pets	Wheelchair	Recreation	Fee	Season	Can reserve	Stay limit
234 Ahtanum Camp and Ahtanum Meadows		•	18			P		•		•		F		year-round		7
235 Bird Creek		•	8			P			•			H		May-mid Oct		7
236 Brooks Memorial State Park	•	•	57	60	WES	F	•	•	•	•		HFR	$$-$$$$	Apr-Oct		10
237 Bumping Lake and Boat Landing		•	45	30		V		•		•		HFBS ROC	$$$	mid May-late Nov	•	14
238 Cedar Springs		•	14	22		P		•	•	•		HF	$$$	late May-late Nov	•	14
239 Clear Lake North		•	36	22		V			•	•	•	HFB	$$	mid Apr-late Nov		14
240 Clear Lake South		•	31	22		V		•	•	•		HFB	$$	mid Apr-late Nov		14
241 Clover Flats		•	9	21		P		•		•		H		year-round		7
242 Columbia Hills State Park		•	13	60		F			•	•		HFB	$$-$$$$	Apr-Oct		14
243 Cottonwood		•	9	22		P		•	•	•		HF	$$$	Apr-Nov	•	14
244 Crow Creek		•	15	30		P		•	•	•		HFO	$	mid Apr-Nov		14
245 Dog Lake		•	8	20		P			•	•		HF	$	late May-late Nov		14
246 Halfway Flat		•	11	27		P			•	•		HFO	$$	Apr-late Nov		14
247 Hause Creek		•	42	30		F		•	•	•	•	HFB	$$$	late May-late Nov	•	14
248 Hells Crossing		•	18	20		P		•	•	•		HF	$$	late May-late Nov	•	14
249 Indian Creek		•	39	32		V		•	•	•		HFSB	$$$$	late May-mid Sept	•	14
250 Island Camp		•	6			P			•	•		H		year-round		7
251 Kaner Flat		•	41	30		F		•	•	•		HFO	$-$$$	mid Apr-Oct		14
252 Lake Easton State Park	•	•	138	60		F	•	•	•	•	•	HFBSC	$$-$$$$	late Apr-mid Oct	•	10
253 Little Naches		•	21	20		V		•	•	•		HF	$$	late May-late Nov	•	14
254 Lodge Pole		•	34	20		V		•	•	•		HF	$$$	mid June-mid Sept	•	14
255 Morrison Creek			12			V			•			HF		July-late Sept		14
256 Moss Creek		•	17	32		V		•	•	•	•	HF	$	mid May-early Sept	•	14

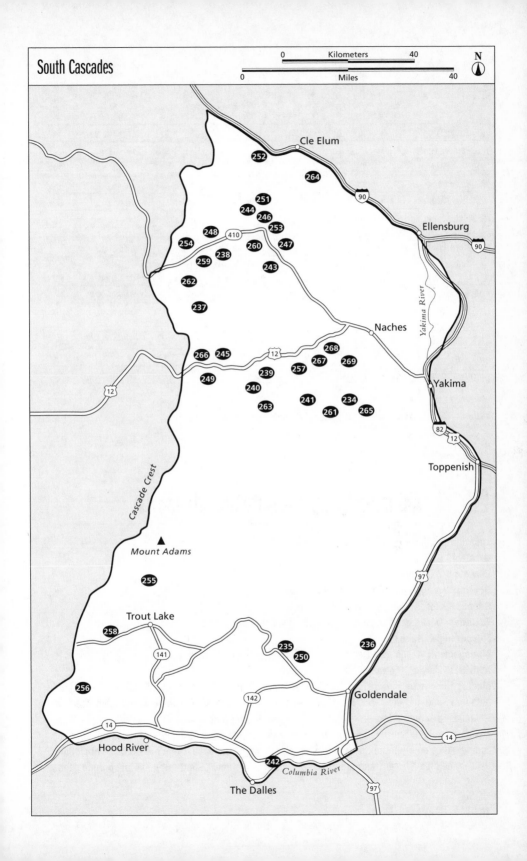

South Cascades

	Group Sites	RV Sites	Total # of sites	Max RV Length	Hookups	Toilets	Showers	Drinking water	Dump station	Pets	Wheelchair	Recreation	Fee	Season	Can reserve	Stay limit
257 Peninsula		•	60	20		V						HFSB	$	mid Apr–late Nov		14
258 Peterson Prairie	•	•	24	32		P		•		•	•	H	$$$	May–late Sept	•	14
259 Pleasant Valley		•	17	32		P		•		•	•	HF	$$$	mid Jun–Nov	•	14
260 Sawmill Flat		•	23	24		V		•	•	•	•	HF	$$$	Apr–Nov	•	14
261 Snow Cabin		•	8			P				•	•	HFRC		year-round		7
262 Soda Springs		•	26	30		V		•	•	•	•	HF	$$$	May–late Nov	•	14
263 South Fork Group Campground	•		15	20		V			•	•		HF	$$$$	late May–mid Sept	•	14
264 Taneum		•	12	21		V		•		•	•	HFO	$$$	May–late Sept		14
265 Tree Phones		•	14			P				•		RC		year-round		7
266 White Pass Lake (Leech Lake)		•	16	20		V			•	•		HF	$	Jun–late Nov		14
267 Wildrose		•	8	22		V			•	•		HF	$	Apr–late Nov		14
268 Willows		•	16	20		V		•		•	•	HF	$$	Apr–late Nov	•	14
269 Windy Point		•	15	22		V		•		•	•	HF	$$	Apr–late Nov	•	14

Hookups: W=Water E=Electric S=Sewer
Toilets: F=Flush V=Vault P=Pit
Recreation: C=Bicycling/Mountain Biking H=Hiking S=Swimming F=Fishing B=Boating
O=Off-highway driving R=Horseback Riding
Maximum Trailer/RV Length given in feet. Stay Limit given in days.
Fee $ = less than $10; $$ = $10–$15; $$$ = $16–20; $$$$ = more than $20.
If no entry under Fee, camping is free.

234 Ahtanum Camp and Ahtanum Meadows

Location: 34 miles west of Yakima on Ahtanum Creek
GPS: N46 31.357' / W121 00.555'
Elevation: 3,071 feet
Season: Year-round, except during heavy snows
Sites: 18 sites for tents or self-contained RVs
Facilities: Drinking water, picnic tables, fire grills, tent pads, pit toilets
Fee per night: None
Management: Washington Department of Natural Resources, Southeast Region, (509) 925-8510
Activities: Fishing, snowmobiling
Finding the campground: From Yakima drive 3 miles south to Union Gap via I-82. Turn west onto Ahtanum Road and drive for 21 miles to Tampico. Continue west on North Fork Ahtanum Road for 9.5 miles to Ahtanum Meadows on the left and Ahtanum Camp on the right.
The campground: Snowmobiling in the winter is one of the main attractions of these primitive campgrounds on Ahtanum Creek in the Ahtanum Multiple Use Area. There are 60 miles of groomed trails in the area. Winter users are required to have a Sno-Park permit (available at sporting goods stores and ranger stations).

235 Bird Creek

Location: About 110 miles southwest of Yakima on Bird Creek, near Goldendale
GPS: N46 03.824' / W121 20.255'
Elevation: 2,569 feet
Season: May to mid-Oct
Sites: 8 sites for tents or self-contained RVs
Facilities: Picnic tables, fire grills, tent pads, pit toilets; no drinking water
Fee per night: None
Management: Washington Department of Natural Resources, Southeast Region, (509) 925-8510
Activities: Hiking, snowmobiling
Finding the campground: From Yakima drive 5 miles south on I-82/US 97 through the town of Union Gap. Stay on US 97 as it leaves I-82 and continue 64 miles southwest to Goldendale. Turn west onto WA 142 and drive about 12 miles. Then turn right (north) onto Glenwood-Goldendale Road and drive about 24 miles to Glenwood. From the post office in Glenwood, continue 0.3 mile west out of town. Then turn right onto Bird Creek Road and drive 0.9 mile. Turn left onto Road K-3000, cross over the cattleguard, and drive 1.2 miles. Turn right onto gravel Road S-4000 and drive 1.3 miles. Turn left onto Road K-4000 and stay left for the next 2 miles. Turn left into the campground.
The campground: This small, rustic campground is in a forested area beside Bird Creek. It is a nice place to relax, or you can use it as a base camp from which to explore the Mount Adams Wilderness.

236 Brooks Memorial State Park

Location: 48 miles south of Yakima, near Goldendale
GPS: N45 56.592' / W120 40.169'
Elevation: 3,000 feet
Season: Apr through Oct
Sites: 23 RV sites with water, sewer, and electrical hookups; 22 sites for tents or self-contained RVs no longer than 60 feet; 7 cabins; 4 tepees; 1 group site for up to 6 motor homes and 50 people
Facilities: Drinking water, picnic tables, fire grills, flush toilets, playground, coin-operated showers, dump station, environmental learning center
Fee per night: $$-$$$$
Management: Washington State Parks and Recreation Commission, (360) 902-8844 (information); (509) 773-4611 (park office); no reservations
Activities: Hiking, fishing, horseback riding, cross-country skiing
Finding the campground: From Yakima drive south on US 97 for 48 miles to the park, which is just south of Satus Pass.
The campground: This forested, 700-acre park memorializes an area citizen, Nelson R. Brooks, who became a local celebrity for his efforts to help build an excellent local road system. The East

Prong Klickitat River is just across the highway, and the trout fishing is reputed to be great. The hiking is good too; there are 3 miles of foot trails in camp.

237 Bumping Lake (upper campground) and Boat Landing (lower campground)

Location: 56 miles northwest of Yakima on the south shore of Bumping Lake
GPS: N46 52.752' / W121 16.980'
Elevation: 3,400 feet
Season: Mid-May to late Nov
Sites: 45 sites for tents or self-contained RVs no longer than 30 feet (50 feet maximum in the lower campground)
Facilities: Drinking water, picnic tables, vault toilets, firewood, boat ramp
Fee per night: $$$
Management: Okanogan-Wenatchee National Forest, Naches Ranger District, (509) 653-1401
Activities: Hiking, bicycling, fishing, horseback riding, educational programs, boating, climbing, hunting, off-highway driving, winter sports, wildlife viewing, waterskiing, swimming
Finding the campground: From I-82 in Yakima take US 12 northwest and drive 17 miles, passing through Naches to the junction with WA 410. Take WA 410 northwest and continue 28 miles to Bumping Lake Road (FR 18). Turn left (southwest) onto Bumping Lake Road and drive 11 miles to the campground on the right.
The campground: This is a very popular campground because of its proximity to the 1,300-acre lake, which holds kokanee salmon and rainbow trout. Some campsites are right at the water's edge. There are also some backpacking routes and day-use trails in the area that lead into the William O. Douglas Wilderness. For a minimal fee you can make reservations by contacting the National Recreation Reservation Service at www.recreation.gov or (877) 444-6777.

238 Cedar Springs

Location: About 45 miles northwest of Yakima on the Bumping River
GPS: N46 58.284' / W121 09.900'
Elevation: 2,800 feet
Season: Late May to late Nov
Sites: 14 sites for tents or self-contained RVs no longer than 22 feet
Facilities: Drinking water, picnic tables, pit toilets, dump station, firewood
Fee per night: $$$
Management: Okanogan-Wenatchee National Forest, Naches Ranger District, (509) 653-1401
Activities: Hiking, trout fishing
Finding the campground: From I-82 in Yakima take US 12 northwest for 17 miles, passing through Naches to the junction with WA 410. Take WA 410 northwest for 28 miles to Bumping

Lake Road (FR 18). Turn left (southwest) onto Bumping Lake Road and drive 0.5 mile to the campground.

The campground: Set on the Bumping River, this small campground is close to good hiking trails and is 11 miles downstream from Bumping Lake. It is also popular with picnickers. For a minimal fee you can make reservations by contacting the National Recreation Reservation Service at www .recreation.gov or (877) 444-6777.

239 Clear Lake North

Location: About 50 miles west of Yakima on Clear Lake
GPS: N46 38.028' / W121 16.080'
Elevation: 3,100 feet
Season: Mid-Apr to late Nov
Sites: 36 sites for tents or self-contained RVs no longer than 22 feet
Facilities: Picnic tables, vault toilets, dump station, firewood, boat ramp, docks; no drinking water
Fee per night: $$
Management: Okanogan-Wenatchee National Forest, Naches Ranger District, (509) 653-1401; no reservations
Activities: Hiking, fishing
Finding the campground: From I-82 in Yakima take US 12 northwest for 17 miles, passing through Naches to the junction with WA 410. Stay on US 12 for another 31 miles to CR 1200 (Tieton Reservoir Road) at the west end of Rimrock Lake. Turn left (south) onto CR 1200 and follow it for 1 mile. Continue on FR 1200-840 for 0.5 mile to the campground.
The campground: This campground is quite primitive but lovely in the spring and early summer when Rimrock and Clear Lakes, created by a dam on the Tieton River, are full. It is not so lovely in the fall when the reservoir is drawn down and much of the lakebed turns to mud. That is when the dirt bikers take over. Swimming is not allowed anytime. The campground is about 5 miles east of the Pacific Crest National Scenic Trail.

240 Clear Lake South

Location: 49 miles west of Yakima on Clear Lake
GPS: N46 37.746' / W121 16.080'
Elevation: 3,100 feet
Season: Mid-Apr to late Nov
Sites: 31 sites for tents or self-contained RVs no longer than 22 feet
Facilities: Drinking water, picnic tables, vault toilets, dump station, boat ramp, docks
Fee per night: $$
Management: Okanogan-Wenatchee National Forest, Naches Ranger District, (509) 653-1401; no reservations
Activities: Hiking, fishing

Finding the campground: From I-82 in Yakima take US 12 northwest for 17 miles, passing through Naches to the junction with WA 410. Stay on US 12 for another 31 miles to CR 1200 (Tieton Reservoir Road) at the west end of Rimrock Lake. Turn left onto CR 1200 and follow it for 1 mile to the campground.

The campground: This campground is a bit nicer than Clear Lake North. The lake is very beautiful when it is full in the spring and early summer. The kokanee fishing is pretty good, and nearby hiking trails lead into the Goat Rocks Wilderness.

241 Clover Flats

Location: 43 miles southwest of Yakima
GPS: N46 30.340' / W121 10.688'
Elevation: 6,345 feet
Season: Year-round, except during heavy snows
Sites: 9 sites for tents or self-contained RVs no longer than 21 feet
Facilities: Drinking water, picnic tables, fire grills, tent pads, pit toilets
Fee per night: None
Management: Washington Department of Natural Resources, Southeast Region, (509) 925-8510
Activities: Hiking, snowmobiling
Finding the campground: From Yakima drive 3 miles south on I-82 to Union Gap. Turn west onto Ahtanum Road and drive for 21 miles to Tampico. Then continue west on North Fork Ahtanum Road for 9.5 miles to Ahtanum Camp. Turn left (south) onto Middle Fork Ahtanum Road and drive for 9.2 miles to the Clover Flats Campground. All of this last stretch of road is one-lane gravel. It becomes very steep, a 12 to 13 percent grade, about 6 miles beyond Ahtanum Camp. The road beyond Clover Flats is impassable.

The campground: Clover Flats is way out there, and therefore it is pretty quiet. It is a good base camp for hikers. Nearby trails head west into the Goat Rocks Wilderness. For winter users there are 60 miles of groomed snowmobiling trails in the area.

242 Columbia Hills State Park (formerly Horsethief Lake State Park)

Location: 90 miles east of Vancouver on the Columbia River, near The Dalles
GPS: N45 38.707' / W121 06.647'
Elevation: 350 feet
Season: Apr through Oct
Sites: 12 sites for tents or self-contained RVs (8 are partial utility) no longer than 60 feet, 1 walk-in site
Facilities: Drinking water, fire grills, picnic tables, flush toilets, firewood, 2 boat ramps, dump station
Fee per night: $$–$$$$

Management: Washington State Parks and Recreation Commission, (360) 902-8844 (information); (509) 767-1159 (park office); no reservations

Activities: Hiking, fishing, boating (nonmotorized on Horsethief Lake), rock climbing, sailboarding

Finding the campground: From I-5 in Vancouver take exit 1 and head east on WA 14 for 90 miles to the campground.

The campground: The campground is on the shore of 90-acre Horsethief Lake, which is actually a backwater created by a railroad jetty on the Columbia River. Sun worshippers will appreciate the campground's lack of shade. This park covers 3,338 acres and is large for the number of sites. Access to the Columbia River is easy, but beginning sailboarders would be safer starting out on the lake. It can be very windy in the Columbia River Gorge. Some of the oldest petroglyphs in the Northwest are upriver, but you can view them only as part of a guided tour with a park ranger. (You can make arrangements in advance by calling the park at 509-767-1159.) The campground was once a Nez Perce campground and burial site, one of the biggest along the river. A small graveyard is just a short walk away.

243 Cottonwood

Location: 35 miles northwest of Yakima on the Naches River
GPS: N46 54.444' / W121 01.800'
Elevation: 2,300 feet
Season: Apr through Nov
Sites: 9 sites for tents or self-contained RVs no longer than 22 feet
Facilities: Drinking water, picnic tables, fire grills, tent pads, pit toilets, dump station
Fee per night: $$$
Management: Okanogan-Wenatchee National Forest, Naches Ranger District, (509) 653-1401
Activities: Hiking, fishing
Finding the campground: From I-82 in Yakima take US 12 northwest and drive 17 miles, through Naches, to the junction with WA 410. Take WA 410 northwest and continue 18 miles to the campground on the left.
The campground: Set on the banks of the Naches River, this wooded campground is just right for sitting around with or without a fishing rod and maybe taking a hike or two. For a minimal fee you can make reservations by contacting the National Recreation Reservation Service at www.recreation.gov or (877) 444-6777.

244 Crow Creek

Location: About 45 miles northwest of Yakima on the Naches River
GPS: N47 00.936' / W121 08.280'
Elevation: 2,900 feet
Season: Mid-Apr to Nov
Sites: 15 sites for tents or self-contained RVs no longer than 30 feet
Facilities: Drinking water, picnic tables, fire grills, tent pads, pit toilets, dump station

Fee per night: $

Management: Okanogan-Wenatchee National Forest, Naches Ranger District, (509) 653-1401; no reservations

Activities: Hiking, fishing, off-road driving

Finding the campground: From I-82 in Yakima take US 12 northwest for 17 miles, passing through Naches to the junction with WA 410. Take WA 410 northwest for 24.5 miles to FR 1900. Turn right (northwest) onto FR 1900 and drive for 2.5 miles. Then turn left (west) onto FR 1904. The campground is 0.5 mile farther on the right.

The campground: Located just 3 miles off the highway, this riverside campground is most popular with off-road driving enthusiasts. The main trail out of camp divides into several others that lead to other rivers and creeks in the area and on to the Norse Peak Wilderness.

245 Dog Lake

Location: 53 miles west of Yakima on Dog Lake
GPS: N46 39.312' / W121 21.600'
Elevation: 3,400 feet
Season: Late May to late Nov
Sites: 8 sites for tents or self-contained RVs no longer than 20 feet
Facilities: Picnic tables, fire grills, tent pads, pit toilets, dump station, boat ramp, docks; no drinking water
Fee per night: $
Management: Okanogan-Wenatchee National Forest, Naches Ranger District, (509) 653-1401; no reservations
Activities: Hiking, fishing
Finding the campground: From I-82 in Yakima go northwest on US 12 for 17 miles, passing through Naches to the junction with WA 410. Stay on US 12 for another 36 miles to reach the campground on the right.

The campground: Dog Lake is favored as a base camp by hikers, but it may be a bit too rustic for everyone else. It is squeezed into a fairly small site between the lakeshore and rugged mountains.

246 Halfway Flat

Location: 41 miles northwest of Yakima on the Naches River
Sites: 11 sites for tents or self-contained RVs no longer than 27 feet
GPS: N46 58.854' / W121 05.760'
Elevation: 2,500 feet
Season: Apr to late Nov
Facilities: Picnic tables, fire grills, tent pads, pit toilets, dump station; no drinking water
Fee per night: $$
Management: Okanogan-Wenatchee National Forest, Naches Ranger District, (509) 653-1401; no reservations

Activities: Hiking, fishing, off-road driving

Finding the campground: From I-82 in Yakima take US 12 and drive northwest for 17 miles, passing through Naches to the junction with WA 410. Take WA 410 northwest for 21 miles. Turn left (northwest) onto FR 1704 and drive 3 miles to the campground on the left.

The campground: This is a pleasant, though primitive, campground on the bank of the Naches River. The fishing is pretty good, and there are plenty of trails in the area to explore.

247 Hause Creek

Location: 35 miles west of Yakima on the Tieton River
GPS: N46 40.512' / W121 04.800'
Elevation: 2,500 feet
Season: Late May to late Nov
Sites: 42 sites for tents or self-contained RVs no longer than 30 feet
Facilities: Drinking water, picnic tables, flush toilets, dump station, boat ramp, docks
Fee per night: $$$
Management: Okanogan-Wenatchee National Forest, Naches Ranger District, (509) 653-1401
Activities: Hiking, fishing, boating on nearby Rimrock Lake
Finding the campground: From I-82 in Yakima take US 12 and drive northwest for 17 miles, passing through Naches to the junction with WA 410. Stay on US 12 for another 18 miles to reach the campground on the right.

The campground: This is one of the nicest campgrounds in the vicinity. Located downstream from Tieton Dam and Rimrock Lake, it is bigger than most and so are the sites. For a minimal fee you can make reservations by contacting the National Recreation Reservation Service at www.recreation .gov or (877) 444-6777.

248 Hells Crossing

Location: 51 miles northwest of Yakima on the American River
GPS: N46 57.942' / W121 15.840'
Elevation: 3,250 feet
Season: Late May to late Nov
Sites: 18 sites for tents or self-contained RVs no longer than 20 feet
Facilities: Drinking water, picnic tables, fire grills, pit toilets
Fee per night: $$
Management: Okanogan-Wenatchee National Forest, Naches Ranger District, (509) 653-1401
Activities: Hiking, fishing
Finding the campground: From I-82 in Yakima take US 12 and drive northwest for 17 miles, passing through Naches to the junction with WA 410. Take WA 410 northwest for 34 miles to the campground.

The campground: This campground is a favorite of tent campers, but small RVs fit in some of the sites. Especially appealing are the nearby hiking trails that connect with higher elevation streams

Family compounds are a common sight at Washington state parks.

and lakes in the William O. Douglas Wilderness. For a minimal fee you can make reservations by contacting the National Recreation Reservation Service at www.recreation.gov or (877) 444-6777.

249 Indian Creek

Location: 44 miles west of Yakima on Rimrock Lake
GPS: N46 38.676' / W121 14.580'
Elevation: 3,000 feet
Season: Late May to mid-Sept
Sites: 39 sites for tents or self-contained RVs no longer than 32 feet
Facilities: Drinking water, picnic tables, fire grills, vault toilets, dump station, boat ramp, docks
Fee per night: $$$$
Management: Okanogan-Wenatchee National Forest, Naches Ranger District, (509) 653-1401
Activities: Hiking, fishing, swimming, boating, waterskiing
Finding the campground: From I-82 in Yakima take US 12 and drive northwest for 17 miles, passing through Naches to the junction with WA 410. Stay on US 12 for another 27 miles to the campground.

The campground: Located next to the Rimrock Lake Marina, this comfy campground offers plenty of water recreation. Nearby trails head into the William O. Douglas Wilderness. For a minimal fee you can make reservations by contacting the National Recreation Reservation Service at www .recreation.gov or (877) 444-6777.

250 Island Camp

Location: About 113 miles southwest of Yakima on Bird Creek
GPS: N46 04.907' / W121 22.805'
Elevation: 3,376 feet
Season: Year-round
Sites: 6 sites for tents or self-contained RVs
Facilities: Picnic tables, fire grills, tent pads, pit toilets, dump station; no drinking water
Fee per night: None
Management: Washington Department of Natural Resources, Southeast Region, (509) 925-8510
Activities: Hiking, snowmobiling
Finding the campground: From Yakima drive 5 miles south on I-82/US 97, through the town of Union Gap. Stay on US 97 as it leaves I-82 and continue southwest for about 64 miles to Goldendale. Turn west onto WA 142 and drive about 12 miles. Turn right onto Glenwood-Goldendale Road and drive about 24 miles to Glenwood. From the post office in Glenwood, go 0.3 mile west; turn right onto Bird Creek Road, and drive 0.9 mile. Turn left onto Road K-3000, cross over the cattleguard, and drive 1.2 miles. Turn right onto Road S-4000 (gravel) and drive 1.3 miles. Turn left onto Road K-4000 and stay left for the next 3.4 miles. Turn left onto K-4200 Road and go 1.1 mile. Turn left into the campground.
The campground: This forested, creekside campground appeals mainly to winter snowmobilers and to summer backpackers who appreciate its proximity to the Mount Adams Wilderness.

251 Kaner Flat

Location: 45 miles northwest of Yakima on the Naches River
GPS: N47 00.660' / W121 07.800'
Elevation: 3,250 feet
Season: Mid-Apr through Oct
Sites: 41 sites for tents or self-contained RVs no longer than 30 feet
Facilities: Drinking water, picnic tables, vault, composting, flush toilets, dump station
Fee per night: $–$$$
Management: Okanogan-Wenatchee National Forest, Naches Ranger District, (509) 653-1401; no reservations
Activities: Hiking, fishing, off-road driving
Finding the campground: From I-82 in Yakima take US 12 and drive northwest for 17 miles, passing through Naches to the junction with WA 410. Take WA 410 northwest for 24.5 miles to FR 1900. Turn right (northwest) onto FR 1900 and drive for 2.5 miles to the campground on the right.

The campground: Located just 2.5 miles off the highway, this riverside campground is on the Old Naches Trail, a nineteenth-century wagon trail. Dirt bikers and off-roaders are the main trail users now. The campground is large and has spacious campsites.

252 Lake Easton State Park

Location: 71 miles southeast of Seattle on Lake Easton
GPS: N47 15.324' / W121 12.055'
Elevation: 2,130 feet
Season: Late Apr through mid-Oct
Sites: 90 developed tent sites, 2 hiker/biker sites, 45 sites for tents or self-contained RVs no longer than 60 feet, 1 group site (capacity 50)
Facilities: Drinking water, picnic tables, fire grills, flush toilets, showers, dump station, playground, boat ramp, boat dock, beach, roped-off swimming section
Fee per night: $$–$$$$
Management: Washington State Parks and Recreation Commission, (360) 902-8844 (information); (509) 656-2230 (park office)
Activities: Hiking, bicycling, fishing, boating, swimming, snowshoeing, snowmobiling, cross-country skiing, mushroom hunting
Finding the campground: From I-5 in Seattle take exit 164 and drive east on I-90 for 70 miles to exit 70 (signed as the Lake Easton State Park exit). Follow the signs for 1 mile to the park.
The campground: The 516-acre park lies in a glacial valley 16 miles southeast of Snoqualmie Pass in the Cascades. It features 24,000 feet of shoreline on man-made Lake Easton and 2,000 feet on the Yakima River. Kachess, Keechelus, and Cle Elum Lakes are nearby. This large, wooded campground offers fun for the whole family. There is a golf course nearby, but the boating is what attracts most campers. The trout fishing is good to excellent. In the winter there are 37 miles of cross-country ski trails to explore. Local wildlife includes marmots, pikas, red-tailed hawks, Steller's jays, whiskey jacks, and black-tailed deer. Sno-Park permit required from November 15 through April 30. Individual campsites can be reserved by visiting https://secure.camis.com/WA/ or calling (888) 226-7688.

253 Little Naches

Location: 42 miles northwest of Yakima on the Little Naches River
GPS: N47 00.660' / W121 07.800'
Elevation: 2,678 feet
Season: Late May to late Nov
Sites: 21 sites for tents or self-contained RVs no longer than 20 feet
Facilities: Drinking water, picnic tables, fire grills, vault toilets, dump station
Fee per night: $$
Management: Okanogan-Wenatchee National Forest, Naches Ranger District, (509) 653-1401; no reservations
Activities: Hiking, fishing

Finding the campground: From I-82 in Yakima take US 12 and drive northwest for 17 miles, passing through Naches to the junction with WA 410. Take WA 410 northwest for 24.5 miles to FR 1900. Turn north onto FR 1900; the campground is right there on the left.

The campground: This is a nice family campground near the confluence of the Little Naches and American Rivers. Some of the campsites are wide enough for two vehicles. For reservations call the National Recreation Reservation Service at (877) 444-6777 or visit www.recreation.gov/.

254 Lodge Pole

Location: 58 miles northwest of Yakima on the American River
GPS: N46 54.984' / W121 23.040'
Elevation: 3,500 feet
Season: Mid-June to mid-Sept
Sites: 34 sites for tents or self-contained RVs no longer than 20 feet
Facilities: Drinking water, picnic tables, vault toilets, dump station
Fee per night: $$$
Management: Okanogan-Wenatchee National Forest, Naches Ranger District, (509) 653-1401
Activities: Hiking, fishing
Finding the campground: From I-82 in Yakima head northwest on US 12 and drive 17 miles, passing through Naches to the junction with WA 410. Take WA 410 northwest for 41 miles to the campground.

The campground: This is the first campground you pass along the American River while driving toward Mount Rainier from the east. The campsites are nestled in the pines. As with most campgrounds in the vicinity, the primary activity is hiking. The Norse Peak Wilderness lies just to the north; the William O. Douglas Wilderness is to the south. For a minimal fee you can make reservations by contacting the National Recreation Reservation Service at www.recreation.gov or (877) 444-6777.

255 Morrison Creek

Location: About 105 miles northeast of Vancouver on Morrison Creek, near the town of Trout Lake
GPS: N46 07.793' / W121 30.926'
Elevation: 4,600 feet
Season: July to late Sept
Sites: 12 tent sites
Facilities: Picnic tables, fire rings, vault toilets; no drinking water
Fee per night: None
Management: Gifford Pinchot National Forest, Mount Adams Ranger District, (509) 395-3400; no reservations
Activities: Hiking, fishing
Finding the campground: From I-5 in Vancouver take exit 1 and drive east on WA 14 for 66 miles. At Bingen turn north onto WA 141 and drive 27 miles to the town of Trout Lake. From there head

north on CR 17 (Mount Adams Recreation Area Road) for 2 miles. Turn left (north) onto FR 80; drive for 3.5 miles and then turn right (north) onto FR 8040. Continue 6 miles to the campground. The access roads can be rough if they have not recently been graded.

The campground: This wooded camp on the banks of Morrison Creek is used mainly by hikers heading into the Mount Adams Wilderness. There are not many amenities or much comfort, but the setting is beautiful.

256 Moss Creek

Location: 58 miles east of Vancouver on the Little White Salmon River
GPS: N45 47.691' / W121 37.976'
Elevation: 1,300 feet
Season: Mid-May to early Sept
Sites: 17 sites for tents or self-contained RVs no longer than 32 feet
Facilities: Drinking water, picnic tables, fire rings, vault toilets, dump station
Fee per night: $
Management: Gifford Pinchot National Forest, Mount Adams Ranger District, (509) 395-3400
Activities: Hiking, fishing
Finding the campground: From I-5 in Vancouver take exit 1 and head east on WA 14 for 50 miles to the town of Cook. Turn north onto CR 1800 and drive 8 miles to the campground. The name of the route will change from Cook-Underwood Road to Willard Road to Oklahoma Road, but it is still CR 1800 the whole way.

The campground: This wooded, creekside campground provides plenty of privacy, and the fishing is good. For a minimal fee you can make reservations by contacting the National Recreation Reservation Service at www.recreation.gov or (877) 444-6777.

257 Peninsula

Location: 39 miles west of Yakima on Rimrock Lake
GPS: N46 38.106' / W121 08.460'
Elevation: 3,000 feet
Season: Mid-Apr to late Nov
Sites: 60 sites for tents or self-contained RVs no longer than 20 feet
Facilities: Picnic tables, fire grills, tent pads, vault toilets, boat ramp, docks; no drinking water
Fee per night: $
Management: Okanogan-Wenatchee National Forest, Naches Ranger District, (509) 653-1401; no reservations
Activities: Hiking, fishing, swimming, waterskiing, cross-country skiing, snowmobiling
Finding the campground: From I-82 in Yakima head northwest on US 12 for 17 miles, passing through Naches to the junction with WA 410. Stay on US 12 for another 18 miles; turn left (south) onto CR 1200/FR 12 (Tieton Reservoir Road) and drive 3 miles. Turn right (west) onto FR 1382 and drive 1 mile to the campground.

The campground: Set on the southeastern shore of Rimrock Lake, this campground offers stunning views of the region's mountain peaks. The amenities are not much, but easy access to the lake counts for a lot.

258 Peterson Prairie

Location: About 100 miles northeast of Vancouver, near the town of Trout Lake
GPS: N45 58.124' / W121 39.474'
Elevation: 2,976 feet
Season: May to late Sept
Sites: 23 sites for tents or self-contained RVs no longer than 32 feet, 1 group site
Facilities: Drinking water, picnic tables, fire rings, pit toilets
Fee per night: $$$
Management: Gifford Pinchot National Forest, Mount Adams Ranger District, (509) 395-3400
Activities: Hiking, berry picking, cross-country skiing, snowmobiling
Finding the campground: From I-5 in Vancouver take exit 1 and head east on WA 14 for 66 miles to Bingen. Turn north onto WA 141 and drive 27 miles to the town of Trout Lake. Continue west and then southwest on WA 141 for 5 miles to the Skamania County line. The road becomes FR 24 at this point. Stay on it for 2.5 miles to the campground on the right.
The campground: This is huckleberry central for the state of Washington. Late August through mid-September is prime time. The campground feels like it is way out on the flats, but it is close to mild adventure—the nearby Ice Cave and Big Lava Bed. The campground is nicely shaded and has spacious sites, but the amenities are primitive. For a minimal fee you can make reservations by contacting the National Recreation Reservation Service at www.recreation.gov or (877) 444-6777.

259 Pleasant Valley

Location: 50 miles northwest of Yakima on the American River
GPS: N46 56.557' / W121 19.522'
Elevation: 3,400 feet
Season: Mid-June to Nov
Sites: 17 sites for tents or self-contained RVs no longer than 32 feet
Facilities: Drinking water, pit toilets, dump station
Fee per night: $$$
Management: Okanogan-Wenatchee National Forest, Naches Ranger District, (509) 653-1401
Activities: Hiking, fishing, cross-country skiing
Finding the campground: From I-82 in Yakima head northwest on US 12 for 17 miles, passing through Naches to the junction with WA 410. Take WA 410 northwest for 33 miles to the campground on the left.
The campground: Popular with RVers, this riverside campground is often used as a base camp for hiking into the nearby Norse Peak and William O. Douglas Wildernesses. It is pretty basic, but the

sites are big. For a minimal fee you can make reservations by contacting the National Recreation Reservation Service at www.recreation.gov or (877) 444-6777.

260 Sawmill Flat

Location: 38 miles west of Yakima on the Naches River
GPS: N46 58.518' / W121 05.700'
Elevation: 2,500 feet
Season: Apr through Nov
Sites: 23 sites for tents or self-contained RVs no longer than 24 feet
Facilities: Drinking water, picnic tables, vault toilets, dump station, Adirondack group shelter
Fee per night: $$$
Management: Okanogan-Wenatchee National Forest, Naches Ranger District, (509) 653-1401
Activities: Hiking, fishing
Finding the campground: From I-82 in Yakima head northwest on US 12 for 17 miles, passing through Naches to the junction with WA 410. Take WA 410 northwest for 21 miles to the campground on the left.
The campground: Popular with families, this campground sits in a pine forest on the Naches River, where the fishing is good. Some campsites are doublewide family sites. Backcountry trails, Horsetail and Devils Creek Falls, and the popular Boulder Cave are nearby. For a minimal fee you can make reservations by contacting the National Recreation Reservation Service at www.recreation .gov or (877) 444-6777.

261 Snow Cabin

Location: About 40 miles southwest of Yakima on the North Fork Ahtanum Creek
GPS: N46 35.033' / W121 04.850' (Gray Rock Trail)
Elevation: 2,950 feet
Season: Year-round, except during heavy snows
Sites: 8 sites for tents or self-contained RVs
Facilities: Picnic tables, fire grills, pit toilets, dump station, horse facilities; no drinking water
Fee per night: None
Management: Washington Department of Natural Resources, Southeast Region, (509) 925-8510
Activities: Hiking, fishing, horseback riding, mountain biking
Finding the campground: From I-82 in Yakima drive 3 miles south to Union Gap. Turn west onto Ahtanum Road and drive for 21 miles to Tampico. Continue west on North Fork Ahtanum Road for 9.5 miles to Ahtanum Camp. From there continue on North Fork Ahtanum Road for 4.5 miles. Keep left for 1.1 miles to the Gray Rock Trailhead. Continue 1.5 miles to the campground on the left.
The campground: Oddly, Snow Cabin Campground does not have a snow shelter, although nearby Tree Phones Campground does. Still, there are plenty of old logging roads for horseback riding and mountain biking, and the campground is equipped for horses.

262 Soda Springs

Location: 50 miles northwest of Yakima on the Bumping River
GPS: N46 55.554' / W121 12.960'
Elevation: 3,100 feet
Season: May to late Nov
Sites: 26 sites for tents or self-contained RVs no longer than 30 feet
Facilities: Drinking water, picnic tables, vault toilets, dump station
Fee per night: $$$
Management: Okanogan-Wenatchee National Forest, Naches Ranger District, (509) 653-1401
Activities: Hiking, fishing
Finding the campground: From I-82 in Yakima head northwest on US 12 for 17 miles, passing through Naches to the junction with WA 410. Take WA 410 northwest for 28 miles to Bumping Lake Road (FR 18). Turn left (southwest) onto Bumping Lake Road and drive 5 miles to the campground on the left.
The campground: RVers consider Soda Springs one of the best campgrounds in the vicinity. It is farther from the road than most and closer to the Bumping River. There is actually a Soda Springs, which burbles up minerals due to the forces that created nearby Mount Rainier and the Cascades. Bumping Lake is just 6 miles upriver. Nearby trails lead into the William O. Douglas Wilderness. For a minimal fee you can make reservations by contacting the National Recreation Reservation Service at www.recreation.gov or (877) 444-6777.

263 South Fork Group Campground

Location: About 40 miles west of Yakima on the South Fork Tieton River
GPS: N46 37.530' / W121 08.100'
Elevation: 3,000 feet
Season: Late May to mid-Sept
Sites: For groups only; 15 sites for tents or self-contained RVs no longer than 20 feet
Facilities: Picnic tables, vault toilets, dump station; no drinking water
Fee per night: $$$$
Management: Okanogan-Wenatchee National Forest, Naches Ranger District, (509) 653-1401
Activities: Hiking, fishing
Finding the campground: From I-82 in Yakima head northwest on US 12 for 17 miles, passing through Naches to the junction with WA 410. Stay on US 12 for another 18 miles; turn left (south) onto CR 1200 (Tieton Reservoir Road) and drive 4 miles to FR 1203. Turn left (south) onto FR 1203 and drive 0.5 mile to the campground.
The campground: More of a parking lot than a campground, South Fork is used mainly by RVers. The attractions here are the nearby natural phenomena, like the Blue Slide, Goose Egg Mountain, and numerous landmasses and waterfalls of giant proportions. For a minimal fee you can make reservations by contacting the National Recreation Reservation Service at www.recreation.gov or (877) 444-6777.

264 Taneum

Location: 103 miles southeast of Seattle on Taneum Creek, near Cle Elum
GPS: N47 06.516' / W120 51.360'
Elevation: 2,400 feet
Season: May to late Sept
Sites: 12 sites for tents or self-contained RVs no longer than 21 feet
Facilities: Drinking water, picnic tables, vault toilets
Fee per night: $$$
Management: Okanogan-Wenatchee National Forest, Cle Elum Ranger District, (509) 852-1100; no reservations
Activities: Hiking, fishing, off-road driving, cross-country skiing
Finding the campground: From I-5 in Seattle head southeast on I-90 and drive 93 miles to exit 93, just beyond Cle Elum. Take the exit, drive over the freeway, and turn south onto Thorp Prairie Road. Drive for 4 miles and cross back over I-90 to Taneum Road. Turn west (right) onto Taneum Road, which becomes FR 33, and drive 6 miles to the campground.
The campground: For a rustic camping experience, this 8-acre campground is just the place. Conditions are basic, but it is still popular because there is so much to do in the area. There are plenty of hiking trails nearby in the L. T. Murray Wildlife Area below the South Cle Elum Ridge, as well as numerous cross-country ski trails for winter recreation.

265 Tree Phones

Location: About 39 miles southwest of Yakima on Middle Fork Ahtanum Creek
GPS: N46 29.824' / W121 07.271'
Elevation: 4,836 feet
Season: Year-round
Sites: 14 sites for tents or small, self-contained RVs
Facilities: Picnic tables, fire grills, tent pads, pit toilets, horse facilities, snow shelter with wood stove; no drinking water
Fee per night: None
Management: Washington Department of Natural Resources, Southeast Region, (509) 925-8510
Activities: Horseback riding, mountain biking, trail biking, snowmobiling
Finding the campground: From I-82 in Yakima drive 3 miles south to Union Gap. Turn west onto Ahtanum Road and drive 21 miles to Tampico. Then continue west on Road A-2000 for 15 miles. Turn left and drive 0.1 mile to the campground.
The campground: Winter and summer trail riders of all stripes are attracted to this campground, with its abundance of trails that crisscross through the Ahtanum Multiple Use Area. The primitive campground sits on the bank of a forest stream.

266 White Pass Lake (Leech Lake)

Location: About 55 miles west of Yakima on Leech Lake
GPS: N46 38.724' / W121 22.800'
Elevation: 4,500 feet
Season: June to late Nov
Sites: 16 sites for tents or self-contained RVs no longer than 20 feet
Facilities: Picnic tables, vault toilets, dump station, boat ramp, docks; no drinking water
Fee per night: $
Management: Okanogan-Wenatchee National Forest, Naches Ranger District, (509) 653-1401; no reservations
Activities: Hiking, fly fishing
Finding the campground: From I-82 in Yakima head northwest on US 12 for 17 miles, passing through Naches to the junction with WA 410. Stay west on US 12 for another 37.7 miles to the campground entrance road on the right.
The campground: White Pass Lake Campground is at the White Pass Summit, across the highway from the White Pass Ski Area. Fly fishing is good when the water warms a bit, but that is also when the mosquitoes swarm at this altitude. The Pacific Crest National Scenic Trail runs right by Leech Lake; other trails lead into the William O. Douglas Wilderness.

267 Wildrose

Location: 34 miles west of Yakima on the Tieton River
GPS: N46 40.422' / W121 02.604'
Elevation: 2,400 feet
Season: Apr to late Nov
Sites: 8 sites for tents or self-contained RVs no longer than 22 feet
Facilities: Picnic tables, vault toilets, dump station; no drinking water
Fee per night: $
Management: Okanogan-Wenatchee National Forest, Naches Ranger District, (509) 653-1401; no reservations
Activities: Hiking, fishing
Finding the campground: From I-82 in Yakima head northwest on US 12 for 17 miles, passing through Naches to the junction with WA 410. Stay west on US 12 for another 17 miles to the campground.
The campground: Wildrose sits on the banks of the Tieton River about 5 miles downstream from Rimrock Lake. The river is not very big, except in fall when the dam is opened to draw down the lake. The campground is small and rudimentary, but the setting is very nice; the camp is usually not crowded.

268 Willows

Location: 33 miles west of Yakima on the Tieton River
GPS: N46 40.357' / W121 02.388'
Elevation: 2,400 feet
Season: Apr to late Nov
Sites: 16 sites for tents or self-contained RVs no longer than 20 feet
Facilities: Drinking water, picnic tables, vault toilets, dump station
Fee per night: $$
Management: Okanogan-Wenatchee National Forest, Naches Ranger District, (509) 653-1401
Activities: Hiking, fishing
Finding the campground: From I-82 in Yakima head northwest on US 12 for 17 miles, passing through Naches to the junction with WA 410. Stay west on US 12 for another 16 miles to the campground.
The campground: Willows occupies a nicer setting than some of the other campgrounds in this area. It is on the banks of the Tieton River, just over 5 miles downstream from Rimrock Lake. Washington is not known for its fall foliage because there are so many evergreens, but this valley is one place where they shine. Local trees include larch, alder, and aspen. For a minimal fee you can make reservations by contacting the National Recreation Reservation Service at www.recreation .gov or (877) 444-6777.

269 Windy Point

Location: 26 miles west of Yakima on the Tieton River
GPS: N46 41.646' / W120 54.420'
Elevation: 2,000 feet
Season: Apr to late Nov
Sites: 15 sites for tents or self-contained RVs no longer than 22 feet
Facilities: Drinking water, picnic tables, vault toilets, dump station
Fee per night: $$
Management: Okanogan-Wenatchee National Forest, Naches Ranger District, (509) 653-1401
Activities: Hiking, fishing
Finding the campground: From I-82 in Yakima head northwest on US 12 for 17 miles, passing through Naches to the junction with WA 410. Stay west on US 12 for another 9 miles to the campground.
The campground: Drinking water is a bonus for campgrounds in the Tieton Valley. Windy Point also feels more isolated than the other camps along the river. The Oak Creek Wildlife Area is just across the road, and trails lead to and through other canyons to the south. For a minimal fee you can make reservations by contacting the National Recreation Reservation Service at www.recreation .gov or (877) 444-6777.

Eastern Region: Columbia Plateau

	Group Sites	RV Sites	Total # of sites	Max RV Length	Hookups	Toilets	Showers	Drinking water	Dump station	Pets	Wheelchair	Recreation	Fee	Season	Can reserve	Stay limit
270 Beebe Bridge Park		•	46		WE	F	•	•	•	•		HFBS	$$	Apr–Oct		10
271 Bridgeport State Park	•	•	35	45	WE	F	•	•	•	•	•	FBS	$$–$$$$	Apr–late Oct	•	10
272 Charbonneau Park		•	52		WES	F	•	•	•	•	•	HFBS	$$–$$$$	year-round	•	
273 Crawfish Lake		•	19	31		V	•			•		HFBS		mid May–mid Sept		14
274 Crow Butte Park	•	•	51	60	WES	F	•	•	•	•	•	HFBS	$$–$$$$	mid Mar–Oct	•	10
275 Curlew Lake State Park		•	84	40	WES	F	•	•	•	•	•	HFBS	$$–$$$$	Apr–Oct	•	10
276 Daroga State Park		•	45	45	WE	V	•	•	•	•	•	HFBSC	$$–$$$$	May–Oct	•	10
277 Entiat City Park		•	81		WES	F	•	•	•			FSB	$$$$	Apr–mid Sept	•	
278 Ferry Lake		•	9	20		V				•		HFSC	$	May–Sept		14
279 Fishhook Park		•	52		WE	F	•	•	•	•	•	HFSB	$$–$$$$	mid May–mid Sept	•	
280 Ginko Petrified Forest State Park		•	51	60	WES	F	•	•		•	•	HFBS	$$$$	Mar–Oct	•	10
281 Hood Park		•	67		E	F	•	•	•	•	•	FB	$$–$$$$	mid May–mid Sept	•	
282 Keller Ferry		•	55	16		F	•	•		•		FBS	$$	year-round		
283 Lincoln Rock State Park		•	98	65	WES	F	•	•	•	•	•	HFBSC	$$–$$$$	Mar–Oct	•	10
284 Long Lake		•	12	21		V	•			•	•	HFSC	$	May–Sept		333
285 Lyman Lake		•	4	31		V				•		F		mid May–mid Sept		
286 Maryhill State Park		•	70	60	WES	F	•	•	•	•	•	HFBS	$$–$$$$	year-round	•	10
287 Osoyoos Lake Veteran's Memorial Park		•	86	45		F	•	•	•	•	•	FBS	$$–$$$$	Apr–Oct	•	10
288 Potholes State Park	•	•	127	50	WES	F	•	•	•	•	•	HFBS	$$–$$$$	year-round	•	10
289 Sherman Pass Overlook		•	10	30		V	•			•		HR	$	mid May–late Sept		10
290 Spring Canyon		•	87	26		F	•	•	•	•		HFBS	$$	year-round	•	14
291 Steamboat Rock State Park		•	142	60	WES	F	•	•		•	•	HFBSR	$$–$$$$	year-round	•	10
292 Sun Lakes–Dry Falls State Park	•	•	192	65	WES	F	•	•	•	•	•	HFBSR	$$–$$$$	Apr–Nov	•	10

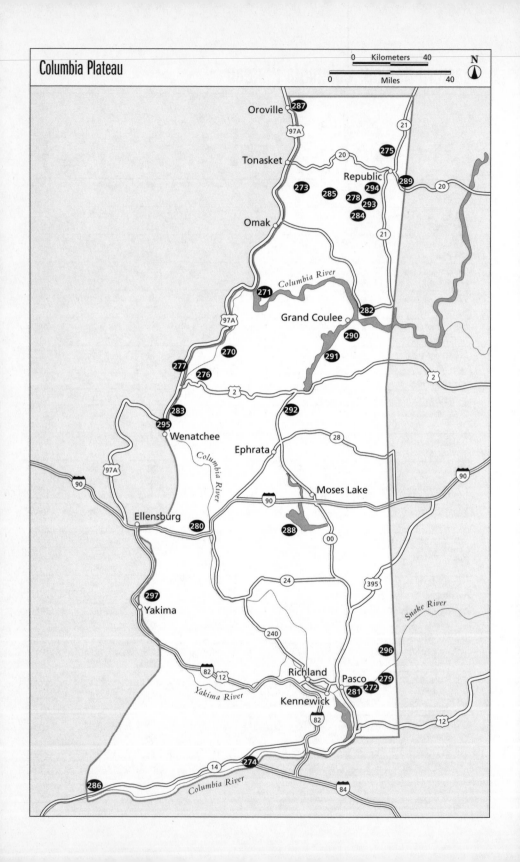

Kilometers 40

Miles 40

N

Oroville 287

97A

21

Tonasket 275

20

Republic

273 285 294 289 20

278 293

284 21

Omak

Columbia River

271

282

97A

Grand Coulee 290

270 291

277

276 2

2

283

295

Wenatchee

292

Columbia River

Ephrata 28

97A

90 Moses Lake 90

90

Ellensburg 00

280

288

24

395

297 Snake River

Yakima

240

296

82 12 Richland Pasco 279

12 281 272

Yakima River Kennewick

82

14 274

286 Columbia River 84

	Group Sites	RV Sites	Total # of sites	Max RV Length	Hookups	Toilets	Showers	Drinking water	Dump station	Pets	Wheelchair	Recreation	Fee	Season	Can reserve	Stay limit
293 Swan Lake	•	•	26	31		V	•		•			HFSC	$$	May–Sept		14
294 Tenmile		•	9	21		V			•			HFC	$	mid May–mid Oct		14
295 Wenatchee Confluence State Park	•	•	60	65	WES	F	•	•	•	•	•	HFBSC	$$–$$$$	year-round	•	10
296 Windust		•	24			F	•	•	•	•		FBS	$$	Apr–Oct	•	
297 Yakima Sportsman State Park		•	67	60	WES	F	•	•	•	•		HF	$$–$$$$	year-round	•	10

Hookups: W = Water E = Electric S = Sewer
Toilets: F = Flush V = Vault P = Pit
Recreation: C = Bicycling/Mountain Biking H = Hiking S = Swimming F = Fishing B = Boating
O = Off-highway driving R = Horseback Riding
Maximum Trailer/RV Length given in feet. Stay Limit given in days.
Fee $ = less than $10; $$ = $10–$15; $$$ = $16–20; $$$$ = more than $20.
If no entry under Fee, camping is free.

270 Beebe Bridge Park

Location: 41 miles northeast of Wenatchee on the Columbia River
GPS: N47 48.617' / W119 58.267'
Elevation: 750 feet
Season: Early Apr to the end of Oct
Sites: 46 sites with electricity and water for tents or RVs
Facilities: Drinking water, restrooms, showers, 2-lane boat ramp, docks, short-term boat moorage, swimming beach, tennis courts, horseshoe pits, playground, dump station
Fee per night: $$
Management: Chelan County Public Utility District, (509) 661-4551; no reservations
Activities: Boating, fishing, swimming, hiking, tennis, volleyball, horseshoes
Finding the campground: From WA 285, 2 miles north of Wenatchee, head north on US 97 for 39 miles to the campground.
The campground: This 56-acre park is great for families who want to spend some quiet time along the mighty Columbia. It is clean, roomy, and only a few miles from Chelan. Chelan Falls and the Chelan Butte Wildlife Area are just across the river. There is plenty to do here, including hiking the trails that run along the riverbank.

271 Bridgeport State Park

Location: About 80 miles north of Wenatchee on Rufus Woods Lake, near Brewster
GPS: N48 00.834' / W119 36.564'

Children enjoy the playground at Bridgeport State Park.

Elevation: 885 feet

Season: Apr to late Oct

Sites: 14 tent sites, 20 sites with water and electrical hookups for RVs no longer than 45 feet, 1 group site for up to 72 people

Facilities: Drinking water, restrooms, showers, dump station, boat ramp, boat docks

Fee per night: $$–$$$$

Management: Washington State Parks and Recreation, (360) 902-8844 (information); (509) 686-7231 (park office)

Activities: Swimming, play area, boating, fishing, waterskiing

Finding the campground: From WA 285, 2 miles north of Wenatchee, head north on US 97 (or use US 97A—the two routes converge after following opposite banks of the Columbia River) for 65 miles to Brewster. From there take WA 173 southeast and drive 12 miles across the Columbia River to Bridgeport and Chief Joseph Dam. Drive over the dam via WA 17 and immediately turn right. Follow the signs for about 2 miles to Bridgeport State Park.

The campground: Ralph Van Slyke, a retired employee of the US Army Corps of Engineers, took it upon himself to create this park in the valley above Chief Joseph Dam in the early 1960s. He used common garden tools to build roads, plant trees and lawn, and install many of the park's amenities. The 800-acre park features 7,500 feet of waterfront and a sandy swimming beach on Rufus Woods Lake, which is actually a section of the Columbia River. The campground is grassy, shady, and very relaxing. There is an adjacent eighteen-hole golf course, clubhouse, and snack bar. A 0.25-mile trail leads to an observation point from where you can look down on the water. Keep an eye out for rattlesnakes. Other local wildlife includes bull snakes, rabbits, mule deer, coyotes, quail, chukars, owls, and songbirds. Don't feed the marmots—there are too many already. Chief Joseph Dam is southwest of the park. Individual campsites can be reserved by visiting https://secure .camis.com/WA/ or calling (888) 226-7688.

272 Charbonneau Park

Location: 15 miles northeast of Pasco on Lake Sacajawea
GPS: N46 15.334' / W118 50.683'
Elevation: 440 feet
Season: Year-round
Sites: 52 sites with electricity for tents or RVs, 2 day-use picnic shelters
Facilities: Drinking water, picnic tables, fire grills, flush toilets, showers, pay phone, dump station, playground, marina, boat docks, boat ramp, marine dump station, campground host
Fee per night: $$–$$$$
Management: US Army Corps of Engineers, (509) 547-2048
Activities: Hiking, fishing, boating, swimming, waterskiing
Finding the campground: From Pasco, drive southeast on US 12 for 5 miles. Just after crossing the Snake River, turn east onto WA 124 at Burbank Heights. Continue east for 8 miles to Sun Harbor Road. Turn left (north) onto Sun Harbor Road and drive 2 miles to the park.
The campground: Located along the historic route of Lewis and Clark, this park is 1.5 miles upriver from Ice Harbor Dam, which turns this stretch of the Snake River into Lake Sacajawea. The 31-mile long reservoir sits amid eastern Washington's channeled scablands and black-rock canyons. The campground is on the eastern shore. At the Ice Harbor Lock and Dam Visitor Center, you can visit the fish viewing room to see salmon migrating upriver. Outside, you can watch barges negotiate the 100-foot-tall locks. Reservations can be made by calling (877) 444-6777 or visiting www.reserveamerica.com.

273 Crawfish Lake

Location: 29 miles northeast of Okanogan on Crawfish Lake
GPS: N48 29.026' / W119 12.875'
Elevation: 4,500 feet
Season: Mid-May to mid-Sept
Sites: 19 sites for tents or self-contained RVs no longer than 31 feet
Facilities: Drinking water, picnic tables, fire grills, vault toilets, firewood
Fee per night: None
Management: Okanogan-Wenatchee National Forest, Tonasket Ranger District, (509) 486-2186; no reservations

Activities: Swimming, boating, fishing, hiking

Finding the campground: From Okanogan drive north on US 97 for 8 miles to Riverside. From there turn northeast across the Okanogan River onto CR 9320, which joins Tunk Creek Road (which in turn becomes Haden Road) and drive 21 miles to the campground.

The campground: If you like isolated and primitive camping with your fishing and hiking, Crawfish Lake Campground is for you. There are plenty of crawfish to catch too. The lake is half in the Okanogan-Wenatchee National Forest and half in the Colville Indian Reservation.

274 Crow Butte Park

Location: 155 miles east of Vancouver on a 1,500-acre island in the Columbia River, near Paterson

GPS: N45 51.281' / W119 51.089'

Elevation: 266 feet

Season: Mid-March through Oct

Sites: 50 sites with full hookups for tents or RVs no longer than 60 feet, primitive campground

Facilities: Drinking water, fire grills, picnic tables, flush toilets, showers, dump station, 3 boat ramps, boat moorage, bathhouse

Fee per night: $$–$$$$

Management: Port of Benton, (509) 375-3060; (509) 875-2644 (caretaker)

Activities: Hiking, fishing, boating (no gas motors), swimming, waterskiing, sailboarding, birding

Finding the campground: From the Tri-Cities (Richland, Pasco, and Kennewick), drive southwest on US 395 for 24 miles. Turn east onto WA 14 and drive 27 miles to the campground on the left.

The campground: Crow Butte is called the "Maui of the Columbia" by campers who return year after year. The winds for sailboarding on the Columbia River are just as reliable as those on Maui, and it is usually as sunny here during the summer months. Like Maui, Crow Butte is even on an island, accessible by bridge from Washington. The park is on the historic Lewis and Clark Trail, adjacent to the McNary (Umatilla) National Wildlife Refuge. Hundreds of thousands of migratory waterfowl spend the winter here each year. Lake Umatilla was created when John Day Dam was built to hold back the Columbia River. The dam flooded some of the original nineteenth-century homesteads, but descendants of the early pioneers still live in the area. The park covers 1,300 acres and features 6.5 miles of shoreline, including 750 feet of unguarded swimming beach. For reservations phone the caretaker at (509) 875-2644.

275 Curlew Lake State Park

Location: 10 miles northeast of Republic on Curlew Lake

GPS: N48 43.182' / W118 39.594'

Elevation: 3,600 feet

Season: Apr through Oct

Sites: 57 tent sites, 25 utility sites (18 full and 7 with water and electric only) for RVs no longer than 40 feet, 2 primitive sites with tie-downs for people who fly in to Ferry County Airport

Facilities: Drinking water, picnic tables, flush toilets, showers, dump station, firewood, 2-lane boat ramp

Fee per night: $$-$$$$

Management: Washington State Parks and Recreation Commission, (360) 902-8844 (information); (509) 775-3592 (park office); no reservations

Activities: Hiking, fishing, boating, waterskiing, swimming, cross-country skiing

Finding the campground: From Republic drive 3 miles east on WA 20; turn north onto WA 21 and drive 7 miles to the campground.

The campground: This 123-acre state park has nearly 1 mile of waterfront on Curlew Lake, including a good swimming beach. This was apparently the site of an early Interior Salish–speaking Indian settlement. Relics, including flint chips, construction tools, and household implements, have been found here and on other parts of the lakeshore. Flint does not exist here naturally, so it was either packed in or acquired through trade with people from another area. The trout and bass fishing are reputed to be excellent here. There is also a 1-mile hiking trail.

276 Daroga State Park

Location: 20 miles north of Wenatchee on the Columbia River, near Entiat

GPS: N47 41.994' / W120 11.631'

Elevation: 708 feet

Season: May 1 through Oct

Sites: 28 sites with water and electrical hookups for RVs no longer than 45 feet, 17 tent sites for campers who boat, bicycle, or walk in

Facilities: Drinking water, picnic tables, vault toilets, moorage space, 2-lane boat ramp, 3 boat docks, restrooms, bathhouse, trailer dump station, boat dump station, basketball and tennis courts, ball field, volleyball area

Fee per night: $$-$$$$

Management: Washington State Parks and Recreation Commission, (360) 902-8844 (information); (509) 664-6380 (park office); no reservations

Activities: Hiking, fishing, boating, waterskiing, sailing, sailboarding, swimming, tennis, basketball, volleyball, baseball, soccer, bicycling, birding, personal watercraft

Finding the campground: From WA 285, 2 miles north of Wenatchee, head north on US 97 for 18 miles to the campground.

The campground: This is a very pleasant campground, with just about everything an active camper would want. It encompasses 90 acres, including 1.5 miles of shoreline on the east side of the Columbia River and a 295-foot swimming beach. Access to the river is easy. Just over 2 miles of trail follow the shoreline.

277 Entiat City Park

Location: 18 miles north of Wenatchee on Lake Entiat, in the town of Entiat
GPS: N47 40.658' / W120 12.789'
Elevation: 708 feet
Season: Apr to mid-Sept
Sites: 50 tent sites, 31 RV sites with full hookups
Facilities: Drinking water, restrooms, showers, boat ramp, docks, playground, swimming area, dump station
Fee per night: $$$$
Management: City of Entiat, (509) 784-1500
Activities: Fishing, swimming, boating
Finding the campground: From WA 285, 2 miles north of Wenatchee, take US 97A north for 16 miles to Entiat. Follow the sign for a right turn to the park.
The campground: This 40-acre park sits on the shore of Lake Entiat, which is actually a portion of the Columbia River that has been dammed. The fish ladders at Rocky Reach Dam, 10 miles farther south, make a fun excursion. Since the campground is essentially in town, grocery shopping is easy, and it is a good place to mingle with the locals. No dogs are allowed in the campground, but motorcycles are permitted. To make reservations visit www.entiat.org/Parks-Recreation/Parks/Entiat-City-Park.aspx.

278 Ferry Lake

Location: About 128 miles northwest of Spokane on Ferry Lake, near Republic
GPS: N48 31.367' / W118 48.583'
Elevation: 3,300 feet
Season: May through Sept
Sites: 9 sites for tents or self-contained RVs no longer than 20 feet
Facilities: Picnic tables, fire grills, vault toilets; no drinking water
Fee per night: $
Management: Colville National Forest, Republic Ranger District, (509) 775-7400; no reservations
Activities: Hiking, fishing, swimming, mountain biking
Finding the campground: From I-90 in Spokane take exit 287 and drive 61 miles west on US 2 to Wilbur. Turn right (north) onto WA 21 and drive 60 miles toward Republic. About 7 miles before Republic, turn left (west) onto FR 53 (Scatter Creek Road) and drive 6 miles to FR 5330. Then turn right (north) and continue a bit over 1 mile to the campground.
The campground: This far into the boonies, campers are thankful for an available campsite no matter what the amenities. This one is on the rustic side; the main appeal is the small lake amid the forest of lodgepole pines. No gas motors are permitted on the lake.

279 Fishhook Park

Location: 25 miles east of Pasco on Lake Sacajawea
GPS: N46 18.900' / W118 45.967'
Elevation: 440 feet
Season: Mid-May to mid-Sept
Sites: 41 sites with water and electricity for tents or RVs, 11 walk-in sites
Facilities: Drinking water, picnic tables, fire grills, flush toilets, dump station, showers, public phone, playground, boat ramp, docks
Fee per night: $$–$$$$
Management: US Army Corps of Engineers, (509) 547-2048
Activities: Hiking, fishing, swimming, boating, waterskiing
Finding the campground: From Pasco drive southeast on US 12 for 5 miles. Just after crossing the Snake River, at Burbank Heights, turn east onto WA 124 and continue for 16 miles east and then northeast on some of the straightest road you will ever see. When WA 124 makes an oblique right turn, take an oblique left onto Fishhook Park Road and continue north for 4 miles to the park.
The campground: This park is truly in the middle of the proverbial nowhere on the eastern shore of the Snake River, where it has been dammed to create Lake Sacajawea. Ice Harbor Dam is 10 miles downriver, Eureka Flat is to the east, and the Juniper Dunes Wilderness is to the west across the river. Any towns nearby are on the other side of the river, so a boat would be good transportation. The wooded campground sits on the historic Lewis and Clark Trail, and water access is easy. Tents on the lawns must be moved every two days. The park gates are locked from 10 p.m. to 6 a.m. To make reservations visit www.recreation.gov or call (877) 444-6777.

280 Ginkgo Petrified Forest State Park

Location: 32 miles east of Ellensburg on Wanapum Lake, near Vantage
GPS: N46 53.996' / W119 59.520'
Elevation: 571 feet
Season: Mar through Oct
Sites: 50 sites with full hookups for RVs no longer than 60 feet, 1 wheelchair-accessible site
Facilities: Drinking water, picnic tables, fire grills, flush toilets, showers, firewood, 2-lane boat ramp, bathhouse, concession stand, binocular rentals, interpretive center
Fee per night: $$$$
Management: Washington State Parks and Recreation Commission, (360) 902-8844 (information); (509) 856-2700 (park office)
Activities: Hiking, waterskiing, boating, swimming, fishing
Finding the campground: From Ellensburg drive east on I-90 for 29 miles; take exit 136 at Vantage and drive 3 miles south on Wanapum Road to the park.
The campground: One of the primary attractions of this park is a petrified forest—the remains of trees that grew here as long as twenty-five million years ago. It was discovered in the early 1930s during highway construction and includes many samples of petrified ginkgo, a tree that no longer grows anywhere in the wild.

The site actually encompasses Wanapum State Recreation Area, where the campsites are located, and Ginkgo State Park, which is 7 miles to the north. The latter is a day-use area where you can view the petrified forest. Wanapum State Recreation Area, named for a now-extinct Native American tribe that once inhabited the area, covers 7,500 acres and features 5 miles of shoreline on man-made Wanapum Lake, a dammed segment of the Columbia River. Three miles of hiking trails and a 1-mile interpretive trail meander through the area. Individual campsites can be reserved by visiting https://secure.camis.com/WA/ or calling (888) 226-7688.

281 Hood Park

Location: About 6 miles southeast of Pasco on the Snake River
GPS: N46 12.823' / W119 00.780'
Elevation: 340 feet
Season: Mid-May to mid-Sept
Sites: 67 sites with electric hookups for tents or self-contained RVs of any length, 1 day-use group picnic shelter
Facilities: Drinking water, fire grills, picnic tables, showers, flush toilets, dump station, electricity, playground, boat ramp, docks
Fee per night: $$-$$$$
Management: US Army Corps of Engineers, (509) 547-2048
Activities: Fishing, boating, basketball, horseshoe pits
Finding the campground: From Pasco drive southeast on US 12 for 5 miles. Just after crossing the Snake River, at Burbank Heights, turn east onto WA 124 and follow the signs for about 1 mile to the park.
The campground: This easy-access campground on the Snake River has all the amenities and is just over a mile from the Snake's confluence with the Columbia. It is well developed and offers good access to both rivers. This is a very pleasant vacation spot, yet close to civilization. The park gates are locked from 10 p.m. to 6 a.m. To make reservations visit www.recreation.gov or call (877) 444-6777.

282 Keller Ferry

Location: 110 miles northeast of Wenatchee on Franklin D. Roosevelt Lake, near Wilbur
GPS: N47 55.605' / W118 41.422'
Elevation: 393 feet
Season: Year-round, weather permitting
Sites: 55 sites for tents or self-contained RVs no longer than 16 feet
Facilities: Drinking water, fire grills, picnic tables, flush toilets, dump station, ice, playground, boat ramp (fee), docks, fuel, marine dump station
Fee per night: $$
Management: Coulee Dam National Recreation Area, (509) 633-3830, ext. 37
Activities: Fishing, boating, swimming, waterskiing, wildlife viewing

Finding the campground: From Wenatchee take US 97 north for 16 miles and then head east on US 2 for 75 miles to Wilbur. From there take WA 21 north for 14 miles to the campground. Alternatively, from Grand Coulee Dam take WA 174 southeast for 19 miles to Wilbur; drive north via WA 21 from there.

The campground: This campground is adjacent to the Keller Ferry, which is a main link between the Colville Indian Reservation and the south side of the Columbia River. The ferry is part of the Washington State Ferries system, and the ride is free. The campground is large, wooded, and right on the lake, which is actually a dammed segment of the Columbia River. The camp feels a bit busy in the summer, but it is still nice to spend a few days here. There is a lifeguard on duty from July through Labor Day weekend. To make reservations visit www.recreation.gov or call (877) 444-6777.

283 Lincoln Rock State Park

Location: 9 miles north of Wenatchee on the Columbia River
GPS: N47 32.148' / W120 17.016'
Elevation: 700 feet

No tent or RV? No problem. This is one of five cabins for rent at Lincoln Rock State Park.

Season: Mar through Oct

Sites: 94 sites including 27 tent sites and 67 utility sites for tents or RVs no longer than 65 feet, 4 cabins

Facilities: Drinking water, restrooms, showers, 3-lane boat ramp, boat trailer parking, short-term moorage, playground, volleyball area, tennis court, horseshoe pits, amphitheater, dump station

Fee per night: $$–$$$$

Management: Washington State Parks and Recreation Commission, (360) 902-8844 (information); (509) 884-8702 (park office)

Activities: Hiking, fishing, swimming, personal watercraft, sailboarding, bicycling, roller-skating, tennis, basketball, volleyball, soccer, softball, horseshoe pits, cross-country skiing

Finding the campground: From WA 285, 2 miles north of Wenatchee, take US 97 north for 7 miles to the campground, which is just north of Rocky Reach Dam.

The campground: Tucked along the east bank of the Columbia, 80-acre Lincoln Rock State Park is a popular place for boaters, swimmers, and anglers to access the river. It has nearly 0.5 mile of waterfront. For walkers and bicyclists, the park has plenty of roads and paved trails, which offer views of Lincoln Rock across the river. This outcropping is said to resemble the profile of Abraham Lincoln. It reportedly got its name in 1889 after a photo of it won first prize in a *Ladies Home Journal* contest. Individual campsites and cabins can be reserved by visiting https://secure.camis .com/WA/ or calling (888) 226-7688.

284 Long Lake

Location: About 130 miles northwest of Spokane on Long Lake, near Republic

GPS: N48 30.050' / W118 48.583'

Elevation: 3,250 feet

Season: May through Sept

Sites: 12 sites for tents or self-contained RVs no longer than 21 feet

Facilities: Drinking water, fire grills, picnic tables, vault toilets, boat ramp

Fee per night: $

Management: Colville National Forest, Republic Ranger District, (509) 447-7300; no reservations

Activities: Hiking, fly fishing, swimming, mountain biking

Finding the campground: From I-90 in Spokane take exit 287 and drive 61 miles west on US 2 to Wilbur. Turn north onto WA 21 toward Republic and drive 60 miles. About 7 miles before you reach Republic, turn left (west) onto FR 53 (Scatter Creek Road). Drive 8 miles, turn left (south) onto FR 400, and drive 1.5 miles to the campground.

The campground: Despite its name, Long Lake is the smallest of the three lakes in this vicinity (Swan and Ferry Lakes are the others). An easy trail runs around the perimeter of this lake, which sits in a forest of lodgepole pines. Fly fishing is the main activity, but there are some good trails in the area for hiking and mountain biking. Boats with gas motors are not allowed on the lake.

285 Lyman Lake

Location: 57 miles northeast of Okanogan on Lyman Lake
GPS: N48 31.621' / W119 01.273'
Elevation: 2,900 feet
Season: Mid-May to mid-Sept
Sites: 4 sites for tents or self-contained RVs no longer than 31 feet
Facilities: Picnic tables, fire grills, vault toilets, firewood; no drinking water
Fee per night: None
Management: Okanogan-Wenatchee National Forest, Tonasket Ranger District, (509) 486-2186; no reservations
Activities: Fishing
Finding the campground: From Okanogan head north on US 97 for 29 miles to Tonasket. Turn east onto WA 20 and drive 12.5 miles. Then turn right (southeast) onto Aeneas Valley Road and go 13 miles. Turn right (south) onto Lyman Lake–Moses Meadow Road and drive 2.5 miles to the campground entrance.
The campground: This campground is very small and very primitive, but for the self-reliant camper it offers a rewarding experience. Plan on being alone, because few people venture this far into the Okanogan-Wenatchee National Forest. The lake appears too small for fish, but they are reputed to be there.

286 Maryhill State Park

Location: 79 miles south of Yakima on the Columbia River, near Goldendale
GPS: N45 40.879' / W120 50.213'
Elevation: 161 feet
Season: Year-round
Sites: 20 tent sites, 50 sites with full hookups for RVs no longer than 60 feet
Facilities: Drinking water, picnic tables, flush toilets, showers, firewood, dump station, boat ramp, docks, unguarded swimming beach, bathhouse
Fee per night: $$–$$$$
Management: Washington State Parks and Recreation Commission, (360) 902-8844 (information); (509) 773-5007 (park office)
Activities: Hiking, boating, fishing, swimming, waterskiing, sailboarding
Finding the campground: From Yakima drive south on US 97 for 79 miles to the park on the Columbia River. To get there from Vancouver, take exit 1 off I-5 onto WA 14 and drive 108 miles east to the campground. The campground is 1 mile south of WA 14 on US 97.
The campground: The park covers nearly 100 acres and features 1 mile of waterfront on the Columbia River, which has been slowed here by breakwaters to make access easier. There is a 10-day limit on camping here during summer because this is such a nice place to take a vacation. Most of the sites are shaded and grassy, and the campground offers more amenities than most in the state. Fishing for salmon and sturgeon is perhaps the most popular activity. Gas stations and

restaurants are right across the river at Biggs Junction. Individual campsites can be reserved year-round by visiting https://secure.camis.com/WA/ or calling (888) 226-7688.

Three miles to the east of the state park, the Maryhill Museum of Art sits well above the river, offering great vistas. Its tree-shaded grounds are a welcome respite on a hot summer day. The museum and its grounds are on the National Register of Historic Places. The museum was built in 1926 by Sam Hill as a home for his wife Mary. She did not take to its location, and Hill's friends convinced him to convert the home to a museum. One of those friends was Queen Marie of Romania, granddaughter of Queen Victoria, and some of her belongings are exhibited in the museum. There are also many authentic sketches and replicas of sculptures by the French artist Auguste Rodin, as well as Native American artifacts.

Hill, who owned 7,000 acres here, also tried to establish a colony of Belgian Quakers before World War II. The plan did not work, but one of his successes is a full-scale model of Stonehenge, which he built between 1918 and 1929. It sits adjacent to the park overlooking the Columbia. Hill was a Quaker who was appalled by the carnage of World War I. He had visited England's Stonehenge and built this replica to honor the fallen WWI soldiers of Klickitat County.

287 Osoyoos Lake Veteran's Memorial Park

Location: 48 miles north of Okanogan on Osoyoos Lake, near Oroville
GPS: N48 56.872' / W119 26.076'
Elevation: 912 feet
Season: Apr through Oct
Sites: 86 sites for tents or self-contained RVs no longer than 45 feet (including 2 that are wheelchair accessible)
Facilities: Drinking water, picnic tables, fire grills, flush toilets, showers, firewood, dump station, store, cafe, playground, bathhouse, concession, boat ramp
Fee per night: $$–$$$$
Management: City of Oroville, (509) 476-2926; (509) 476-3321 (park office)
Activities: Swimming, boating, fishing, waterskiing, ice skating, sledding, ice fishing
Finding the campground: From Okanogan head north on US 97 for 47 miles to Oroville. Continue north for 1 mile to the campground.
The campground: Osoyoos Lake stretches across the US-Canadian border and is advertised in Canada as that country's warmest freshwater lake. The 47-acre park has nearly 1.5 miles of shoreline and 300 feet of swimming beach. This site has been a gathering place for as long as people have known about it. Native American tribes from all over the Northwest rendezvoused at this part of the lake. Later, much later, it became the site of the Okanogan County and International Fair, which featured an Indian encampment, a grandstand show with local talent, horse races, a rodeo, and an exhibition hall. Migrant orchard workers were housed here during World War II to alleviate labor shortages. Until the 1950s, when the site became a state park, travelers and Oroville residents flocked here to relax and be rejuvenated. To make a reservation visit https://secure.camis.com/Osoyoos/ or call the City of Oroville at (509) 476-2926.

288 Potholes State Park

Location: 24 miles south of Moses Lake on Potholes Reservoir
GPS: N46 58.684' / W119 21.272'
Elevation: 1,040 feet
Season: Year-round
Sites: 60 sites with full hookups for RVs no longer than 50 feet, 61 tent sites, 5 cabins, 1 group site for up to 50 people
Facilities: Drinking water, picnic tables, fire grills, flush toilets, coin-operated showers, dump station, store, playground, firewood (fee), boat ramp
Fee per night: $$–$$$$
Management: Washington State Parks and Recreation Commission, (360) 902-8844 (information); (509) 346-2759 (park office)
Activities: Hiking, boating, swimming, waterskiing, fishing
Finding the campground: From Moses Lake drive 3 miles east on I-90. Take exit 179 and head southeast onto WA 17. Drive 10 miles, turn right (west) onto WA 262, and drive 11 miles to the park entrance on the right.
The campground: Potholes State Park covers 640 acres and features over 1 mile of shoreline that includes a good swimming beach. Potholes is named for, well, the potholes—great big ones. They are actually depressions in the sand dunes that were created by glaciers during the ice age and subsequently flooded. Some of them are large enough to be called lakes. This desert park is near the center of the Columbia Basin—a terrain consisting of sand dunes, lakes, and rocky canyons. A good hiking trail follows the Frenchman Hills Wasteway. Local birdlife includes white pelicans, sandhill cranes, and great blue herons. Fish include largemouth and smallmouth bass, rainbow trout, crappie, bluegill, and perch. Individual campsites can be reserved year-round by visiting https://secure.camis.com/WA/ or calling (888) 226-7688.

289 Sherman Pass Overlook

Location: About 100 miles northwest of Spokane, near Republic
GPS: N48 36.300' / W118 27.767'
Elevation: 5,400 feet
Season: Mid-May to late September
Sites: 10 sites for tents or self-contained RVs no longer than 30 feet
Facilities: Drinking water, fire grills, picnic tables, vault toilets
Fee per night: $
Management: Colville National Forest, Three Rivers/Kettle Falls Ranger District, (509) 738-7700; no reservations
Activities: Hiking, trail riding
Finding the campground: From I-90 in Spokane take exit 281 and head north and then northwest on US 395 for 81 miles to Kettle Falls. Continue west on WA 20 for about 20 miles to the campground.

The campground: This is a very basic campground, but it is an excellent stopover if you come to enjoy the views from the highest elevation highway open year-round in the state. From 5,575-foot Sherman Pass, trails lead along both sides of the highway and out to some of the high peaks.

290 Spring Canyon

Location: 3 miles east of Grand Coulee Dam on Franklin D. Roosevelt Lake
GPS: N47 55.984' / W118 56.344'
Elevation: 393 feet
Season: Year-round
Sites: 87 sites for tents or self-contained RVs no longer than 26 feet
Facilities: Drinking water, fire grills, picnic tables, flush toilets, dump station, playground, boat ramp (fee), docks, cafe
Fee per night: $$
Management: Lake Roosevelt National Recreation Area, (509) 633-3830, ext. 37
Activities: Hiking, fishing, boating, swimming, waterskiing, wildlife viewing, free ranger-guided canoe trips, historical tours, campfire talks
Finding the campground: From the town of Grand Coulee, drive east on WA 174 for 3 miles to the campground entrance.
The campground: You cannot go wrong camping on Franklin D. Roosevelt Lake in the Lake Roosevelt National Recreation Area. The "lake" is actually a segment of the Columbia River, held back by Grand Coulee Dam 2.5 miles downriver. This is a great campground, with lots of ranger support services. It is very popular with families, and there are plenty of things to do in the nearby towns of Grand Coulee, Coulee Dam, and Electric City. Coulee City is 34 miles south of the campground, at the south end of Banks Lake. To make reservations visit www.recreation.gov or call (877) 444-6777.

291 Steamboat Rock State Park

Location: 15 miles southwest of Grand Coulee Dam on Banks Lake
GPS: N47 51.138' / W119 07.986'
Elevation: 1,571 feet
Season: Year-round; limited services in winter
Sites: 100 sites with full hookups for RVs no longer than 60 feet, 26 tent sites, 2 wheelchair-accessible sites, 2 primitive tent sites, 12 nonreservable boat-in sites
Facilities: Drinking water, picnic tables, fire grills, flush toilets, cafe, playground, coin-operated showers, swimming beach, 4 boat ramps, handling docks, 6 mooring buoys, 2 fish-cleaning stations, public phones, bathhouse, concession
Fee per night: $$–$$$$
Management: Washington State Parks and Recreation Commission, (360) 902-8844 (information); (509) 633-1304 (park office)

Activities: Hiking, boating, fishing, swimming, climbing, horseback riding, waterskiing, scuba diving, sailboarding, cross-country skiing, snowshoeing, ice fishing, kite flying, metal detecting. Hunting with shotguns is allowed on adjacent lands administered jointly by the Washington Department of Fish and Wildlife and the parks commission. A permit, available at most sporting goods stores, is required.

Finding the campground: From the town of Grand Coulee, drive southwest on WA 155 for 8 miles along Banks Lake to the park entrance on your right. Follow the signs to the camping area 2 miles ahead.

The campground: This park covers 3,520 acres, including 9.5 miles of shoreline on Banks Lake, a 26-mile-long, 27,000-acre reservoir of irrigation water. The campground is located on a large peninsula that juts into the lake, and prominent on this peninsula is 800-foot Steamboat Rock, a flat-topped butte made of columnar basalt. Banks Lake is a wildlife preserve, and there are two bald eagle roosts on the butte. The park also attracts American white pelicans, one of the largest and most spectacular birds, according to John James Audubon. Keep an eye out for bobcats, cougars, and rattlesnakes. Fish in the lake include largemouth and smallmouth bass, yellow perch, rainbow trout, walleye, kokanee, black crappie, bullhead, and whitefish. Thirty-four miles of hiking trails crisscross the park, and equestrian trails can be found in nearby Northrup Canyon State Park. Winter here at Steamboat attracts snowmobilers, cross-country skiers, snowshoers, and ice fishers.

Steamboat requires advance reservations. Individual campsites can be reserved year-round by visiting https://secure.camis.com/WA/ or calling (888) 226-7688. There are no drop-in sites except for a boat-in tent area that is inaccessible by car. There is a large day-use area.

292 Sun Lakes–Dry Falls State Park

Location: 38 miles north of the town of Moses Lake, near Coulee City
GPS: N47 35.402' / W119 23.672'
Elevation: 918 feet
Season: Apr through Nov
Sites: 152 tent sites, 39 sites (with full hookups) for RVs no longer than 65 feet, 1 tent-only group site for up to 75 people
Facilities: Drinking water, picnic tables, flush toilets, showers, dump station, laundry room, ice, swimming pool, firewood, stables, visitor center, boat ramp, environmental learning center, golf course, cafe, general store, boat rentals
Fee per night: $$–$$$$
Management: Washington State Parks and Recreation Commission, (360) 902-8844 (information); (509) 632-5291 (park office)
Activities: Hiking, mountain biking, rock climbing, swimming, boating, fishing, golf, canoeing, horseback riding
Finding the campground: From I-90 in the town of Moses Lake, head north on WA 17 for 35.5 miles. Turn right (east) onto Park Lake Road and drive 2.5 miles along the east shore of Park Lake to the park.
The campground: Sun Lakes State Park is located in the Lower Grand Coulee, below and including Dry Falls. Four of the seven lakes in the park were originally plunge pools formed by the falls. The campground is on Park Lake, which has a paved boat ramp and is the most popular with

boaters, personal watercraft users, and water-skiers. There is also a 300-foot beach. Motorized watercraft are prohibited on Dry Falls Lake. The park covers 4,000 acres and offers 14 miles of freshwater shoreline. The lakes are stocked with rainbow and German brown trout and are popular fly-fishing destinations. For hikers the park has about 15 miles of trails through the rocky desert and canyons. More than 5 miles of trails are open to mountain bikers. Local wildlife includes deer, yellow-bellied marmots, pheasants, and quail. The canyons, called channeled scablands, were carved by the Columbia River during the last ice age. Rock climbing is permitted, but rattlesnakes are common in the area. Sun Lakes State Park also includes the Lake Lenore Caves, where visitors may view petroglyphs, ancient Native American cave drawings. Reservations are available April 15 through October 15 and are advised for the summer months. Individual campsites can be reserved by visiting https://secure.camis.com/WA/ or calling (888) 226-7688.

Sun Lakes State Park Resort (509-632-5291), a separate park within Sun Lakes State Park, is operated by a concessionaire. The facilities are more developed. Cabins and trailers are available for rent, and there are 110 sites for RVs of any length. The concessionaire also runs the golf course and marina, which rents boats. The nine-hole golf course, built on a dredged lakebed, is the only one located within a Washington state park.

293 Swan Lake

Location: 129 miles northwest of Spokane on Swan Lake, near Republic
GPS: N48 30.767' / W118 50.017'
Elevation: 3,700 feet
Season: May through Sept
Sites: 25 sites for tents or self-contained RVs no longer than 31 feet, 1 group site
Facilities: Drinking water, picnic tables fire grills, vault toilets, firewood, boat docks, boat ramp
Fee per night: $$
Management: Colville National Forest, Republic Ranger District, (509) 775-7400; no reservations
Activities: Hiking, fishing, swimming, mountain biking
Finding the campground: From I-90 in Spokane take exit 287 and drive west for 61 miles to Wilbur. Turn north onto WA 21 toward Republic and drive 60 miles. About 7 miles before you reach Republic, turn left (west) onto FR 53 (Scatter Creek Road) and drive 8 miles west and south to the campground.
The campground: There are some lakefront campsites at Swan Lake, a bonus for anglers. This camp is more comfortable than others in the area (Ferry Lake and Long Lake), and so it is more popular. It is nestled in a lodgepole pine forest in the Sanpoil River drainage. Boats with gas motors are not permitted on the lake.

294 Tenmile

Location: 118 miles northwest of Spokane on the Sanpoil River, near Republic
GPS: N48 31.083' / W118 44.217'
Elevation: 2,170 feet

Season: Mid-May to mid-Oct
Sites: 9 sites for tents or self-contained RVs no longer than 21 feet
Facilities: Picnic tables, vault toilets, dump station; no drinking water
Fee per night: $
Management: Colville National Forest, Republic Ranger District, (509) 775-7400; no reservations
Activities: Hiking, fishing, mountain biking
Finding the campground: From I-90 in Spokane take exit 287 and drive west for 61 miles to Wilbur. Turn north onto WA 21 toward Republic and drive 57 miles to the campground entrance.
The campground: Situated where Tenmile Creek enters the Sanpoil River, this campground makes a good overnight stop between Wilbur and Republic. It is rustic, but you cannot beat camping along the river.

295 Wenatchee Confluence State Park

Location: 2 miles north of Wenatchee on the Wenatchee River
GPS: N47 27.480' / W120 19.674'

An apple orchard blooms near Wenatchee. Fruit trees flourish in eastern Washington, and the rest of the nation reaps the benefits.

Elevation: 630 feet

Season: Year-round

Sites: 8 tent sites, 51 sites with full hookups for tents or RVs no longer than 65 feet, 1 group site for up to 300 people

Facilities: Drinking water, restrooms, showers, dump station, 2-lane boat ramp, ball field, picnic shelter, playground, sport courts

Fee per night: $$–$$$$

Management: Washington State Parks and Recreation Commission, (360) 902-8844 (information); (509) 664-6373 (park office)

Activities: Hiking, fishing, boating, waterskiing, sailing, sailboarding, swimming, tennis, basketball, volleyball, baseball, soccer, bicycling, birding, interpretive walks, cross-country skiing

Finding the campground: Simply take the main road (WA 285/Wenatchee Avenue) north out of Wenatchee for 2 miles to the Wenatchee River. Follow signs to the park at the end of Olds Station Road.

The campground: This 200-acre park has a 2-mile shoreline trail and a 97-acre natural area and wetland wildlife habitat. The campground is on one side of the Wenatchee River, and the preserve is on the other. They are connected by a pedestrian bridge near the Wenatchee's confluence with the Columbia. The nature trail has 16 viewing stations. This is a park with a lot of variety. It is relatively peaceful, yet all kinds of activities are right at hand. Individual campsites and the group site can be reserved year-round by visiting https://secure.camis.com/WA/ or calling (888) 226-7688.

296 Windust

Location: About 40 miles northeast of Pasco on Lake Sacajawea

GPS: N46 31.984' / W118 35.000'

Elevation: 540 feet

Season: Apr to Oct—scheduled to reopen May 2013

Sites: 24 primitive sites for tents or self-contained RVs

Facilities: Drinking water, picnic tables, fire grills, flush toilets, dump station, pay phone, playground, boat ramp, docks

Fee per night: $$

Management: US Army Corps of Engineers, (509) 547-2048

Activities: Swimming, boating, fishing

Finding the campground: From the interchange of US 12 and US 395 in Pasco, drive southeast on US 12 for 2 miles. Turn left (east) onto the Pasco-Kahlotus Road. Drive 30 miles to Burr Canyon Road; turn right and drive 6 miles to the park.

The campground: They do not call this campground in the coulees of southeastern Washington Windust for nothing. The lake, actually a dammed segment of the Snake River, provides great relief from the hot weather, and the park is right at the water's edge, 3 miles downriver from Lower Monumental Dam. There is a three-day minimum stay on holiday weekends, and tents set up on lawns must be moved every two days. To make reservations visit www.recreation.gov or call (877) 44-6777.

297 Yakima Sportsman State Park

Location: 1 mile east of Yakima on the Yakima River
GPS: N46 35.736' / W120 27.156'
Elevation: 1,100 feet
Season: Year-round
Sites: 30 tent sites, 37 sites (with full hookups) for RVs no longer than 60 feet
Facilities: Drinking water, picnic tables, fire grills, flush toilets, coin-operated showers (fee), dump station, playground
Fee per night: $$–$$$$
Management: Washington State Parks and Recreation Commission, (360) 902-8844 (information); (509) 575-2774 (park office)
Activities: Hiking, fishing, birding
Finding the campground: From I-82 in Yakima take exit 34 and drive less than 1 mile east on WA 24 to the park.
The campground: This 50-acre park has 3.6 miles of waterfront on the east side of the Yakima River, just across the water from the city of Yakima. Swimming is not allowed in the river, but kayaking and rafting are popular. There is a variety of ponds and vegetation in the park, nurtured first by the Yakima Sportsman Association, then by Yakima County, and now by the state. Fishing ponds in the park are for children under age 16. The river is open seasonally to adult anglers. The Yakima Canyon, through which the river passes on its way toward Yakima, is a shrubby steppe that hosts rare Washington birds including the sage thrasher, long-billed curlew, and sage sparrow. The Bureau of Land Management considers this a vanishing habitat. Individual campsites can be reserved year-round by visiting https://secure.camis.com/WA/ or calling (888) 226-7688.

Eastern Region: Spokane and Northeastern Washington

	Group Sites	RV Sites	Total # of sites	Max RV Length	Hookups	Toilets	Showers	Drinking water	Dump station	Pets	Wheelchair	Recreation	Fee	Season	Can reserve	Stay limit
298 Big Meadow Lake		•	16	32	V					•	•	HF		May–Sept		14
299 Boundary Dam		•	4		V					•		HFBRC		year-round		14
300 Browns Lake		•	18	21	V					•	•	HFB	$$	late May–late Sept		14
301 Canyon Creek		•	12	30	V	•				•	•	HF	$	mid Apr–late Oct		14
302 Clover Leaf			9		V	•		•				FBS	$–$$	year-round		14
303 Douglas Falls Grange Park		•	8		F	•	•	•				H		Apr–Nov		7
304 Dragoon Creek		•	22		V	•		•				F		Apr–Sept		3
305 East Sullivan		•	38	55	V	•	•	•		•	•	HFBS	$$$	mid May–Sept	•	14
306 Edgewater		•	23	20	V	•		•				FB	$$$	late May–early Sept	•	14
307 Evans		•	43	26	F	•	•	•				FBS	$–$$	year-round		14
308 Flodelle Creek		•	8	20	V	•		•				HFC		year-round		7
309 Fort Spokane		•	67	26	F	•		•		•		FBS	$$	year-round	•	14
310 Gifford		•	42	20	P	•		•				FBS	$$	year-round		14
311 Gillette		•	30	31	V	•		•		•	•	HFBSO	$$	mid May–late Sept		14
312 Haag Cove		•	16	26	P	•		•				FBS	$–$$	year-round		14
313 Hawk Creek		•	21	16	P	•		•				HFBS	$$	year-round		14
314 Hunters		•	39	26	F	•		•				FBS	$–$$	year-round		14
315 Kamloops Island			14		P			•				HFSB	$–$$	year-round		14
316 Kettle Falls		•	75	26	F	•	•	•		•	•	FSB	$$	year-round		14
317 Lake Ellen		•	15	22	V					•	•	FS	$	mid Apr–mid Oct		14
318 Lake Gillette		•	14	31	V	•		•		•	•	HFBSO	$$–$$$	mid May–late Sept		14
319 Lake Leo		•	8	15	P	•		•				HFS	$$	mid May–mid Sept		14
320 Lake Thomas		•	16		V	•		•				HFBCO	$$	mid May–late Sept		14
321 Little Twin Lakes		•	20	16	P			•				FBO		mid May–late Sept		14
322 Marcus Island		•	21	20	P	•		•				FSB	$–$$	year-round		14
323 Mill Pond		•	10	21	V	•		•				HFB	$$$	late May–early Sept		14
324 Mount Spokane State Park	•	•	9	30	F	•		•				HRC	$$–$$$$	Snowmelt–Sept 15		10

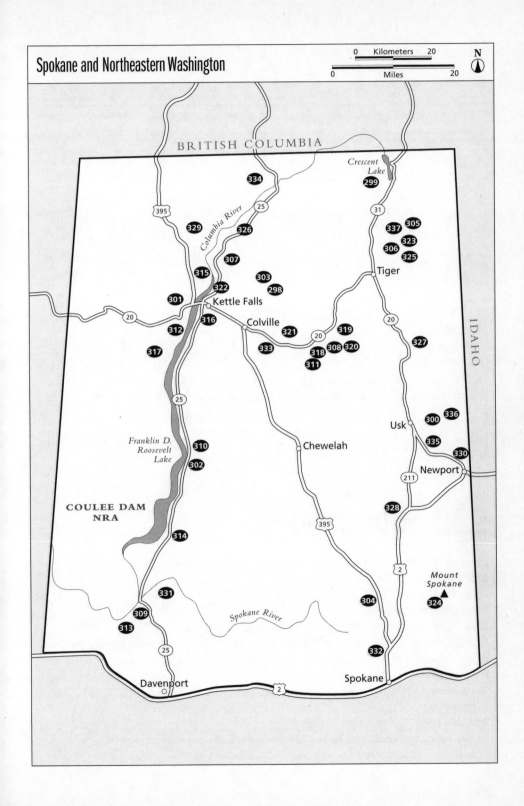

Spokane and Northeastern Washington

0   Kilometers   20

0   Miles   20

N

BRITISH COLUMBIA

Crescent Lake

334

299

395

25

31

329   Columbia River   326

337   305

307

306   323

315

325

322   303

Tiger

301   298

20   Kettle Falls

316   Colville   20

312   321   319

317   333   327

318   308   320

311

25

300   336

Franklin D. Roosevelt Lake   310   Usk   335

302   330

Chewelah   Newport

COULEE DAM NRA   211

328

314   395

2

Mount Spokane

331   324

309

313   304

25   Spokane River

332

Davenport   2   Spokane

IDAHO

	Group Sites	RV Sites	Total # of sites	Max RV Length	Hookups	Toilets	Showers	Drinking water	Dump station	Pets	Wheelchair	Recreation	Fee	Season	Can reserve	Stay limit
325 Noisy Creek	•	19		35		V		•		•		HFB	$$$	late May–early Sept	•	14
326 North Gorge	•	12		26		P		•		•		FBS	$–$$	year-round		14
327 Panhandle	•	13		30		V		•		•		HFSBCO	$	late May–late Sept	•	14
328 Pend Oreille County Park	•	36				F	•	•		•		H	$$	Mem Day–Lab Day	•	
329 Pierre Lake	•	16		24		V				•		HFBS	$	mid Apr–mid Oct		14
330 Pioneer Park	•	17		24		V		•		•	•	FBS	$$$	late May–late Sept	•	14
331 Porcupine Bay	•	31		25		F		•		•	•	HFBS	$$	year-round		14
332 Riverside State Park	•	32		45		F	•	•		•	•	HFBROC	$$–$$$$	year-round	•	10
333 Rocky Lake	•	7				V		•		•		FB		year-round		7
334 Sheep Creek	•	11		20		V		•		•		HFO		year-round		7
335 Skookum Creek	•	10				V		•		•		HFB		year-round		7
336 South Skookum Lake	•	25		30		V		•		•	•	HFB	$$$	late May–late Sept		14
337 West Sullivan	•	10		30		V		•		•		HFB	$$$	mid May–Sept	•	14

Hookups: W = Water E = Electric S = Sewer
Toilets: F = Flush V = Vault P = Pit
Recreation: C = Bicycling/Mountain Biking H = Hiking S = Swimming F = Fishing B = Boating
O = Off-highway driving R = Horseback Riding
Maximum Trailer/RV Length given in feet. Stay Limit given in days.
Fee $ = less than $10; $$ = $10–$15; $$$ = $16–20; $$$$ = more than $20.
If no entry under Fee, camping is free.

298 Big Meadow Lake

Location: 99 miles north of Spokane on Big Meadow Lake, near Colville
GPS: N48 43.733' / W117 33.717'
Elevation: 3,400 feet
Season: May through Sept
Sites: 16 sites for tents or self-contained RVs no longer than 32 feet
Facilities: Fire grills, picnic tables, vault toilets, boat ramp, fishing pier, wheelchair-accessible nature trail, wildlife viewing platform, environmental education lab; no drinking water
Fee per night: None
Management: Colville National Forest, Three Rivers/Kettle Falls Ranger District, (509) 738-7700; no reservations
Activities: Hiking, fishing, wildlife viewing
Finding the campground: From I-90 in Spokane take exit 281 and head north on US 395. Drive 71 miles to Colville and turn east onto WA 20. Drive for 1 mile and turn left (north) onto

Colville-Aladdin-Northport Road. Drive 20 miles to Meadow Creek Road, which is 1 mile past Aladdin. Turn right (east) onto rough and rocky Meadow Creek Road and drive 7 miles to the campground.

The campground: The amenities are not much at this campground, and the road may give your passengers fits, but the location is idyllic. The campground sits at the edge of 70-acre Big Meadow Lake and is quiet and pristine. It is rarely full.

299 Boundary Dam

Location: About 105 miles north of Spokane on the Pend Oreille River, near Metaline Falls
GPS: N48 59.229' / W117 20.848'
Elevation: 2,130 feet
Season: Year-round
Sites: 4 primitive sites for tents or self-contained RVs
Facilities: Picnic tables, vault toilet; no drinking water
Fee per night: None
Management: Bureau of Land Management, (509) 536-1200; no reservations
Activities: Hiking, fishing, boating, bicycling, climbing, horseback riding, berry picking
Finding the campground: From Spokane take US 2 north for 32 miles to WA 211. Turn left (north) onto WA 211 and follow it for 15 miles to Usk and its junction with WA 20. Continue north, now on WA 20, for 31 miles to Tiger. From Tiger drive north for another 13 miles on what is now WA 31. Continue 0.5 mile past Metaline and turn left onto Boundary Road (CR 62). There should be signs for Gardner Cave and Crawford State Park (day use only). Drive 11.5 miles to reach the access road to the dam.
The campground: The Boundary Dam area covers about 1,000 acres of wilderness terrain in northeastern Washington. The campground is in a beautiful forested setting on the west bank of the Pend Oreille River, which is hemmed in by precipitous rock walls that rise 100 to 200 feet. The Salmo Priest Wilderness is on the east side of the river. Local wildlife includes elk, bears, and deer. Rainbow trout are not too hard to catch. Huckleberries are ready to pick beginning in early July.

300 Browns Lake

Location: About 57 miles north of Spokane on Browns Lake, near Newport
GPS: N48 26.167' / W117 11.717'
Elevation: 3,800 feet
Season: Late May to late Sept
Sites: 18 sites for tents or self-contained RVs no longer than 21 feet
Facilities: Picnic tables, vault toilets, boat ramp; no drinking water
Fee per night: $$
Management: Colville National Forest, Newport Ranger District, (509) 447-7300; no reservations.
Activities: Hiking, fly fishing, canoeing

Finding the campground: Drive north from Spokane on US 2 for 32 miles to WA 211. Turn left (north) onto WA 211 and continue for 15 miles to Usk. Cross the Pend Oreille River via Kings Lake Road (which eventually becomes FR 5030) and stay on it all the way to Browns Lake, a distance of about 10 miles.

The campground: You pass both South and North Skookum Lakes on the way to Browns Lake, but this campground is worth the extra few miles. It is basic but peaceful, and the lake is very nice. No motorized boats are permitted on the water. There are myriad forest service roads and trails in the area to explore if the fish are not biting. There is also a barrier-free interpretive trail nearby.

301 Canyon Creek

Location: 91 miles northwest of Spokane on Canyon Creek, near Colville
GPS: N48 34.650' / W118 14.383'
Elevation: 2,050 feet
Season: Mid-April to late Oct
Sites: 12 sites for tents or self-contained RVs no longer than 30 feet
Facilities: Drinking water, fire grills, picnic tables, vault toilets
Fee per night: $
Management: Colville National Forest, Three Rivers/Kettle Falls Ranger District, (509) 738-7700; no reservations
Activities: Hiking, fishing
Finding the campground: From I-90 in Spokane take exit 281 and head northwest on US 395. Drive 81 miles to Kettle Falls, which is 10 miles past Colville. Continue west on WA 20 for 10 miles and cross the Columbia River to reach the campground.
The campground: Situated where Canyon Creek flows into Sherman Creek, this campground offers some good fishing opportunities. The highway here is the Sherman Pass Scenic Byway, and the region is upholstered in forest and meadows. A mile-long barrier-free trail runs along Canyon Creek. FR 136 runs along the other side.

302 Clover Leaf

Location: 91 miles northwest of Spokane on Franklin D. Roosevelt Lake, near Gifford
GPS: N48 17.811' / W118 08.814'
Elevation: 1,289 feet
Season: Year-round; limited winter services
Sites: 9 tent sites, all walk-in or boat-in
Facilities: Drinking water, fire grills, picnic tables, vault toilets, boat ramp (fee), dock
Fee per night: $–$$
Management: Lake Roosevelt National Recreation Area, (509) 633-3830; no reservations
Activities: Fishing, boating, swimming

Finding the campground: From I-90 in Spokane take exit 277 and head west on US 2 for 32 miles to Davenport. Turn north onto WA 25 and drive 59 miles to the campground, just south of Gifford.

The campground: There is not much to do at this small and rustic campground except fish and enjoy the water. The Gifford-Inchelium Ferry is just 2 miles south of camp. It offers free passage across the Columbia River to the Colville Indian Reservation every half hour.

303 Douglas Falls Grange Park

Location: About 77 miles northwest of Spokane on Mill Creek, near Colville
GPS: N48 36.900' / W117 53.802'
Elevation: 1,870 feet
Season: Apr through Nov
Sites: 8 sites for tents or self-contained RVs
Facilities: Drinking water, tent pads, picnic tables, fire grills, restrooms, dump station, baseball field
Fee per night: None
Management: Washington Department of Natural Resources, Northeast Region, (509) 684-7474; no reservations
Activities: Hiking
Finding the campground: From I-90 in Spokane take exit 281 and head northwest on US 395. Drive 71 miles to Colville and turn east onto WA 20. Drive for 1 mile and turn left (north) onto Colville-Aladdin Road (which becomes Douglas Falls Road). Drive just over 5 miles to the campground on the left.

The campground: Set on the edge of Douglas Falls Grange County Park, this wooded campground is a delight. There are hiking trails nearby, but the main activity seems to be sitting in camp and enjoying the company of the other campers. And somebody always seems to be getting a baseball game together. Douglas Falls presents a fine photo opportunity.

304 Dragoon Creek

Location: About 16 miles north of Spokane on Dragoon Creek
GPS: N47 52.560' / W117 22.147'
Elevation: 2,100 feet
Season: Apr through Sept
Sites: 22 sites for tents or self-contained RVs
Facilities: Drinking water, picnic tables, fire grills, tent pads, vault toilets
Fee per night: None
Management: Washington Department of Natural Resources, Northeast Region, (509) 684-7474; no reservations
Activities: Fishing

Finding the campground: From I-90 in Spokane take exit 281 and head north on US 395. Drive 16 miles; turn left onto Dragoon Creek Road and drive 0.5 mile to the campground entrance.

The campground: This is a nice little forested campground on the Half Mile Prairie. It sits next to Dragoon Creek about 4 miles from its confluence with the Little Spokane River. Camp conditions are on the rustic side, but the place is relaxing.

305 East Sullivan

Location: 95 miles north of Spokane on Sullivan Lake, near the town of Metaline Falls
GPS: N48 50.317' / W117 16.783'
Elevation: 2,200 feet
Season: Mid-May through Sept
Sites: 38 sites for tents or self-contained RVs no longer than 55 feet
Facilities: Drinking water, fire grills, picnic tables, vault toilets, dump station, boat ramp, dock
Fee per night: $$$
Management: Colville National Forest, Sullivan Lake Ranger District, (509) 446-7500; no reservations
Activities: Hiking, fishing, boating, swimming, waterskiing
Finding the campground: From I-90 in Spokane take exit 281 and head north on US 2/395. The two highways split in 6 miles. Branch right with US 2 and stay on it for 28 miles to the junction with WA 211. Turn left (north) onto WA 211 and continue for 15 miles to Usk. There join WA 20 and drive north for 31 miles to Tiger. From Tiger go north on WA 31 for 3 miles and then turn right onto Sullivan Lake Road. Cross the Pend Oreille River and drive 12 miles to the campground at the north end of Sullivan Lake. Or you can simply fly in, landing at Sullivan Lake Airport next to the campground. It has a grass airstrip.

The campground: The East Sullivan Campground is separated from the West Sullivan Campground by an airstrip. Four-mile-long Sullivan Lake is surrounded by the mountains of the Colville National Forest. The Salmo Priest Wilderness, just to the north and east, offers some good hiking trails. A foot trail also runs down the east side of the lake, which is very popular with anglers and water-skiers. This good family campground is quite nice and clean. For a minimal fee you can make reservations by contacting the National Recreation Reservation Service at www.recreation.gov or (877) 444-6777.

306 Edgewater

Location: About 86 miles north of Spokane on the Pend Oreille River, near Ione
GPS: N48 45.250' / W117 24.317'
Elevation: 2,200 feet
Season: Late May to early Sept
Sites: 23 sites for tents or self-contained RVs no longer than 20 feet
Facilities: Drinking water, fire grills, picnic tables, vault toilets, boat ramp
Fee per night: $$$

Management: Colville National Forest, Sullivan Lake Ranger District, (509) 446-7500

Activities: Fishing, boating, waterskiing

Finding the campground: From I-90 in Spokane take exit 281 and head north on US 2/395. Drive 6 miles to where the two highways split, bear right with US 2, and stay on it for 28 miles to its junction with WA 211. Turn left (north) onto WA 211 and continue for 15 miles to Usk. There you join WA 20 and drive north for 31 miles to Tiger. From there go north on WA 31 for 3 miles and then turn right onto Sullivan Lake Road. You cross the Pend Oreille River within 0.5 mile. Immediately turn left (north) onto Box Canyon–LeClerc Road and drive 2 miles to the campground entrance on the left.

The campground: This 10-acre campground lies 2 miles upstream from Box Canyon Dam on the Pend Oreille River, at its confluence with Exposure Creek. It is a nice setting, and the camp faces west across the river toward Cement Mountain. Access to the river is easy. For a minimal fee you can make reservations by contacting the National Recreation Reservation Service at www.recreation.gov or (877) 444-6777.

307 Evans

Location: About 90 miles northwest of Spokane on Franklin D. Roosevelt Lake, near Colville

GPS: N48 41.880' / W118 01.050'

Elevation: 1,290 feet

Season: Year-round

Sites: 43 sites for tents or self-contained RVs no longer than 26 feet

Facilities: Drinking water, fire grills, picnic tables, flush toilets, dump station, store, boat ramp (fee), dock, playground

Fee per night: $–$$

Management: Lake Roosevelt National Recreation Area, (509) 633-3830, ext. 37; no reservations

Activities: Fishing, boating, swimming, waterskiing

Finding the campground: From I-90 in Spokane take exit 281 and head north on US 395 for 81 miles to Kettle Falls. A half mile beyond Kettle Falls, turn right (north) onto WA 25 and drive 8 miles to the campground.

The campground: This 16-acre campground is in a wonderful setting, on a small promontory that juts into Franklin D. Roosevelt Lake. It is a pretty comfortable camp—roomy without being too big.

308 Flodelle Creek

Location: About 92 miles north of Spokane on Flodelle Creek, near Colville

GPS: N48 32.736' / W117 34.306'

Elevation: 3,100 feet

Season: Year-round

Sites: 8 sites for tents or self-contained RVs no longer than 20 feet

Facilities: Drinking water, picnic tables, fire grills, tent pads, vault toilets

Fee per night: None

Management: Washington Department of Natural Resources, Northeast Region, (509) 684-7474; no reservations

Activities: Hiking, fishing, mountain biking, trail biking, snowmobiling

Finding the campground: From I-90 in Spokane take exit 281 and head north on US 395. Drive 71 miles to Colville and turn east onto WA 20. Drive for 20.4 miles and turn right (south) onto a two-lane gravel road. Go 0.3 mile; stay left at a junction and continue 0.1 mile to the campground.

The campground: This small rustic campground is not far off the highway, but it is not well known by the camping public. It sits right along forested Flodelle Creek, and there are plenty of trails to explore nearby. Trail biking on motorcycles is popular here, so be prepared for the noise.

309 Fort Spokane

Location: About 54 miles northwest of Spokane on Franklin D. Roosevelt Lake

GPS: N47 54.377' / W118 19.509'

Elevation: 1,289 feet

Season: Year-round; limited winter services

Sites: 67 sites for tents or self-contained RVs no longer than 26 feet

Facilities: Drinking water, picnic tables, fire grills, flush toilets, playground, dump station, boat docks, boat ramps (fee), marine dump station

Fee per night: $$

Management: Lake Roosevelt National Recreation Area, (509) 633-3830, ext. 37

Activities: Fishing, boating, swimming, waterskiing

Finding the campground: From I-90 in Spokane take exit 277 and head west on US 2 for 32 miles to Davenport. Turn right (north) onto WA 25 and drive 21 miles to the intersection with Miles-Creston Road. Turn left (south) onto Miles-Creston Road; the campground is within 0.5 mile. The actual Fort Spokane is a little farther west on WA 25, near the bridge over the Spokane River.

The campground: This modern, 22-acre campground sits at the confluence of the Spokane and Columbia Rivers, along a segment of the Columbia that has been dammed to create Franklin D. Roosevelt Lake. The camp offers ranger-guided daytime activities and evening campfire programs.

Fort Spokane was completed in 1894; the post comprised 45 buildings. At the height of army occupation, more than 300 soldiers lived there, but it was emptied at the outbreak of the Spanish-American War in 1898. In subsequent years the Bureau of Indian Affairs used the post as a boarding school, tuberculosis sanatorium, and general hospital for local Indians. Now operated by the National Park Service, four of the fort's buildings remain. The guardhouse serves as the visitor center. For reservations visit www.recreation.gov or call (877) 444-6777.

310 Gifford

Location: 90 miles northwest of Spokane on Franklin D. Roosevelt Lake, near Gifford

GPS: N48 17.160' / W118 08.566'

Elevation: 1,289 feet

Season: Year-round; limited winter services

Sites: 42 sites for tents or self-contained RVs no longer than 20 feet

Facilities: Drinking water, fire grills, picnic tables, pit toilets, boat docks, boat ramp (fee), moorage

Fee per night: $$

Management: Lake Roosevelt National Recreation Area, (509) 633-3860; no reservations

Activities: Fishing, boating, swimming, waterskiing

Finding the campground: From I-90 in Spokane take exit 277 and drive west on US 2 for 32 miles to Davenport. Turn right (north) onto WA 25 and drive 58 miles to the campground.

The campground: This large, nice campground sometimes seems like a water-ski camp for children. It is an excellent facility for boaters, and the fishing is rumored to be good on this stretch of the Columbia, where it has been dammed to form Franklin D. Roosevelt Lake. The Gifford-Inchelium Ferry is just 1 mile south of camp. It offers free passage across the Columbia to the Colville Indian Reservation every half hour.

311 Gillette

Location: About 92 miles north of Spokane on Lake Gillette, near Colville

GPS: N48 36.750' / W117 32.050'

Elevation: 3,200 feet

Season: Mid-May to late Sept

Sites: 30 sites for tents or self-contained RVs no longer than 31 feet

Facilities: Drinking water, picnic tables, fire grills, vault toilets, dump station, boat ramp, moorage, docks, boat rentals

Fee per night: $$

Management: Colville National Forest, Three Rivers/Kettle Falls Ranger District, (509) 738-7700; no reservations

Activities: Hiking, fishing, boating, swimming, off-road driving

Finding the campground: From I-90 in Spokane take exit 281 and head north on US 395. Drive 71 miles to Colville and turn east onto WA 20. Drive for 20 miles; turn right (east) onto FR 200 and drive 0.5 mile to the campground.

The campground: Located on 7-acre, glacier-formed Lake Gillette, this campground is very popular and often full. It is right across the road from the Lake Gillette Campground. The lake offers wonderful recreational opportunities, and the nearby forest roads and trails are heavily used by off-road vehicle enthusiasts—so it can get noisy here. Trout fishing is good, and an interpretive trail meanders through the area.

312 Haag Cove

Location: 91 miles northwest of Spokane on Franklin D. Roosevelt Lake, near Kettle Falls

GPS: N48 33.677' / W118 09.100'

Elevation: 1,285 feet

Season: Year-round

Sites: 16 sites for tents or self-contained RVs no longer than 26 feet
Facilities: Drinking water, fire grills, picnic tables, pit toilets, boat dock
Fee per night: $-$$
Management: Lake Roosevelt National Recreation Area, (509) 633-9441; no reservations
Activities: Fishing, boating, swimming, waterskiing
Finding the campground: From I-90 in Spokane take exit 281 and head north on US 395 for 81 miles to Kettle Falls. Continue west through town for 3 miles; cross the bridge over the Columbia and immediately turn left (south) with WA 20. Continue for 4 miles; turn left (south) onto Kettle Falls Road and drive 3 miles to the campground.
The campground: This campground, located on the segment of the Columbia River dammed to create Franklin D. Roosevelt Lake, is farther off the beaten track than others in the area. This quite comfortable campground is pleasantly situated near a long, narrow cove that is fun to explore.

313 Hawk Creek

Location: 61 miles northwest of Spokane on Franklin D. Roosevelt Lake
GPS: N47 48.906' / W118 19.500'
Elevation: 1,289 feet
Season: Year-round; limited winter services
Sites: 21 sites for tents or self-contained RVs no longer than 16 feet
Facilities: Drinking water, picnic tables, fire grills, pit toilets, boat docks, boat ramp (fee)
Fee per night: $$
Management: Lake Roosevelt National Recreation Area, (509) 633-3830, ext. 37; no reservations
Activities: Hiking, fishing, swimming, boating, waterskiing
Finding the campground: From I-90 in Spokane take exit 277 and drive west on US 2 for 32 miles to Davenport. Turn right (north) onto WA 25 and drive 21 miles to the intersection with Miles-Creston Road. Turn left (south) onto Miles-Creston Road and drive 8 miles to the campground at the mouth of Hawk Creek.
The campground: This campground is on the north side of a 2.5-mile-long bay of Franklin D. Roosevelt Lake, which was created by damming a segment of the Columbia River. The bay is fed by Hawk Creek, and Hawk Creek Falls is about 0.5 mile to the east, at the head of the bay. This is a nice camp, away from the hubbub on the Columbia River.

314 Hunters

Location: 79 miles northwest of Spokane on Franklin D. Roosevelt Lake
GPS: N48 07.332' / W118 13.556'
Elevation: 1,289 feet
Season: Year-round; limited services in winter
Sites: 39 sites for tents or self-contained RVs no longer than 26 feet
Facilities: Drinking water, picnic tables, fire grills, flush toilets, store, ice, boat docks, boat ramp (fee)

Fee per night: $-$$
Management: Lake Roosevelt National Recreation Area, (509) 738-6266; no reservations
Activities: Fishing, boating, swimming, waterskiing
Finding the campground: From I-90 in Spokane take exit 277 and drive west on US 2 for 32 miles to Davenport. Turn right (north) onto WA 25 and drive 47 miles to Hunters. Hunters Park is 1.5 miles west of Hunters via a signed access road.
The campground: This is a good family camp near an estuary formed by Hunters Creek as it flows into Franklin D. Roosevelt Lake, which is actually a dammed segment of the Columbia River. The camp is comfortable and offers a bit of shopping and fine access to the water.

315 Kamloops Island

Location: About 88 miles northwest of Spokane on Franklin D. Roosevelt Lake, near Colville
GPS: N48 40.744' / W118 07.033'
Elevation: 1,289 feet
Season: Year-round
Sites: 14 tent sites
Facilities: Picnic tables, pit toilets, boat docks; no drinking water
Fee per night: $-$$
Management: Lake Roosevelt National Recreation Area, (509) 738-6266, ext. 109; no reservations
Activities: Hiking, fishing, swimming, boating, waterskiing
Finding the campground: From I-90 in Spokane take exit 281 and head north on US 395 for 81 miles to Kettle Falls. Continue west through town for 4 miles, crossing the bridge over the Columbia, and immediately turn right (north) with US 395. Continue 3.5 miles to the campground entrance on the right, and cross the bridge to Kamloops Island.
The campground: This island camp is perfect for tenters who can appreciate the primitive conditions. Kamloops Island is at the mouth of the Kettle River Arm of this segment of the Columbia River, which has been dammed to form Franklin D. Roosevelt Lake.

316 Kettle Falls

Location: About 86 miles northwest of Spokane on Franklin D. Roosevelt Lake, near Colville
GPS: N48 17.183' / W118 07.202'
Elevation: 1,200 feet
Season: Year-round, limited services in winter
Sites: 75 sites for tents or self-contained RVs no longer than 26 feet
Facilities: Drinking water, picnic tables, fire grills, restrooms, dump station, boat ramp (fee), docks, playground, cafe
Fee per night: $$
Management: Lake Roosevelt National Recreation Area, (509) 633-3830, ext. 37
Activities: Fishing, swimming, boating, waterskiing, campfire programs

Finding the campground: From I-90 in Spokane take exit 281 and head north on US 395 for 81 miles to Kettle Falls. Continue through town, still on US 395, for 3 miles. The campground access road branches off to the left just before you cross the bridge over the Columbia River; the campground is 1.5 miles south on this road.

The campground: This 22-acre park sits right on the shore of Franklin D. Roosevelt Lake, which was created with the damming of the Columbia River. It is a popular park with local residents. The layout and amenities are good; so is the water access. Lions Island, directly south of the campground, is fun to explore. For reservations visit www.recreation.gov or call (877) 444-6777.

317 Lake Ellen

Location: About 98 miles northwest of Spokane on Lake Ellen, near Colville
GPS: N48 30.133' / W118 14.767'
Elevation: 2,500 feet
Season: Mid-April to mid-Oct
Sites: 15 sites for tents or self-contained RVs no longer than 22 feet
Facilities: Picnic tables, fire grills, vault toilets, boat docks; no drinking water
Fee per night: $
Management: Colville National Forest, Three Rivers/Kettle Falls Ranger District, (509) 738-7700; no reservations
Activities: Fishing, swimming
Finding the campground: From I- 90 in Spokane take exit 281 and head north and then northwest on US 395 for 81 miles to the town of Kettle Falls. Continue west through town for 3 miles; cross the bridge over the Columbia River and immediately turn left (south) with WA 20. Drive 4 miles; turn left (south) onto Kettle Falls Road and drive 4.5 miles. At Lake Ellen Road turn right (west) and drive 5 miles to the campground.
The campground: This is a small campground on a small lake, but the amenities are okay. This is a wonderful place to kick back and enjoy the water in forested surroundings.

318 Lake Gillette

Location: About 92 miles north of Spokane on Lake Gillette, near Colville
GPS: N48 36.750' / W117 32.317'
Elevation: 3,200 feet
Season: Mid-May to late Sept
Sites: 14 sites for tents or self-contained RVs no longer than 31 feet
Facilities: Drinking water, picnic tables, fire grills, vault toilets, dump station, boat ramp, moorage, docks, boat rentals
Fee per night: $$–$$$
Management: Colville National Forest, Colville Ranger District, Three Rivers/Kettle Falls Ranger District, (509) 738-7700; no reservations
Activities: Hiking, fishing, boating, swimming, off-road driving

This trailer has two spare bedrooms.

Finding the campground: From I- 90 in Spokane take exit 281 and head north on US 395. Drive 71 miles to Colville and turn east onto WA 20. Drive for 20 miles to FR 200; turn right (east) and drive 0.5 mile to the campground.

The campground: This campground sits on the shore of 7-acre, glacier-formed Lake Gillette, right across the road from the Gillette Campground. It is very popular and is often full. The lake offers wonderful recreational opportunities. The nearby forest roads and trails are heavily used by off-road vehicle enthusiasts—so it can get noisy here. The trout fishing is good, and an interpretive trail meanders through the area.

319 Lake Leo

Location: 95 miles north of Spokane on Lake Leo, near Colville
GPS: N48 38.950' / W117 29.800'
Elevation: 3,200 feet
Season: Mid-May to mid-Sept
Sites: 8 sites for tents or self-contained RVs no longer than 15 feet
Facilities: Drinking water, picnic tables, fire grills, pit toilets, firewood, boat ramp

Fee per night: $$

Management: Colville National Forest, Three Rivers/Kettle Falls Ranger District, (509) 738-7700; no reservations

Activities: Hiking, fishing, swimming, cross-country skiing

Finding the campground: From I-90 in Spokane take exit 281 and head north on US 395 for 71 miles to Colville. Turn right (east) onto WA 20 and drive 24 miles to the campground.

The campground: This is a small, quiet campground on one of the glacially carved Little Pend Oreille Lakes. It is pretty basic, but its lakeside location counts for a lot.

320　Lake Thomas

Location: 92 miles north of Spokane on Lake Thomas, near Colville

GPS: N48 37.433' / W117 32.083'

Elevation: 3,200 feet

Season: Mid-May to late Sept

Sites: 16 tent/small RV sites

Facilities: Drinking water, picnic tables, fire grills, vault toilets, dump station, boat ramp, docks, boat rentals, groceries

Fee per night: $$

Management: Colville National Forest, Three Rivers/Kettle Falls Ranger District, (509) 738-7700; no reservations

Activities: Hiking, fishing, boating, waterskiing, mountain biking

Finding the campground: From I-90 in Spokane take exit 281 and head north on US 395 for 71 miles to Colville. Turn right (east) onto WA 20. Drive for 20 miles; turn right (east) onto FR 200 and drive 1 mile to the campground.

The campground: This 2-mile-long glacial lake sits in the midst of a thick forest. The campground amenities are pretty good, and the recreational opportunities are impressive. There are even some places nearby to drive off-road vehicles, especially the Radar Dome ORV Trail, which is open summer and winter. It is located across WA 20 from the campground, 0.5 mile toward Colville. There are camping and fishing spots all along the Little Pend Oreille River, but nothing beats camping on a lake.

321　Little Twin Lakes

Location: 89 miles north of Spokane on Little Twin Lakes, near Colville

GPS: N48 34.450' / W117 38.650'

Elevation: 3,800 feet

Season: Mid-May through Sept

Sites: 20 sites for tents or self-contained RVs no longer than 16 feet

Facilities: Picnic tables, fire grills, pit toilets, boat docks, boat ramp; no drinking water

Fee per night: None

Management: Colville National Forest, Three Rivers/Kettle Falls Ranger District, (509) 738-7700; no reservations

Activities: Fishing, boating, off-road driving

Finding the campground: From I-90 in Spokane take exit 281 and head north on US 395. Drive 71 miles to Colville and turn right (east) onto WA 20. Drive for 12.5 miles to Black Lake-Squaw Creek Road; turn left (north) and go 4.5 miles to the junction with FR 150. Go straight onto FR 150 and drive 1 mile to the campground.

The campground: The road to this remote, 20-acre site is rough, but the campground is worth the effort. A four-wheel-drive vehicle is a good idea but not always necessary, depending on recent weather conditions. If the access road is not enough of a challenge, there are miles and miles of old logging roads in the area for you to try. The wooded camp is rustic, but the setting is beautiful.

322 Marcus Island

Location: About 85 miles northwest of Spokane on Franklin D. Roosevelt Lake, near Colville

GPS: N48 40.144' / W118 03.449'

Elevation: 1,290 feet

Season: Year-round

Sites: 21 sites for tents or self-contained RVs no longer than 20 feet

Facilities: Drinking water, fire grills, picnic tables, pit toilets, dock

Fee per night: $–$$

Management: Lake Roosevelt National Recreation Area, (509) 633-3830, ext. 37; no reservations

Activities: Fishing, boating, swimming, waterskiing

Finding the campground: From I-90 in Spokane take exit 281 and head northwest on US 395 for 81 miles to the town of Kettle Falls. A half mile beyond town, turn right (north) onto WA 25 and drive 4 miles to the campground on Marcus Island.

The campground: This is a fair-size campground on a segment of the Columbia River that has been dammed to form Franklin D. Roosevelt Lake. Because of its close proximity to the water, the campground offers plenty of recreational opportunities. It is a bit less comfortable and more rustic than Evans Campground, 4 miles to the north.

323 Mill Pond

Location: 96 miles north of Spokane on Mill Pond, near Ione

GPS: N48 51.250' / W117 17.433'

Elevation: 2,200 feet

Season: Late May to early Sept

Sites: 10 sites for tents or self-contained RVs no longer than 21 feet

Facilities: Drinking water, picnic tables, fire grills, vault toilets, boat ramp

Fee per night: $$$

Management: Colville National Forest, Sullivan Lake Ranger District, (509) 446-7500; no reservations

Activities: Hiking, fishing, boating, waterskiing

Finding the campground: From I-90 in Spokane take exit 281 and head north on US 2/395. In 6 miles the two highways split. Branch right with US 2 and stay on it for 28 miles to the junction with WA 211. Turn left (north) onto WA 211 and continue for 15 miles to Usk. There you join WA 20 and continue north for another 31 miles to Tiger. From there go north on WA 31 for 3 miles and turn right (east) onto Sullivan Lake Road. Cross the Pend Oreille River and drive 13 miles to the campground, just beyond Sullivan Lake.

The campground: This sparse campground is favored by backpackers, who use it as a base camp. The pond is nice, but the real action is on Sullivan Lake, 1 mile to the south.

324 Mount Spokane State Park

Location: 30 miles northeast of Spokane on Mount Spokane
GPS: N47 55.511' / W117 06.979'
Elevation: Mount Spokane is 5,880 feet; the campground is lower.
Season: From snowmelt (300 inches annually) to Sept 15
Sites: 8 sites for tents or self-contained RVs no longer than 30 feet, 1 group site (capacity 60). Skiers may park self-contained RVs in the day-use area during winter.
Facilities: Drinking water, picnic tables, flush toilets, 2 horse feeding stations, ski resort, restaurant
Fee per night: $$–$$$$
Management: Washington State Parks and Recreation Commission, (360) 902-8844 (information); (509) 238-4258 (park office); no reservations
Activities: Hiking, horseback riding, huckleberry picking, picnicking, mountain biking, downhill and cross-country skiing, sledding, snowmobiling
Finding the campground: From I-90 in Spokane take exit 281 and drive north on US 2 for 6 miles. Turn right (east) onto WA 206 and drive 24 miles to the campground.
The campground: Encompassing 13,643 acres and providing parking for 1,588 vehicles, this park is obviously more than your ordinary campground. In fact, Mount Spokane is also a 2,000-foot-vertical-drop ski area with five double chairlifts and a lodge. Built by the Civilian Conservation Corps in the 1930s, Mount Spokane was the first Washington state park east of the Cascades. By 1950 the mountain had become popular with skiers. It also offers 50 miles of hiking and equestrian trails and sweeping views of the Inland Empire. The park, the city, and the campground all derive their name from a Spokane Indian word that means "sun."

325 Noisy Creek

Location: 90 miles north of Spokane on Sullivan Lake, near Ione
GPS: N48 47.433' / W117 16.933'
Elevation: 2,200 feet
Season: Late May to early Sept
Sites: 19 sites for tents or self-contained RVs no longer than 35 feet
Facilities: Drinking water, picnic tables, fire grills, vault toilets, boat ramp

Fee per night: $$$
Management: Colville National Forest, Sullivan Lake Ranger District, (509) 446-7500
Activities: Hiking, fishing, boating, waterskiing
Finding the campground: From I-90 in Spokane take exit 281 and head north on US 2/395. In 6 miles the two highways split. Branch right with US 2 and stay on it for 28 miles to the junction with WA 211. Turn left (north) onto WA 211 and continue for 15 miles to Usk. From there join WA 20 and continue north for 31 miles to Tiger. From Tiger go north on WA 31 for 3 miles. Turn right (east) onto Sullivan Lake Road; The campground is in 7 miles on the south end of Sullivan Lake.
The campground: Situated where Noisy Creek enters Lake Sullivan, this primitive campground has great access to the southern end of the 4-mile-long lake. Fishing and waterskiing are the most popular activities. The hiking is good, too. There is a trail that runs along the eastern shore of the lake to the campgrounds at the other end. For a minimal fee you can make reservations by contacting the National Recreation Reservation Service at www.recreation.gov or (877) 444-6777.

326 North Gorge

Location: About 100 miles northwest of Spokane on Franklin D. Roosevelt Lake, near Colville
GPS: N48 47.196' / W118 00.180'
Elevation: 1,290 feet
Season: Year-round
Sites: 12 sites for tents or self-contained RVs no longer than 26 feet
Facilities: Drinking water, fire grills, picnic tables, pit toilets, boat ramp (fee), dock, playground
Fee per night: $-$$
Management: Lake Roosevelt National Recreation Area, (509) 633-3830, ext. 37; no reservations
Activities: Fishing, boating, swimming, waterskiing
Finding the campground: From I-90 in Spokane take exit 281 and head northwest on US 395 for 81 miles to the town of Kettle Falls. A half mile beyond town, turn right (north) onto WA 25 and drive 20 miles to the campground.
The campground: This is the best of three campgrounds along this section of the Columbia River, which has been dammed to form Franklin D. Roosevelt Lake. The amenities at North Gorge are serviceable, and the camp is relatively small and isolated. Bass, sunfish, trout, and walleye await anglers.

327 Panhandle

Location: About 64 miles north of Spokane on the Pend Oreille River, near Ione
GPS: N48 30.517' / W117 13.083'
Elevation: 2,200 feet
Season: Late May to late Sept
Sites: 13 sites for tents or self-contained RVs no longer than 30 feet
Facilities: Drinking water, picnic tables, vault toilets
Fee per night: $

Management: Colville National Forest, Newport Ranger District, (509) 447-7300

Activities: Hiking, fishing, boating, swimming, waterskiing, mountain biking, off-road driving

Finding the campground: From I-90 in Spokane take exit 281 and head north on US 2/395. In 6 miles the two highways split. Branch right with US 2 and stay on it for 28 miles to the junction with WA 211. Turn left (north) onto WA 211 and continue for 15 miles to Usk. Continue through town and across the Pend Oreille River. Immediately after crossing the bridge, turn left onto LeClerc Creek Road and drive 15 miles north to the campground on the left.

The campground: Adjacent to the LeClerc Creek Wildlife Area, this small rustic campground is a good place for water sports enthusiasts. Nearby are some good trails for hiking, mountain biking, and off-road driving. For a minimal fee you can make reservations by contacting the National Recreation Reservation Service at www.recreation.gov or (877) 444-6777.

328 Pend Oreille County Park

Location: 31 miles north of Spokane
GPS: N48 04.824' / W117 19.602'
Elevation: 2,200 feet
Season: Memorial Day through Labor Day
Sites: 34 standard tent sites, 2 sites for tents or self-contained RVs
Facilities: Drinking water, picnic tables, fire grills, flush toilets, showers
Fee per night: $$
Management: Pend Oreille County Department of Public Works, (509) 447-4513; no reservations.
Activities: Hiking

Finding the campground: From I-90 in Spokane take exit 281 and head north on US 2/395. In 6 miles the two highways split. Branch right with US 2 and stay on it for 25 miles to the campground on the left.

The campground: This campground makes a better layover than a destination. It is perfectly nice, but there is not a lot to do. Trails in the nearby Fertile Valley are a good possibility.

329 Pierre Lake

Location: 104 miles northwest of Spokane on Pierre Lake, near Kettle Falls
GPS: N48 54.267' / W118 08.367'
Elevation: 2,150 feet
Season: Mid-Apr to mid-Oct
Sites: 16 sites for tents or self-contained RVs no longer than 24 feet
Facilities: Picnic tables, fire grills, vault toilets, boat ramp, docks; no drinking water
Fee per night: $
Management: Colville National Forest, Kettle Falls Ranger District, Three Rivers/Kettle Falls Ranger District, (509) 738-7700; no reservations
Activities: Hiking, fishing, boating, swimming

Finding the campground: From I-90 in Spokane take exit 281 and head north on US 395 for 81 miles to the town of Kettle Falls. Continue another 14 miles north on US 395 to Barstow. Turn right (east) onto CR 4013 (Barstow-Pierre Lake Road) and continue 9 miles to the campground.

The campground: Located about 7 miles from the Canadian border, Pierre Lake is very nice indeed. The campground is used mostly by anglers, but it is fine for families too. There is an easy hike along the west shore of the lake, as well as a bit tougher one up Hungry Hill. The campground is on the rustic side but perfectly adequate.

330 Pioneer Park

Location: About 50 miles northeast of Spokane on the Pend Oreille River, near Newport
GPS: N48 12.750' / W117 03.250'
Elevation: 2,200 feet
Season: Late May to late Sept
Sites: 17 sites for tents or self-contained RVs no longer than 24 feet
Facilities: Drinking water, picnic tables, vault toilets, boat docks, boat ramps, nearby boat rentals
Fee per night: $$$
Management: Colville National Forest, Newport Ranger District, (509) 447-7300
Activities: Fishing, boating, swimming, waterskiing
Finding the campground: From I-90 in Spokane take exit 281 and head north on US 2/395. In 6 miles the two highways split. Branch right with US 2 and stay on it for 41 miles to Newport on the Idaho border. Stay on US 2 through town and over the bridge into Idaho, but take an immediate left onto LeClerc Creek Road and drive for 2 miles to the park. It is on the Washington side of the border.

The campground: The Pend Oreille River flows smooth and wide here, a consequence of Box Canyon Dam 50 miles to the north. A barrier-free interpretive trail with a boardwalk allows campers to enjoy the beautiful waterway. There is a protected inlet, and Cooks Island is just offshore. Native Americans lived along the river as long as 9,000 years ago, and an archaeological dig at the campground provides a glimpse of early life. For a minimal fee you can make reservations by contacting the National Recreation Reservation Service at www.recreation.gov or (877) 444-6777.

331 Porcupine Bay

Location: 54 miles northwest of Spokane on the Spokane River
GPS: N47 53.778' / W118 10.614'
Elevation: 1,289 feet
Season: Year-round, weather permitting
Sites: 31 sites for tents or self-contained RVs no longer than 25 feet
Facilities: Drinking water, picnic tables, fire grills, flush toilets, playground, boat docks, boat ramp (fee)
Fee per night: $$

Management: Lake Roosevelt National Recreation Area, (509) 633-3830, ext. 37; no reservations.

Activities: Hiking, fishing, boating, swimming

Finding the campground: From I-90 in Spokane take exit 277 onto US 2 West and drive 32 miles to Davenport. Turn north onto WA 25 and drive 13.5 miles. At Porcupine Bay Road and the sign for the Coulee Dam National Recreation Area, turn right (north) and drive 6.5 miles to the campground.

The campground: This 7-acre riverside campground is popular with boaters. It is rather isolated in the small hills that border the Spokane River.

332 Riverside State Park

Location: 6 miles northwest of downtown Spokane on the Spokane River
GPS: N47 41.754' / W117 29.577'
Elevation: 1,640 feet
Season: Year-round
Sites: 32 sites (16 with water and electricity hookups) for tents or RVs no longer than 45 feet
Facilities: Drinking water, picnic tables, fire grills, flush toilets, showers, boat ramp, riding stables, off-road vehicle park
Fee per night: $$-$$$$
Management: Washington State Parks and Recreation Commission, (360) 902-8844 (information); (509) 456-3964 (park office)
Activities: Boating, fishing, hiking, bicycling, horseback riding, motorcycle and ATV riding, snowmobiling, cross-country skiing, birding
Finding the campground: From downtown Spokane take the Maple Street Bridge Route north to Northwest Boulevard. Turn left onto Northwest Boulevard and continue 2.5 miles to H Street. Turn left as the brown Riverside State Park sign directs, and follow park signs past Downriver Golf Course to the park entrance.
The campground: This 10,000-acre park with 37 miles of freshwater shoreline feels like it is way out in the country, but it is easily accessible from Spokane. The ponderosa forest along the Spokane River extends to a ridge with great views of the city. A concession operates equestrian facilities in the Fort George Wright portion of the park, and there is a 600-acre motorcycle and off-road vehicle park. Horseback riding is a great way to see the park, and the park stables rents mounts by the hour or day. There are 37 miles of foot and horse trails to explore. A lava formation in the park, called the Bowl and Pitcher, attracts photography classes from local colleges. You can reach it via a 218-foot-high pedestrian suspension bridge over the Spokane River. Individual campsites can be reserved year-round by visiting https://secure.camis.com/WA/ or calling (888) 226-7688.

333 Rocky Lake

Location: About 82 miles north of Spokane on Rocky Lake, near Colville
GPS: N48 29.811' / W117 52.332'

Elevation: 1,620 feet

Season: Year-round

Sites: 7 sites for tents or self-contained RVs

Facilities: Drinking water, picnic tables, fire grills, tent pads, vault toilets, boat ramp

Fee per night: None

Management: Washington Department of Natural Resources, Northeast Region, (509) 684-7474

Activities: Fishing, canoeing

Finding the campground: From I-90 in Spokane take exit 281 and head north and then northwest on US 395 for 71 miles to Colville. Turn east onto WA 20 and drive 5.9 miles. Then turn right (south) onto Artman-Gibson Road and continue 3.2 miles. Turn right (northwest) again onto a one-lane gravel road and drive 0.3 mile. Stay to the left at the junction and continue another 2 miles to the site.

The campground: This small rustic campground is an ideal place to kick back and maybe do a bit of canoe fishing on a big pond. Just remember, it is named Rocky Lake for a reason. The campground is very close to the Little Pend Oreille Habitat Management Area, which offers good hiking and fishing.

334 Sheep Creek

Location: About 120 miles northwest of Spokane on Sheep Creek, near Northport

GPS: N48 54.967' / W117 46.784' (town of Northport)

Elevation: 1,960 feet

Season: Year-round

Sites: 11 sites for tents or self-contained RVs no longer than 20 feet

Facilities: Drinking water, picnic tables, fire grills, tent pads, vault toilets, group shelter

Fee per night: None

Management: Washington Department of Natural Resources, Northeast Region, (509) 684-7474

Activities: Hiking, fishing, off-road driving

Finding the campground: From I-90 in Spokane take exit 281 and head north and then northwest on US 395 for 81 miles to the town of Kettle Falls. A half mile beyond Kettle Falls, turn right (north) onto WA 25 and drive 33 miles to Northport. Continue 0.7 mile north on WA 25, cross the Columbia River, turn left onto Sheep Creek Road and drive 4.3 miles. Turn right into the campground.

The campground: This is a very basic campground but nicely positioned along forested Sheep Creek. There are plenty of nearby hiking trails and four-wheel-drive routes.

335 Skookum Creek

Location: About 50 miles north of Spokane on Skookum Creek, near Newport

GPS: N48 22.161' / W117 10.980'

Elevation: 2,290 feet

Season: Year-round

Sites: 10 sites for tents or self-contained RVs
Facilities: Drinking water, picnic tables, fire grills, tent pads, vault toilets
Fee per night: None
Management: Washington Department of Natural Resources, Northeast Region, (509) 684-7474
Activities: Hiking, fishing, boating
Finding the campground: From I-90 in Spokane take exit 281 and head north and then northwest on US 2 for 32 miles to the intersection with WA 211. Turn left onto WA 211 and continue for 15 miles to Usk. Cross the Pend Oreille River via Kings Lake Road. In 0.9 mile turn right onto LeClerc Creek Road and drive 2.2 miles. Turn left onto a one-lane gravel road; drive just 0.1 mile and turn left for 0.3 mile to the campground.
The campground: This is a nice place for canoeing or kayaking. The campsites are wooded and are close to the creek.

336 South Skookum Lake

Location: About 55 miles north of Spokane on South Skookum Lake, near Newport
GPS: N48 23.500' / W117 10.967'
Elevation: 3,800 feet
Season: Late May to late Sept
Sites: 25 sites for tents or self-contained RVs no longer than 30 feet
Facilities: Drinking water, picnic tables, vault toilets, small boat ramp, wheelchair-accessible fishing dock
Fee per night: $$$
Management: Colville National Forest, Newport Ranger District, (509) 447-7300; no reservations
Activities: Hiking, fishing, boating
Finding the campground: From I-90 in Spokane take exit 281 and head north and then northwest on US 2 for 32 miles to the intersection with WA 211. Turn left (north) onto WA 211 and continue for 15 miles to Usk. Cross the Pend Oreille River via Kings Lake Road and stay on it for 7 miles. Then turn right (northeast) onto FR 50. It swings around the north end of King Lake for 1.5 miles. Turn right (south) onto the campground access road.
The campground: This medium-size campground is a very pleasant respite from the workaday world. There is an easy walking trail around the small lake and a more ambitious one up 4,383-foot Kings Mountain.

337 West Sullivan

Location: 95 miles north of Spokane on Sullivan Lake, near Ione
GPS: N48 50.350' / W117 17.067'
Elevation: 2,200 feet
Season: Mid-May through Sept
Sites: 10 sites for tents or self-contained RVs no longer than 30 feet
Facilities: Drinking water, picnic tables, fire grills, vault toilets

Fee per night: $$$
Management: Colville National Forest, Sullivan Lake Ranger District, (509) 446-7500
Activities: Hiking, fishing, boating, waterskiing
Finding the campground: From I-90 in Spokane take exit 281 and head north on US 2/395. In 6 miles the two highways split. Branch right with US 2 and stay on it for 28 miles to the junction with WA 211. Turn left (north) onto WA 211 and continue for 15 miles to Usk. From there join WA 20 and continue north for 31 miles to Tiger. From Tiger go north on WA 31 for 3 miles and then turn right onto Sullivan Lake Road. The campground is 12 more miles at the north end of Sullivan Lake. Or you can simply fly in, landing at Sullivan Lake Airport next to the campground. It has a grass airstrip.

The campground: Four-mile-long Sullivan Lake is surrounded by the mountains of the Colville National Forest. The Salmo Priest Wilderness is just to the north and east. It offers some good hiking trails. A foot trail also runs down the east side of the lake, which is very popular with anglers and water-skiers. The campground is nice and clean. It is a good family campground. For a minimal fee you can make reservations by contacting the National Recreation Reservation Service at www.recreation.gov or (877) 444-6777.

	Group Sites	RV Sites	Total # of sites	Max RV Length	Hookups	Toilets	Showers	Drinking water	Dump station	Pets	Wheelchair	Recreation	Fee	Season	Can reserve	Stay limit
338 Alder Thicket		•	5	15		V			•	•		H		mid May–mid Nov		7
339 Big Springs		•	10			V			•	•		H		mid May–mid Nov		7
340 Central Ferry Park	•	•	69	45	WES	F	•	•	•	•	•	HFSB	$$–$$$$	Apr–Sept	•	10
341 Chief Timothy Park		•	66	60	WE	F	•	•	•	•	•	HFB	$$–$$$$	Apr–Sept	•	10
342 Fields Spring State Park	•	•	31	30		F	•	•	•	•		H	$$–$$$$	year-round		10
343 Godman		•	8	15		V				•		HR		mid Jun–late Oct		7
344 Lewis and Clark Trail State Park	•	•	41	28		F		•	•	•		HF	$–$$$	Apr–Sept 14		10
345 Lyons Ferry Park and Marina		•	58	45	WES	F	•	•	•	•		HFBS	$$$–$$$$	Apr–Sept	•	10
346 Palouse Falls State Park		•	10	40		P		•	•	•	•	H	$$	year-round		10
347 Teal Spring		•	7	15		V		•	•	•		H	$	Jun–mid Nov		7
348 Tucannon		•	18	15		V				•		HF	$	May–late Nov		7
349 Wickiup		•	7	15		V		•	•			H		mid June–late Oct		7

Hookups: W = Water E = Electric S = Sewer
Toilets: F = Flush V = Vault P = Pit
Recreation: C = Bicycling/Mountain Biking H = Hiking S = Swimming F = Fishing B = Boating
O = Off-highway driving R = Horseback Riding
Maximum Trailer/RV Length given in feet. Stay Limit given in days.
Fee $ = less than $10; $$ = $10–$15; $$$ = $16–20; $$$$ = more than $20.
If no entry under Fee, camping is free.

338 Alder Thicket

Location: About 130 miles south of Spokane, near Pomeroy
GPS: N46 15.550' / W117 33.988'
Elevation: 5,100 feet
Season: Mid-May to mid-Nov
Sites: 5 sites for tents or self-contained RVs no longer than 15 feet
Facilities: Picnic tables, fire grills, vault toilets, dump station; no drinking water
Fee per night: None
Management: Umatilla National Forest, Pomeroy Ranger District, (541) 278-3716; no reservations
Activities: Hiking

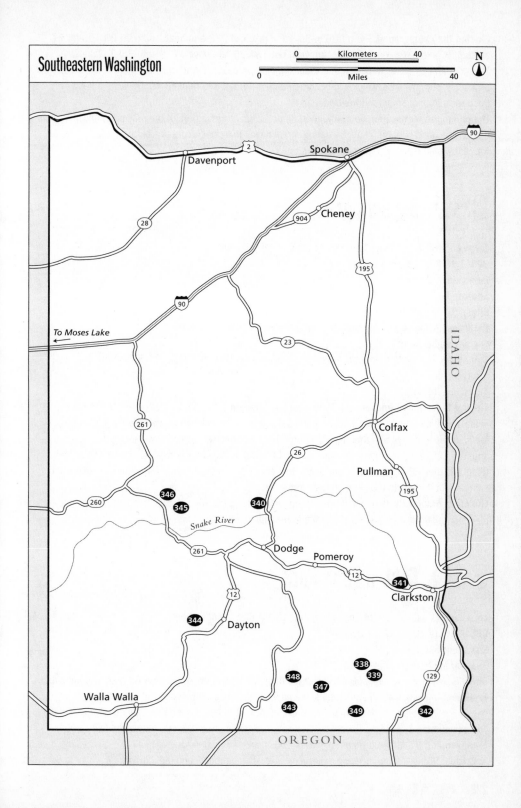

Southeastern Washington

Finding the campground: From I-90 in Spokane take exit 279 and head south on US 195 for 57 miles. Just before you reach Colfax, turn west onto WA 26 and drive 17 miles to Dusty. Take WA 127 south for 27 miles to Dodge and then turn east onto US 12 and drive 13 miles to Pomeroy. Turn south onto WA 128, which will become Mountain Road and then FR 40. Drive 17 miles from the turnoff to the campground entrance.

The campground: Located, naturally, in an alder thicket in the middle of the proverbial nowhere, this campground is quite rustic, bordering on primitive. The choices are to kick back and commune with nature or go hiking and commune with nature.

339 Big Springs

Location: About 137 miles south of Spokane, near Pomeroy
GPS: N46 13.772' / W117 32.567'
Elevation: 4,970 feet
Season: Mid-May to mid-Nov
Sites: 10 tent/RV sites
Facilities: Picnic tables, vault toilets, dump station; no drinking water
Fee per night: None
Management: Umatilla National Forest, Pomeroy Ranger District, (541) 278-3716; no reservations
Activities: Hiking
Finding the campground: From I-90 in Spokane take exit 279 and head south on US 195 for 57 miles. Just before Colfax, turn west onto WA 26 and drive 17 miles to Dusty. Take WA 127 south for 27 miles to Dodge and then turn east onto US 12 and drive 13 miles to Pomeroy. Turn south onto WA 128 and drive about 20 miles to the Clearwater Lookout. The road will become Mountain Road and then FR 40 along the way. At the lookout turn left (east) onto FR 42 (Ruchert Road) and continue for 3 miles to the campground on the left.

The campground: Nestled below Unfried Ridge, Big Springs is a very basic campground—a good place for roughing it. Hunters use the site in the fall.

340 Central Ferry Park

Location: 91 miles south of Spokane on the Snake River, near Pomeroy
GPS: N46 37.702' / W117 48.650'
Elevation: 640 feet
Season: Apr through Sept
Sites: 8 primitive tent sites, 60 sites with full hookups for RVs no longer than 45 feet, 1 group site
Facilities: Drinking water, picnic tables, fire grills, flush toilets, showers, dump station, group fire ring, 3 horseshoe pits, 3 boat docks, 2 ski docks, 4 boat ramps, fishing pier, marine dump station
Fee per night: $$-$$$$
Management: US Army Corps of Engineers, (509) 547-7781 (information)
Activities: Hiking, fishing, boating, swimming, waterskiing, beachcombing, birding

Finding the campground: From I-90 in Spokane take exit 279 and head south on US 195 for 57 miles. Just before you reach Colfax, turn west onto WA 26 and drive 17 miles to Dusty. From there take WA 127 south for 17 miles to the park.

The campground: Central Ferry encompasses 185 acres, including 6,500 feet of shoreline on Lake Bryan, backwater of the Little Goose Dam on the Snake River. The water frontage includes 775 feet of unguarded swimming beach. The park is tucked into the wheat fields of southeastern Washington. High bluffs border the park on one side. Resident birds include meadowlarks, bluebirds, Chinese pheasants, killdeer, and swans. The brushy countryside just beyond the park harbors some dangerous wildlife, including rattlesnakes and black widow spiders. Individual campsites can be reserved by visiting https://secure.camis.com/WA/ or calling (888) 226-7688.

341 Chief Timothy Park

Location: 111 miles south of Spokane on an island in Lower Granite Lake, near Clarkston
GPS: N46 25.112' / W117 06.267'
Elevation: 900 feet
Season: Apr through Sept
Sites: 33 tent sites, 33 sites with water and electrical hookups for RVs no longer than 60 feet
Facilities: Drinking water, picnic tables, fire grills, flush toilets, showers, complete disposal facilities, interpretive center, 4 boat ramps and docks, playground, snack bar
Fee per night: $$–$$$$
Management: US Army Corps of Engineers, (509) 547-7781 (information); (509) 758-9580 (park office)
Activities: Hiking, fishing, boating, waterskiing, interpretive programs
Finding the campground: From I-90 in Spokane take exit 279 and head south on US 195 for 94 miles to the Idaho border. US 195 joins US 95 as the route enters Idaho and continues for 6 miles to Lewiston. At Lewiston turn west onto US Highway 12 and drive 11 miles back into Washington to the park.
The campground: This 282-acre park is on an island in a segment of the Snake River that has been dammed to create Lower Granite Lake. The dam is more than 20 miles downstream. The park features 11,500 feet of shoreline, including an unguarded swimming area that is protected from boat traffic. The Alpowai Interpretive Center is built near the original site of a mid-nineteenth century Nez Perce village called Alpowai. Individual campsites can be reserved by visiting https://secure.camis.com/WA/ or calling (888) 226-7688.

342 Fields Spring State Park

Location: 29 miles south of Clarkston, near the Grande Ronde River
GPS: N46 04.878' / W117 10.224'
Elevation: 4,500 feet
Season: Year-round; limited services in winter

Sites: 20 sites for tents or self-contained RVs no longer than 30 feet, 2 8-person tepees, 1 cabin, 1 lodge for up to 20 people, 1 lodge with 6 cabins that sleep 10 people each

Facilities: Drinking water, picnic tables, fire grills, flush toilets, dump station, playground, coin-operated showers, firewood (fee), 7.5 miles of cross-county ski trails, 3 miles of hiking trails, sled run, lighted tubing hill

Fee per night: $$–$$$$

Management: Washington State Parks and Recreation Commission, (360) 902-8844 (information); (509) 256-3332 (park office); no reservations except for the tepees, cabins, and lodges. Phone the office for details.

Activities: Hiking, birding, cross-country skiing, sledding, tubing, snowmobiling

Finding the campground: From Clarkston, on the Idaho border, head south on WA 129 for 29 miles to the park.

The campground: This idyllic site in the Blue Mountains encompasses nearly 800 acres on Puffer Butte. It is situated 4,000 feet above the Grande Ronde River on an old Native American route between Oregon and Idaho. The Indians stopped in the area to dig roots. There is a hiking trail to the top of the butte, which offers wondrous views into three states. In 1974 about 70 percent of the Douglas and white firs in this area was damaged by an infestation of tussock moths and subsequently removed.

343 Godman

Location: About 150 miles south of Spokane, near Dayton

GPS: N46 06.000' / W117 46.998'

Elevation: 6,050 feet

Season: Mid-June to late Oct

Sites: 8 sites (5 tent-only, 3 for tents or RVs no longer than 15 feet)

Facilities: Picnic tables, fire grills, vault toilets, dump station, horse facilities; no drinking water

Fee per night: None

Management: Umatilla National Forest, Pomeroy Ranger District, (541) 278-3716; no reservations

Activities: Hiking, horseback riding, snowmobiling

Finding the campground: From I-90 in Spokane take exit 279 and head south on US 195 for 57 miles. Just before you reach Colfax, turn west onto WA 26 and drive 17 miles to Dusty. From there take WA 127 south for 27 miles, crossing the Snake River, to Dodge. Turn west onto US 12 and drive 24 miles west and south to Dayton. Leave US 12 and turn left (southeast) into town. In 0.5 mile turn left (east) onto Mustard Hollow Road; drive almost 4 miles and turn east onto Eckler Mountain Road. Stay on it (as it becomes Skyline Drive and FR 46) for 24 miles to the campground.

The campground: This is definitely the end of the road in the Blue Mountains, but it is also where the trails begin. The campground makes a good base for backpacking into the Wenaha Tucannon Wilderness. It is used a lot by horseback riders too and by snowmobilers in winter. The campground is connected by a trail to the Ski Bluewood ski area, 3 miles west.

344 Lewis and Clark Trail State Park

Location: 130 miles south of Spokane on the Touchet River, near Walla Walla
GPS: N46 17.298' / W118 04.338'
Elevation: 1,610 feet
Season: Year-round for primitive sites; rest of park closed Sept 15 to Mar 31
Sites: 24 sites for tents or self-contained RVs no longer than 28 feet, 17 primitive tent sites in the day-use area
Facilities: Drinking water, picnic tables, fire grills, flush toilets, dump station, amphitheater
Fee per night: $–$$$
Management: Washington State Parks and Recreation Commission, (360) 902-8844 (information); (509) 337-6457 (park office); no reservations
Activities: Birding, fishing, hiking, picnicking, sledding, hunting
Finding the campground: From I-90 in Spokane take exit 279 and head south on US 195 for 57 miles. Just before you reach Colfax, turn west onto WA 26 and drive 17 miles to Dusty. From there take WA 127 south for 27 miles to Dodge. Turn west onto US 12 and drive 29 miles to the campground, which is 5 miles beyond Dayton. From Walla Walla drive northeast on US 12 for 24 miles to the park.
The campground: This 37-acre campground is on the Touchet River, which eventually joins the Walla Walla River on its way to the Columbia. The route that Lewis and Clark took on their return journey in 1806 runs right through the park and gives the park its name. Homesteaders used this site to hold post-harvest picnics and games. Today park rangers host campfire interpretive programs in summer. There is a 1-mile interpretive trail and a 0.75-mile bird watching trail in the camp.

345 Lyons Ferry Park and Marina

Location: 126 miles southwest of Spokane on the Snake River, near Pomeroy
GPS: N46 31.056' / W118 07.164'
Elevation: 545 feet
Season: Apr through Sept
Sites: 58 sites for tents or self-contained RVs no longer than 45 feet (including 18 full hookup sites in the lower area)
Facilities: Drinking water, picnic tables, fire grills, flush toilets, showers, dump station, 2 boat ramps
Fee per night: $$$–$$$$
Management: Port of Columbia, (509) 382-2577 (information)
Activities: Hiking, fishing, boating, swimming, waterskiing
Finding the campground: From I-90 in Spokane take exit 279 and head south on US 195 for 57 miles. Just before you reach Colfax, turn west onto WA 26 and drive 17 miles to Dusty. From there take WA 127 south for 27 miles to Dodge. Head west on US 12 for 9 miles to the junction with WA 261. Turn right (west) onto WA 261 and drive 16 miles to the campground, which is 8 miles past Starbuck.

The campground: Now a KOA, this 1,282-acre park, located at the confluence of the Snake and Palouse Rivers, features 10 miles of Snake riverfront, including 428 feet of unguarded swimming beach. The park also encompasses the Marmes Rock Shelter Heritage Area, site of an ancient burial cave. Archaeologists found human remains dating back 10,000 years in the valley now flooded by Lower Monumental Dam. More recently the Palouse Indians used the site as a burial grounds. About 400 graves were moved before the flooding. The Lewis and Clark expedition passed through here, and the Lyons Ferry, propelled by the river current, has been crossing the Snake River here for 108 years. Early settlers and the US Army used the ferry to reach the Palouse country. It is currently berthed in the park. For reservations visit https://koa.com/campgrounds/starbuck/reserve/ or call (509) 399-8020.

346 Palouse Falls State Park

Location: 134 miles southwest of Spokane on the Palouse River, near Dayton
GPS: N46 39.820' / W118 13.633'
Elevation: 560 feet
Season: Year-round; water turned off Oct through Apr
Sites: 10 primitive sites for tents or self-contained RVs no longer than 40 feet
Facilities: Drinking water, picnic tables, fire grills, pit toilets, observation shelter, barrier-free trail to overlook
Fee per night: $$
Management: Washington State Parks and Recreation Commission, (360) 902-8844 (information); (509) 646-9218 (park office)
Activities: Hiking, picnicking, viewing of falls
Finding the campground: From I-90 in Spokane take exit 279 and head south on US 195 for 57 miles. Just before you reach Colfax, turn west onto WA 26 and drive 17 miles to Dusty. From there take WA 127 south for 27 miles to Dodge. Head west on US 12 for 9 miles to the junction with WA 261. Turn right onto WA 261 and drive 22 miles west and north to Palouse Falls Road. Turn right (northeast) and drive 2 miles to the campground.
The campground: Palouse Falls is the only remaining waterfall on the Palouse River that was formed by glacial floods. It is 198 feet high and is most spectacular in the spring and early summer. The park is more popular with day-trippers than campers, but the campground is serviceable if you do not expect too much. There is plenty of shade, and the park is located near the confluence of the Snake and Palouse Rivers.

347 Teal Spring

Location: 134 miles south of Spokane, near Pomeroy
GPS: N46 11.315' / W117 34.318'
Elevation: 5.600 feet
Season: June to mid-Nov
Sites: 7 sites for tents or self-contained RVs no longer than 15 feet

Facilities: Drinking water, picnic tables, fire grills, vault toilets, snow shelter
Fee per night: $
Management: Umatilla National Forest, Pomeroy Ranger District, (541) 278-3716; no reservations
Activities: Hiking
Finding the campground: From I-90 in Spokane take exit 279 and head south on US 195 for 57 miles. Just before you reach Colfax, turn west onto WA 26 and drive 17 miles to Dusty. From there take WA 127 south for 27 miles to Dodge. Head southeast on US 12 for 13 miles to Pomeroy; turn south onto WA 128 and drive about 20 miles. The route will become Mountain Road and then FR 40 along the way. The campground turnoff is on the right 0.5 mile past the Clearwater Lookout.
The campground: This is a very basic and pleasant campground just off FR 40, the main thoroughfare in these parts. A pack trail leads from camp to and beyond Diamond Peak (elevation 6,415 feet). The campground's snow shelter is used by hunters in the fall.

348 Tucannon

Location: 138 miles south of Spokane, near Dayton
GPS: N46 14.559' / W117 41.237'
Elevation: 2,600 feet
Season: May to late Nov
Sites: 18 sites for tents or self-contained RVs no longer than 15 feet
Facilities: Picnic tables, fire grills, vault toilets; no drinking water
Fee per night: $
Management: Umatilla National Forest, Pomeroy Ranger District, (541) 278-3716; no reservations
Activities: Hiking, fishing
Finding the campground: From I-90 in Spokane take exit 279 and head south on US 195 for 57 miles. Just before you reach Colfax, turn west onto WA 26 and drive 17 miles to Dusty. From there take WA 127 south for 27 miles to Dodge. Turn left (west) onto US 12 and drive 9 miles to Tucannon. Bear left on Tucannon Road, which eventually becomes FR 47, and drive 28 miles east and south to the campground.
The campground: This is certainly the backcountry, way back. Roughing it is your only option here, but the wooded setting is very peaceful. The campground is close to the Tucannon River.

349 Wickiup

Location: About 145 miles south of Spokane, near Pomeroy
GPS: N46 08.218' / W117 26.124'
Elevation: 5,100 feet
Season: Mid-June to late Oct
Sites: 7 sites for tents or self-contained RVs no longer than 15 feet
Facilities: Drinking water, picnic tables, fire grills, vault toilets

Fee per night: None

Management: Umatilla National Forest, Pomeroy Ranger District, (541) 278-3716; no reservations

Activities: Hiking

Finding the campground: From I-90 in Spokane take exit 279 and head south on US 195 for 57 miles. Just before you reach Colfax, turn west onto WA 26 and drive 17 miles to Dusty. From there take WA 127 south for 27 miles to Dodge. Turn left (east) onto US 12 and drive 13 miles to Pomeroy. Turn right (south) onto WA 128 and drive about 27 miles. WA 128 will become Mountain Road and then FR 40 along the way. When you reach the junction with FR 44; turn left (east) and drive 3 miles to the campground.

The campground: This campground is way, way down the road, but you are sure to have the place pretty much to yourself when you get there. It is quite primitive, and there is not a lot to do besides relax. Of course if you get bored, you could always hike up Hogback Ridge, which is 1 mile or so east of camp.

Index

About the Author

Steve Giordano began camping at age 5 with his adventurous mother and father in army surplus mummy bags on the beaches of Northern California. Since moving to Washington many years ago, he has been hitting the highways and byways in search of memorable camping experiences. He has tried motor homes, campers, station wagons, trucks, tents, and even bicycle camping. But he still thinks nothing quite matches the ol' feather-leaking sleeping bag under the open sky.

Steve is the author of three previous books, including *Scenic Driving Washington* (FalconGuides, 1997). He writes columns for *RV Life* magazine, contributes to and edits skiing guidebooks and websites skisnowboard.com and highonadventure.com, and writes for travel magazines and online publications. With his wife and five Pacific Northwest friends, he co-owns, contributes to, and manages the technical headaches for highonadventure.com, a website of outdoor adventure writers. He is a member of the North American Snowsports Journalists Association and the Society of American Travel Writers, which he will serve as president in 2013–14.